TENNYSON
The Muses' Tug-of-War

TENNYSON
The Muses' Tug-of-War

by
Daniel Albright

UNIVERSITY PRESS OF VIRGINIA

Charlottesville

This is a title in the series

VIRGINIA
VICTORIAN
STUDIES

THE UNIVERSITY PRESS OF VIRGINIA
Copyright © 1986 by the Rector and Visitors
of the University of Virginia

First published 1986

Library of Congress Cataloging-in-Publication Data
Albright, Daniel, 1945–
Tennyson : the muses' tug-of-war.
(Virginia Victorian studies)
Includes index.
1. Tennyson, Alfred Tennyson, Baron, 1809–1892—
Criticism and interpretation. I. Title. II. Series.
PR5588.A38 1986   821'.8   86-1546
ISBN 0-8139-1100-1

Printed in the United States of America

Contents

Idealist" and the dissolution of Arthur; "Guinevere"
and the failure of panpsychism

Part Two: PERSONAE

Part Three: THE THREE MAJOR POEMS

Acknowledgments

It has been great luck to have as my friends and colleagues two top Tennysonians, Cecil Y. Lang and Edgar F. Shannon, the editors of Tennyson's letters. Their advice and good will have meant much to me. Traces of their wisdom linger, all too faintly, on many pages of this book.

I also owe an intellectual debt to Christopher Ricks and Robert Bernard Martin. Christopher Ricks's edition, *The Poems of Tennyson* (Longmans, Green, 1969)—referred to as *Ricks* in this text—is to scholars of Tennyson a labor-saving device roughly comparable to the invention of electric light. Robert Bernard Martin's biography, *Tennyson: The Unquiet Heart* (Oxford University Press, 1980)—referred to as *Martin* in this text—has also been of lasting help.

Finally I must thank someone who is difficult to thank within a text that she has herself shaped, someone easier to thank in daily working life, by trying to imitate her immense kindness and resourcefulness, Karin Larson.

INTRODUCTION

I

Three Struggles

MANY STUDENTS OF ENGLISH POETRY do not enjoy the works of
Tennyson. One hears complaints about his sanctimoniousness, his
collusion with complacent authority, his deplorable attitude toward the Crimean war, his prolonged virginity, his Technicolor
synthetic medievalism. I admire Tennyson almost without reservation, but I too find in his work something off-key or irresolute,
wobbly. It is not just that Tennyson's genius sometimes fails him;
it is that his genius, even at its strongest, is divided and frustrated,
self-impeding.

A study of Tennyson's life makes it possible to conclude that
Tennyson was a neurotic whose conflicting desires both energized
and weakened his poetry. But this conclusion may be too simple,
for I believe that Tennyson's aesthetic goals were themselves in
conflict, and that this impasse, as well as his psychological difficulties, is responsible for the strangeness of his achievement. Tennyson tried to unite two incompatible poetics, one governed by a
heavenly muse who disdained the homely details of life, the other
governed by an earthly muse suspicious of the ideal and vague; and
because he could not effect a full synthesis, a certain lingering stress
can be found everywhere in his work, a headache of inaccurate
focus. These two poetics can be defined by three different polar-
ities, pertaining (1) to his life, (2) to his notions of personality, and
(3) to literary history.

1. *Tennyson vs. namelessness.* Tennyson was given to fits of
intuition, "a kind of 'waking trance' . . . I have frequently had quite
up from boyhood when I have been all alone. This has often come
upon me through repeating my own name to myself silently . . . &
this not a confused state but the clearest of the clearest" (Letter to
B. P. Blood, cited Martin, pp. 28–29; cf. Hallam Tennyson, *Alfred*

Lord Tennyson: A Memoir, 1:320). In his late poem "The Ancient Sage" (1885) Tennyson versified this passage:

> "for more than once when I
> Sat all alone, revolving in myself
> The word that is the symbol of myself,
> The mortal limit of the Self was loosed,
> And past into the Nameless, as a cloud
> Melts into Heaven. I touched my limbs, the limbs
> Were strange not mine—and yet no shade of doubt,
> But utter clearness, and through loss of Self
> The gain of such large life as matched with ours
> Were Sun to spark."

(ll. 229–38)

Loss of self is the motto of choice in many of Tennyson's poems: in "Vastness" (1885) Christ nails himself to the cross until "Self died out in the love of his kind" (l. 28); and in "The Holy Grail" (1869) the pure Sir Galahad cries out, "If I lose myself, I save myself!" (l. 178).

Tennyson was attracted to the hope that this state of high anonymity could be made to speak. Many of his poems can be described as the attempts of a great poet, employing all his resourcefulness, to utter the nonself, to lapse into an unconscious and almost inhuman zone of being. And yet a certain honesty, a certain obligation to be faithful to the friends, the family, the society, the self that he knew, compelled Tennyson to retreat from namelessness into the comfortable and secure. Among Tennyson's poems we find many whose author is clearly Alfred Tennyson dealing with his historical troubles—the death of Hallam, the souring of his relation to Rosa Baring, the stillbirth of his son, and so forth—poems trying to define, to make explicit, some precise emotional content. But, as in some sections of *In Memoriam,* Alfred Tennyson cannot always stay named, and may show a disquieting tendency to slip into a region of superhuman feelings, unimaginable intensities of grief or elation, amorphous states that resist exact formulation. T. S. Eliot has said that *Hamlet* is disfigured by Shakespeare's fascination with "the inexpressibly horrible" (*Selected Essays,* p. 126), an emotion too vast and vague to find any proper objective correlative. One might say instead that the works of Shakespeare, and Tennyson, and for that matter T. S. Eliot, are given a certain tensile strength by their attempts to express the inexpressible. Indeed much of Tennyson's best poetry is a kind of contest of authorship between Tennyson and his shadow, a lurking anonymity.

2. *Personae vs. clouds.* As with the author, so with his characters. Many of the rhetorical personages in Tennyson's works are, from one perspective, well defined and well inflected, pungent characters; yet from another perspective they are nearly incoherent loci of extravagances. In "Œnone" (1832), for example, the heroine is given a certain gravity and steadiness by the monotony of her lamentation, but when examined closely she dissolves into a cloud, too oversaturated and shifty to constitute a human being. Even the most prosaic and idyllic of Tennyson's characters can suddenly undo himself, veer into namelessness. "Enoch Arden" (1862) is the story of a good-hearted sailor, long shipwrecked on a deserted island and at last found, restored to England to become a furtive witness of his loving wife, now married to his best friend, and of her children by two husbands. Much of the poem is workmanlike narrative, as rich in circumstantial detail as a story in prose:

Enoch Arden, a rough sailor's lad
Made orphan by a winter shipwreck, played
(ll. 14–18)   Among the waste and lumber of the shore,
Hard coils of cordage, swarthy fishing-nets,
Anchors of rusty fluke, and boats updrawn.

But when Enoch is marooned he finds himself disoriented, in a world in which he can no longer sustain any precision of identity:

No sail from day to day, but every day
The sunrise broken into scarlet shafts
Among the palms and ferns and precipices;
(ll. 587–95)   The blaze upon the waters to the east;
The blaze upon his island overhead;
The blaze upon the waters to the west;
Then the great stars that globed themselves in Heaven,

The hollower-bellowing ocean, and again
The scarlet shafts of sunrise—but no sail.

The tropical vehemence dazzles him, and he slips away into paralysis, loss of self. At last Enoch is discovered by a crew strayed off course, and he approaches them

(ll. 634–36) Brown, looking hardly human, strangely clad,
Muttering and mumbling, idiotlike it seemed,
With inarticulate rage, and making signs.

All that blazing has, it seems, burned away his brain until he has lost every human faculty, undergone what Samuel Beckett calls loss of species. Enoch Arden slowly is assimilated back into European society; the gibberer evolves into a man with a name, with complicated social relations, with a restrained and carefully qualified personality.

The case of Enoch Arden shows that anonymity is not necessarily a pleasant state, though it has a certain Gauguin charm to it. In "The Lotos-Eaters" (1832) the fall from history into choral drugged euphoria is not accidental but willed; and the willfulness suggests better Tennyson's ambivalence about the depersonalization extolled in "The Ancient Sage." In "Merlin and Vivien" (1859) Merlin is trapped forever by magical means in a prison without walls, in which he is "lost to life and use and name and fame" (l. 212 and, with minor changes, ll. 302, 372, 435, and 968). Here it is clear that the slide from history into anonymity is a descent into hell. On one hand namelessness is a condition of ecstasy, a passing-away into larger-than-human energies; on the other hand it is blindness, numbness, involution, anesthesia, thinghood. We cannot long endure the banality of having a name, nor the peril of doing without one; and so we vacillate uncomfortably between the two states, unable to affirm either. The characters in Tennyson's poems cannot decide whether to be men or ghosts, so they hover restlessly in an uncertain middle ground.

3. *The commonplace vs. the sublime.* Historically some aspects of Tennyson's predicament arise from the shift from Romantic sublimity, the state in which the mind's capacity for feeling

attains its limit, to Victorian appreciation of the particular. There was a tendency in Romantic poetry and criticism to extend the domain of the sublime from a response appropriate to certain rare and exalted experiences to a general heightening of the pitch of responsiveness to every mean, paltry, or grand event of life. This tendency comported well with Tennyson's desire to exalt the minute particulars around him, to endow slight things with an aura of glory:

("'Flower in the Crannied Wall,'" ll. 3–6)

> I hold you here, root and all, in my hand,
> Little flower—but *if* I could understand
> What you are, root and all, and all in all,
> I should know what God and man is.

Such lines of rumination are derived from Wordsworth:

(*The Excursion*, 1.230–34, 3.437–39)

> the least of things
> Seemed infinite; and there his spirit shaped
> Her prospects, nor did he believe,—he *saw*.
> What wonder if his being thus became
> Sublime and comprehensive! . . .
>
> what good is given to men,
> More solid than the gilded clouds of heaven?
> What joy more lasting than a vernal flower?

Tennyson's flower is a little grubbier, a little more tangible, but there is no great difference. Yet Tennyson was attracted to another, more radical movement in Romantic aesthetics, associated less with Wordsworth than with Coleridge, according to which the sublime is not a nimbus or iridescence that plays about pedestrian things, but instead a vertigo, a reeling, a state of imagelessness; not a flower in a crannied wall but the shadow of a flower dissolving in water. Both Burke (*A Philosophical Enquiry* II.iii) and Coleridge (*Lecture VII*, 1811–12) quote with great approval Milton's description of Death, a shapeless shape and a shadowy substance, as the epitome of the sublime; but whereas Burke finds Milton's Death an example of the appropriateness of obscurity in describing sublime entities, Coleridge sees it leading to a general recommendation of imagelessness in art; as if it would be a good thing if every epic and drama and panegyric and little exclamation of feeling appealed to a higher and more vivid indeterminacy. Sublimity is at last a kind of exercise of the eye, a willed unfocusing, or a focusing on a spiritual penumbra, a tremulousness in the circumambient ether. If this doctrine were taken to its extreme, as in Coleridge's poem "Limbo," it would require a poem to contain no objects whatsoever, only swirls and smears and smudges. Tennyson, as we shall see, was in a number of his poems as excited by the possibility of thinglessness as by the possibility of namelessness. The protagonist of "The Mystic" (1830) is not only anonymous but dwells in a fully unreified domain. The stress in Tennyson's poetic between the desire to construct beautiful images and the desire to dissolve, to dislimn them, is only another aspect of the stresses in his personae, or in his sense of the lyric subject. The personae and the objects they handle, the visions they behold, all show a disconcerting tendency to turn spectral, unreal.

What is probably the most sublime passage in all Tennyson's works occurs at the climax of his great project *In Memoriam,* and it will illustrate the strange desire for contentlessness that comes upon Tennyson at his peak moments. Here Tennyson is meditating outdoors, at night, after a lawn party; the green fallen leaves strewn on the grass start to form themselves, under the pressure of his gaze, into letters, letters that spell out the "silent-speaking words" of Hallam's noble proclamations of faith:

> So word by word, and line by line,
>   The dead man touched me from the past,
>   And all at once it seemed at last
> The living soul was flashed on mine,
>
> And mine in this was wound, and whirled
>   About empyreal heights of thought,
>   And came on that which is, and caught
> The deep pulsations of the world,
>
> Aeonian music measuring out
>   The steps of Time—the shocks of Chance—
>   The blows of Death. At length my trance
> Was cancelled, stricken through with doubt.

(95.33–44)

The trance fades, and the glimmering cattle and the large leaves of the sycamore reappear; only the vestiges of this transfiguration remain to encourage the poet. This passage is perhaps as impressive as the high moments in Milton's work or Wordsworth's spots of time, but its confidence in its ability to sustain its imaginative vigor is far lower, and those prosaic forces antagonistic to vision have gained in power. Also, while the sublime has always been expressed by vague billowy abstractions, this imagery here is unusually evacuated; Hallam and Tennyson and the landscape all whirl out into a condition of imagelessness. In this extreme confusion the content of the poetry refines itself almost to nothing; and what replaces the content, after this delirium of deletion, is pure rhythm, rhythm naked and heavy, inorganic, extenuated by no variance in beat or syncopation. It is as if Tennyson had stopped writing words and simply transcribed a pattern of macrons and breves onto the page, plain marks of emphasis, steps, shocks, blows. At the moment of greatest intensity the metrical ictus becomes the subject of the poem; but the landscape that has turned into letters, stressed iambs, is, disturbingly, no longer a landscape in any ordinary sense, and must cool from this state of superheated meaningfulness if the moths and the trees, the teapot, are to be visible at all. Doubt had better enter the poem, or the poem would be unable to continue. Here music is the enemy of grace, and wit, and design, and even thought; and the sublime is a hammer likely to destroy what it hits.

To Tennyson, the sublime is an ecstasy and a danger; an ecstasy because the sublime is a state of overstimulated consciousness designed to heighten thought and feeling beyond every ordinary bound, as if the acuity of presentation of every external object were keenly felt as an attribute of the mind; and a danger because the sublime, in another mode, is a state of overtranquilized consciousness designed to entertain the poet with his own brain rhythms, exclusive of any outer world, as if the dead lumpishness of external nature infected the mind with its own ponderous inanition. These extremes converge, in that the delirium of heightening cannot be long sustained and tends to recoil into numbness and obtuseness. The Romantic poets, having proved that every flower, or every grain of sand, was an aperture opening to infinity, bequeathed to their successors a dangerously unstable world in which the least pebble was conducive to a painful hyperaesthesia, and the most scraggly weed was lotos. It was Tennyson's problem to reconcile the sublime aspect of things with the nonsublime: to show that each fading violet was an emblem, a miracle, and yet at the same time nothing more than a fading violet.

In Tennyson's age the sublime no longer excited much controversy or speculation; there are no significant Victorian treatises on sublimity; and yet the old poetical hyperventilations continue to be a temptation to the best writers. If we look back to Duff's *An Essay on Original Genius* (1767)—"Longinus maintains that a high degree of sublimity is utterly inconsistent with accuracy of imagination"— the first poem we think of is perhaps no eighteenth-century poem but Browning's "Andrea del Sarto" (1855), the "faultless painter" anxious that his accuracy of imagination may be the mark of Cain, the stigma of mediocrity. It may be generally true that the poets of the nineteenth century do not discuss the sublime, but dramatize it. To Tennyson the urge toward the sublime at once enables and disables; and much of the drama of his finest poems is a dialectic of a poet tempted to every giddy height of self-distention, yet fearing that poet and poetry alike will founder in willful distortions, annulments of the homely actuality of things. Indeed it may be said that sublimity, under the name of the Soul in "The Palace of Art," actually appears herself as a character in Tennyson's work—" 'I take possession of man's mind and creed' "—as if the extreme of poetic aspiration had been reduced to a kind of caricature, a raving female Herod.

Several critics have discussed Tennyson's career as a struggle between competing aesthetics. As James R. Kincaid says, "We have seen for some time that Tennyson was caught between the worlds of *Pride and Prejudice* and *Hyperion,* between the practical, novelistic world and the visionary, mythical world" (*Tennyson's Major Poems,* p. 12). Kincaid has done better than many of Tennyson's critics at exploring the various irreconcilable and reconcilable tensions—he calls the former ironic, the latter comic—between the two worlds, but it should be noted that there are certain extremes of elevation or depression, as in the case of Merlin, which may efface the visionary and the novelistic alike, cause a complete cessation of faculty. I prefer the term *sublime* to *visionary* or *mythical,* for I believe that Tennyson found himself tantalized by psychic experiences that were nearly inexpressible, that resisted mythology and mimesis alike, experiences so difficult to confront that only the idea of the sublime is sufficiently urgent, undescriptive, yawning. It is true that Tennyson was a mythmaker; but he is usually critical of his own mythopoeia, as if he understood what a poet like Shelley never could, that myths tend to damage, to violate the world of precious small actualities, by their very attempts to control it. At times he vacillates between a smooth, stylized, attractively passionate mythology and those precise finitudes that give the lie to it; but at other times he seems eager to sweep his canvas clear of both, as if no definite shapely thing could satisfy. A. Dwight Culler is one critic who has appreciated Tennyson's appetite for the shapeless and the unintelligible: "This element of indeterminacy in Tennyson's religion created a problem. . . . if he attempted visionary poetry, he could not have a clear vision" (*The Poetry of Tennyson,* p. 26); but not even Culler, I think, has explored the extent to which Tennyson's aesthetic depends upon some reverberation from the abyss to give significance even to the humblest subjects.

I shall try to show that the most productive tension in Tennyson's imagination was between two forces, either one of which, indulged to an extreme, would make poetry impossible: the urge to the sublime, or the nameless, and the urge to the commonplace; and I shall try to show that Tennyson's poetry is happiest when he can dress up the one in the vestments of the other, make the ineffable seem part of our usual furniture—and invest the ordinary with a tinge of eeriness. Much of the distinctive character of his poetry comes from this continual readjustment of focus and depth of field. The story of *Hyperion* must turn into a domestic squabble—this is almost what happens in "Demeter and Persephone"—and *Pride and Prejudice* must reveal itself as a competition among Titans.

Tennyson wrote before he was twenty-four years old a body of poetry so distinguished that only Keats, among English poets of comparable youth, will not suffer by comparison; then Tennyson engaged himself with three major projects for more than twenty years; and afterwards he wrote poems which, while not necessarily inferior in quality to his early work, continually restate, modify, or correct the themes, the characters, and the plots he used in his youth. Often one can make a pairing between an early poem and a late poem: "Œnone" and "The Death of Œnone," "Ulysses" and "Columbus," "The Lady of Shalott" and "Lancelot and Elaine" are only a few of the many pairs that present themselves. Therefore I have chosen to discuss Tennyson's early poems and his late poems together, under the large topics of art (whether resisting nature or aiding nature) and personae (whether coherent or incoherent). This method seemed to offer the fullest statement of the competing imaginative possibilities that Tennyson contemplated in his attempts to reconcile the too-bright or the too-dark, the smeary or the self-engrossed, with the honest mimesis of the poet's common life; and I have concluded with his longest, most subtle, and complicated poems, *Maud, In Memoriam A. H. H.,* and *The Princess.* (I could not bring myself to regard the *Idylls of the King* as an effort as coherent as these three masterpieces, so I have treated the *Idylls* as individual poems written in Tennyson's later period and discussed many of them in the earlier sections.) In *Maud* Tennyson carries his experimentation with personae to an extreme, develops an anonymous speaker continually in danger of falling into a vague, awful mythicality, almost storyless and pointless, impinging on the speechless sublime. In *In Memoriam* the elegist is pulled in opposing directions by two muses, Melpomene and Urania, the muse of the commonplace and the muse of the sublime—but, strangely, he is not sure which is the more valuable to him. And in *The Princess* he gives us two competing worlds, a world of high-flown fable in which all sexual and social distinctions move toward a collapse into plasm, light, and a world of homely love persisting in spite of mutability and death, revealed in the interspersed songs. I end with *The Princess* because it will serve as the most complete statement of Tennyson's conflicts, for in it the celestial and fantastic elements are at last exposed as a kind of suggestive heavenly folderol; while the dark, low, honest life, lived close to the bone, subdued and passionate, becomes invested with grave nobility, meaningfulness—as if the sublime and its opposite had at last traded places, as if the heavenly muse had at last stepped down to earth, and the earthly muse sprouted wings.

II

Derangement and
Disengagement

THE FIRST STAGE OF TENNYSON'S CAREER was a series of experiments
by which the poet proved to himself the inadequacy of the sublime,
the need for a more earthly muse. In Tennyson's early work one
finds competing modes of sublimity, some attractive, some appalling, all fascinating, as if a sorority of celestial muses were vying for
the poet's attention.

The notion that the sublime constituted a single phenomenon,
an idea that reached its high point in Burke's *Philosophical Enquiry*
(1757), started breaking down rapidly in the late eighteenth century.
According to Burke's realpolitik, what has power over you is
sublime; what you have power over is beautiful; and the emotion
associated with the presence of the sublime is terror:

(2.1)
> *The passion caused by the great and sublime in* nature, *when those
> causes operate most powerfully, is Astonishment; and astonish-
> ment is that state of the soul, in which all its motions are suspended,
> with some degree of horror. In this case the mind is so entirely filled
> with its object, that it cannot entertain any other, nor by conse-
> quence reason on that object which employs it. Hence arises the
> great power of the sublime, that far from being produced by them, it
> anticipates our reasonings, and hurries us on by an irresistible
> force. Astonishment, as I have said, is the effect of the sublime in its
> highest degree; the inferior effects are admiration, reverence and
> respect.*

A mind so stricken, so overfilled, so agitated to the point of paralysis, cannot write a poem, cannot think, can scarcely even be said to
feel. As T. S. Eliot says, describing immediate experience—his
term for that state of point-blank, undifferentiated feeling out of

which crystallize a perceiver and a world to be perceived—immediate experience is so immediate that no one has ever experienced it. One makes a poem only while approaching toward or retreating from such a zone of being: at one end is gossip, at the other, catatonia.

And yet there are several strategies by which a poem may approximate this condition of total engagement of poet and world. Each of these strategies has a somewhat different emotional tenor; and so the sublime, as a subject for poetry, shows itself not as stark complete terror, the dentist's drill hitting the nerve, but as a bundle of related techniques and themes. Wordsworth, in a fragmentary essay on the sublime and the beautiful, distinguished between a sublime experience in which the mind roused all its energies to try to grasp what was beyond its capacity, and a sublime experience in which the mind fell prostrate, abject, before a force that overwhelmed it (*Prose Works,* 2:354); and in such ways the sublime starts to acquire a range of emotional colors, from exhilaration to humiliation, any of which might be useful to a poet.

The two chief sublimities for the early Tennyson may be called derangement and disengagement. Derangement is the shattering of the world of experience into a state of extreme expressiveness, in which the poet can study his feelings and thoughts manifested in all that he sees, hears, touches; the psychological equivalent of derangement is narcissism. Disengagement is the state of lofty withdrawal, revulsion against the world of sensuous experience, in which the poet entertains himself with his own worldless fantasy; its psychological equivalent is schizophrenia. The deranged poet is his own muse, for he conceives the existence of no agency other than himself; while the disengaged poet takes for his muse the Soul in "The Palace of Art." Much of Tennyson's best work shows the poet half-conquering, half-succumbing to one or the other of these temptations.

It has often happened in the history of poetry that a great poet will begin his career by writing poems that closely imitate the great poetry of the previous generation, but in such a manner that his imitation calls attention to certain disquieting aspects of the earlier generation's poetry, exactly the aspects that his mature work will attempt to overcome. Tennyson's first major poem is "Armageddon," written when he was about fifteen years old and never published in his lifetime, though some of it was incorporated in his Cambridge prize poem, "Timbuctoo." "Armageddon" begins with the poet standing on Milton's perch, thanking the Spirit of Prophecy for granting him a vision of the end of time—a vision even loftier than Milton's, for whereas Urania was sufficient to inspire Milton to write Book 7 of *Paradise Lost,* no "fabled Muse" or other agency is capable of providing the poet with "Utterance to things unutterable," expression to "Deeds inexpressible" (1.17, 23). What follows this invocation is a pastiche of many favorite sublimities— Milton's seraphs, Shelley's apocalyptic volcanoes, perhaps Coleridge's iridescent fleeting horrors—but there is one element that is Tennyson's own, as this description of the sunset may suggest:

> Spirits of discord seemed to weave across
> His fiery disk a web of bloody haze,
> Through whose reticulations struggled forth
> His ineffectual, intercepted beams,
> Curtaining in one dark terrific pall
> Of dun-red light heaven's azure and earth's green.

(1.36–41)

Where could Tennyson have got this image? I cannot think of any effect of cloud or atmosphere that seems to cast a web over the disk of the sinking sun; nor can I remember any similar passage in literature. But I have noticed that, when an ophthalmologist shines his intolerable light into my eye, my visual field suffuses with bloodred; and I seem to see a network of veins projected over the walls of his office. What Tennyson seems to be describing in this passage is a complicated intraoptical response; the poet claims to be talking about the sun, but he is really talking about his own eye. Burke said that one physiological cause of sublime feeling was the mounting vibration of nerves in the eye when a huge object was beheld, a vibration that approached the level of pain (*Philosophical Enquiry,* 4.9); and it seems as if Tennyson wished to explore sublimity in its quickest state. We are near the ultimate in narcissism: an eye staring into an eye.

Later in "Armageddon," when the poet beholds the descent of

the young seraph and looks into "his inutterable shining eyes," he puts his hands over his face and sees "Such coloured spots as dance athwart the eyes / Of those that gaze upon the noonday sun" (2.8–9). It is a sign of sophistication, perhaps of decay as well, this insistence that visionary poetry is nothing but an elaboration of the minute processes of vision itself; it is a simple step from Tennyson's sunset to the sunset described in Gerard Manley Hopkins's "A Vision of the Mermaids":

(ll. 7–12)
> Plum-purple was the west; but spikes of light
> Spear'd open lustrous gashes, crimson-white;
> (Where the eye fix'd, fled the encrimsoning spot,
> And, gathering, floated where the gaze was not;)
> And through their parting lids there came and went
> Keen glimpses of the inner firmament.

Here Hopkins employs retinal afterimages to establish the veracity of his conceit that the sun is a big eyeball: light streams from the sun, and suns stream from the eye. If Wordsworth alleged that the eye half creates, half perceives, his successors could prove the proposition by studying the actual mechanism of seeing; thus in Victorian poetry there comes a fascination with mirrors, lenses, atmospheric distortion, optical illusions, retinal floaters, and so forth. What the eye manufactures is more visionary than what the eye sees. As early as 1829, when he was twenty, Tennyson noted that he was "distressed by a determination of blood to the Head . . . which . . . affected my eyes with 'muscae volitantes' "; never in his life did he see the stars as other than concentric rings; well may he have made paintings of landscapes as indistinct and swirling as Turner's (Martin, pp. 77, 93, 379). If Milton is the poet of blindness, Tennyson is the poet of myopia and astigmatism; and his career may be described as a long refocusing of his eyes from sublime vacancy to a painful, squinty distinguishing of the precise lineaments of things.

In "Armageddon" the adolescent Tennyson holds a mirror a half-inch from his eyes and describes what he sees; his eyeball is dazzled, pummeled, knuckled, coerced into an interesting simulation of a landscape. W. D. Paden discovered that the source of

Tennyson's reference to the eruption of the volcano Cotopaxi was Ulloa's *Voyage to South America;* Paden describes its illustration of the eruption as follows: "In the foreground rises Cotopaxi, in eruption. While the sun rises, a man looks west to see his own image, reflected from invisible Andean vapors; the apparition is surrounded by three concentric rainbows and a white outer arch" (Ricks, p. 65). There is a strong feeling in "Armageddon" that the poet sees his own image wherever he looks:

> In the East
> Broad rose the moon, first like a beacon-flame
> Seen on the far horizon's utmost verge,
> Or red eruption from the fissured cone
> (1.96–104)   Of Cotopaxi's cloud-capt altitude;
> Then with dilated orb and marked with lines
> Of mazy red athwart her shadowy face,
> Sickly, as though her secret eyes beheld
> Witchcraft's abominations.

Just as the sun earlier seemed like an eye engorged with blood, so now the moon is a "dilated orb," a dilated eye crisscrossed with veins, the poet's eye lifted into the heavens and made a sad spectator of "Obscene, unutterable phantasies." The converse process also happens: when the poet describes the rapid passage of "piercing, trackless, thrilling thoughts" through his "riven rapt brain" ("Timbuctoo," ll. 113, 119), he compares his brain to a large lake into which rocks keep dropping; there is little or no distinction between the landscape of the simile, felt inside the poet's body, and the external landscape, which is a magnified image of his optic nerve. The poet turns inside his own brain for the field of action of the poem, screws himself up into tighter and tighter involution, anonymity.

Keats—who would have been, if he had lived, the first great Victorian poet—derided Wordsworth's "egotistical sublime"; Tennyson, in "Armageddon," has succeeded in making explicit the egotism latent in Romantic sublimity. If Wordsworth is egotistical it is because he has no model for investigating the general operations of our faculties other than his own mind; in "Armageddon" this reflexiveness, this self-interested quality, is accepted, elaborated, coaxed, decorated with a whole aurora borealis of floodlights. At the climax of the poem the seraph commands the poet to open his eyes; his vision, no longer "clogged with dull Mortality," expands until it approaches omniscience:

I seemed to stand
Upon the outward verge and bound alone
Of God's omniscience. Each failing sense,
As with a momentary flash of light,
Grew thrillingly distinct and keen. I saw
The smallest grain that dappled the dark Earth,
The indistinctest atom in deep air,
The Moon's white cities, and the opal width
Of her small, glowing lakes.

(2.25–33)

Suddenly the poet's mind grows coextensive with the universe; this dizzying sensation of being "part of the Unchangeable, / A scintillation of Eternal Mind," (2.46–47) leads the poet to a state of self-idolatry: "Yea! in that hour I could have fallen down / Before my own strong soul and worshipped it" (2.49–50). "Armageddon" is a serious, even overserious, visionary poem, yet it is hard not to think of such states of mind as pathological or evil. Indeed, in Tennyson's play *The Devil and the Lady,* written even before "Armageddon" at the age of fourteen, the Devil, taking up a theme in Marlowe's *Dr. Faustus,* tells the adulterous heroine Amoret that she need not look up when she prays; downward and upward are equally heavenly:

Dost think that Heaven is local, and not rather
The omnipresence of the glorified
And liberated Spirit—the expansion
Of man's depressed and fettered faculties
Into omniscience?

(1.5.21–25)

It is as if the Devil himself were warning Tennyson not to become too engrossed with such visions as "Armageddon." The inculcation of sublimity is perilous to the soul's good; and vision is likely to be a disease of the eye.

All the states of transcendence that evoke awe or exultation in Blake, Wordsworth, or Shelley, evoke in Tennyson fear. The very ground on which he walks trembles with suppressed ferocity. "Armageddon" presents a fully deranged landscape in which every detail is disturbingly expressive, a headache of overwrought feeling; and such fractured and undone places are susceptible to earthquake. In Tennyson's first surviving poem, a schoolboy translation of a passage from Claudian's *Rape of Proserpine,* he describes how the hundred-handed giant Aegaeon bursts his "brazen chain," and, with other monsters, rises out of the deep recesses of the earth to see the light of day; a few years later this will be the plot of his first masterpiece, "The Kraken"; by 1832 these subterranean breakthroughs are explicitly used as an emblem of the poet's psychological processes:

> Pierced through with knotted thorns of barren pain,
>   Deep in forethought of dark calamities,
>   Sick of the coming time and coming woe,
> As one that tramples some volcanic plain
>   And through the yawning rifts and chasms hears
>   The scummy sulphur seething far below
> And dares not to advance or to retire
>   But with a wan discoloured countenance
>   Remaining still, lamenteth bitterly
> For fear the hidden wells of scorching fire
>   Should spout between the clefts and shower flame
>   And flicker round his body that he die.

("'Pierced through with knotted thorns of barren pain,'" ll. 1–12)

Wordsworth found much that was valuable in the overflow of powerful emotions; Byron found such overflow ruinous, though capable of conferring a degraded nobility upon the sufferer; Tennyson imagines himself a little boy paralyzed because his thumb is incapable of stanching the flow behind the crumbling dyke.

Everywhere in his early poems Tennyson considers himself a creature split in two: on the one hand, a great emotional surge or intellectual exaltation, equally scary, and, on the other, an infant overwhelmed alike by body and by soul. The irruption of Krakens, polyps, giants, "Mammoth and Mastodonte" ("'Pierced through,'"

l. 31) is usually associated with the poet's preoccupation with his own body, with nervous convulsive forces that impinge and threaten; in "'Pierced through,'" just after he imagines his precarious position on the volcanic plain, he shows himself

(ll. 16–18)
> Walled round, shut up, imbarred, moaning for light,
> A carcase in the coffin of this flesh,
> Pierced through with loathly worms of utter death.

The last two lines appear in an earlier poem, "Perdidi Diem," in which they continue: "My soul is but the eternal mystic lamp, / Lighting that charnel damp." The poet's body, then, is a corpse, but preternaturally alive with the fever of its decomposition; his soul stands above, illuminating, a detached observer, like the moony eye of "Armageddon," but curiously sinister:

(ll. 19–28)
> I must needs pore upon the mysteries
> Of my own infinite Nature and torment
> My spirits with a fruitless discontent:
> As in the malignant light
> Of a dim, dripping, moon-enfolding night,
> Young ravens fallen from their cherishing nest
> On the elm-summit, flutter in agony
> With a continual cry
> About its roots, and fluttering trail and spoil
> Their new plumes on the misty soil.

Mother does not come. As an ego, a striver, a maker of choices, a reasonable and finite being, the poet is a ruined baby bird; he can imagine what is infinite in him only as an upwelling of chaos or as a malevolent state of self-detachment, self-inspection, self-loathing. Two sublimities beckon, epileptic seizure and schizophrenic distraction—derangement and disengagement.

As "Perdidi Diem" continues, the poet attempts to convert the soul's "mystic lamp" from the agency of a morbid introspection, self-torture, to the agency of religious vision; the poet declaims, in his most Romantic, incantatory manner, upon "Heaven, an inconceivable cone / Of vision-shadowing vans and claspèd palms" (ll. 58–59), upon the beat of the thunder of God's heart that informs even the outer bounds of the universe. But, as we have seen in "Armageddon," these extremities of vision never come without peril, the peril of self-effacement or self-idolatry; Tennyson is never comfortable in such altitudes of the soul, never convinced of the propriety of such affectation of loftiness. Again and again, when the poet attempts to be ringing, confident, secure in his belief or his vision, a mocking, debunking voice will beset him. Tennyson is, as Auden has said, the poet of the nursery, the poet of weakness, of the infant crying in the night (*In Memoriam* 54); the fantasy of oneself as a gurgling boy—"Thrice happy state again to be / The trustful infant on the knee" ("Supposed Confessions," ll. 40–41)—is never far from his mind, and always yields to a kind of fantastic self-pity: the little lamb is led to the slaughter,

> and his native slope,
> Where he was wont to leap and climb,
> Floats from his sick and filmèd eyes,
> And something in the darkness draws
> His forehead earthward, and he dies.

("Supposed Confessions," ll. 164–68)

Psychologists refer to the condition of our inability to remember anything in the first years of our life as infantile amnesia. To Wordsworth, infantile amnesia provided a blank tablet on which he could trace intricate fancies of antenatal glory, after which he stiffened into prosaic numb adulthood; to Tennyson, infantile amnesia was a condition of divine oblivion, an unattainable refuge from the terror of too much feeling and the terror of too little feeling. Never can a man reenter his mother's womb; he is expelled into a "damnèd vacillating state" ("Supposed Confessions," l. 190), vacillating between the monsters of the body and the soul's lunar remoteness, apathy.

Perhaps it is the general fate of the most original and powerful mythopoeic imaginations to be able to invent one, and only one, class of myth. Tennyson's great myth, stated in a dozen poems, has to do with the inadequacy of retreat, the impropriety of living in private fantasies. It is a myth that condemns the soul's presumption in wrapping itself in its own images. In its simplest form it presents the poet's love of overkeen sensations, images of such rare splendor that they tend to exclude whatever is lower, grosser, coarser than they; and then the myth shows this engrossment as a kind of depravity, a state of being impossible to sustain; and at last the myth offers some hint of an alternative orientation for the poet, by which he can confront what he had previously ignored, turn his imagination downward to the humble, the natural. It is as if Tennyson knew only one thing, that Romantic self-absorption was a state of damnation and must be rejected; but that, at the same time, such dangerous magnificence was still the supreme matter of poetry and therefore not entirely capable of repudiation. He developed his peculiar myth in order to write high visionary poetry while at the same time escaping the taint of sublimity; the sin had to be committed before it could be proved sinful. The celestial muse is more a demon than an angel, insofar as she leads the poet to consider worthless the honest palpable reality that surrounds him; yet he cannot comfortably espouse the muse of banalities, either.

Tennyson's first attempt to state his major myth is probably the long narrative poem "The Lover's Tale" (1828–32), in which a story by Boccaccio is ingeniously twisted into a psychological romance. The narrator, Julian, loves his cousin and foster-sister, Camilla, who loves not him but Lionel; the marriage of Camilla and Lionel provokes in Julian all manner of edifying hallucination. Julian is the first of Tennyson's important narcissists; his love for Camilla is an everted self-love:

> She was my foster-sister: on one arm
> The flaxen ringlets of our infancies
> Wandered, the while we rested: one soft lap
> Pillowed us both: a common light of eyes
> Was on us as we lay: our baby lips,
> Kissing one bosom, ever drew from thence
> The stream of life, one stream, one life, one blood,
> One sustenance, which, still as thought grew large,
> Still larger moulding all the house of thought,
> Made all our tastes and fancies like, perhaps—
> All—all but one.

(1.227–37)

Camilla is a surrogate identical twin; Julian wishes to share with her a womblike felicity, unconscious, involved, indistinct; it is the other side of the Tristan and Isolde story, the wish of lovers to be inextricable not in death but before birth. Camilla, alas, is exogamous and not taken with Julian's fantasies of metaphysical incest; Narcissus moons after his image on a film of water, but that image spurns his kisses.

The specular, self-infatuated character of Julian's love is clearest in a deleted passage:

Eye feeding upon eye with deep intent;
And mine with love too high to be exprest,
Arrested in its sphere, and ceasing from
All contemplation of all forms, did pause
To worship mine own image, laved in light,
The centre of the splendours, all unworthy
Of such a shrine—mine image in her eyes
By diminution made most glorious,
Moved with their motions, as those eyes were moved
With motions of the soul, as my heart beat
Time to the melody of her's.

(Ricks,
p. 304,
ll. [6]–[16])

As Christopher Ricks has noticed, there is an echo here of the passage in "Armageddon" in which the poet speaks of falling down before his own soul and worshiping it. In each poem the narrator beholds his own image beginning to saturate all of creation, beginning to exclude all that is not itself; to Julian, Camilla is not a person, with her own will, her own traits, but a vehicle for apotheosis, a living mirror upon which little Julians tremble, dance, multiply. It is easy to see why she does not wish to surrender to his annihilating embrace; but her assertion of her independence drives Julian mad. The poem is full of suggestions of the unhealthiness of Julian's narcissism; for example, when Julian thinks of how he and Camilla slept in the same cradle, mouth against mouth, dreaming the same dream, clasped in uncanny intimacy, he swoons and languishes at the idea,

as though
A man in some still garden should infuse
Rich atar in the bosom of the rose,
Till, drunk with its own wine, and overfull

(1.262–67)

> Of sweetness, and in smelling of itself,
> It fall on its own thorns.

The rose, drunk on its own fragrance, falls on its own thorns; it is a remarkably hermetic, involved simile of the collapse and self-destruction of the self-preoccupied man.

But the inevitable result of Romantic experimentation with overextended, swollen states of being is not manifest until a passage in which Julian describes his fainting after Camilla's confession that she loves Lionel:

> Would I had lain
> Until the plaited ivy-tress had wound
> Round my worn limbs, and the wild brier had driven
> Its knotted thorns through my unpaining brows,
> (1.606–14)   Leaning its roses on my faded eyes.
> The wind had blown above me, and the rain
> Had fallen upon me, and the gilded snake
> Had nestled in this bosom-throne of Love,
> But I had been at rest for evermore.

A character like Wordsworth's leech-gatherer is only half discriminated from the landscape over which he wanders; but here Julian's absorption into nature is a sign, not of noble unanimity, but of fatal self-surrender, a dispersal, an incoherence, a descent into the inhuman, the inorganic. All through Tennyson's career we meet these creatures who, through excess of feeling, have slipped into a state of woozy torpor, barbarian but harmless, subhuman but not crude— as if Tennyson believed that all men who surrendered to their natural selves would become innocent and childish, languageless like Enoch Arden, dim and shapeless like the Lotos-Eaters, no longer sufficiently defined to be beset by pain. (Tennyson's villains are never of this sort but are instead typically stiffs, swells, and dandies, calculating and overcivilized, like Maud's fiancé.) Such emblems as the rose that blossoms through Julian's brain, or the snake that uncurls itself from Julian's heart, constitute the tangible expressions of the emotions that were balked, repressed, as long as he remained an integral man; his dissolution at once gives body to his feelings and releases him from them. Similarly, the Lotos-Eaters make such a fetish of their favorite flower because it not only controls and specifies what they feel—mild-minded melancholy— but also embodies their feeling as well, acts as a kind of totem, a communal exterior soul; the lotos blossoms everywhere, its pollen saturates the air, and the men wander through this affective landscape, this ubiquity of mollifying, as if through some vast softened brain. This is the pleasure of living in a deranged landscape: where one's identity is inscribed at large, over the whole of nature, there one is relieved of the obligation to act, the fret of being.

The theme of pan-natural narcissism is still clearer in a late poem, "The Voyage of Maeldune" (1880), in which the several islands embody diverse styles of self-indulgence; a man can make himself individual, distinct, incisive, man-shaped, only by self-restraint, taciturnity, abstraction, holding back; while preoccupation with one's feelings leads to a smeared, gregarious, cloudy state of being, in which the line of demarcation between oneself and one's environment grows faint. Nature bulges, grows charged with emotion, thick and clogged with significant emblem, while the men within it grow oddly depleted, nerveless, rapt at the spectacle of the expressive landscape. The sentient heart blanches, fades, perishes, so that the emotion it contains may become strong, spectacular; it is this that gives such force to the end of the first part of *Maud,* when the speaker imagines Maud walking over the dust of his decomposed body, imagines how the dust "Would start and tremble under her feet, / And blossom in purple and red." A man cannot be characterized by the emotion he feels; his emotion slips out of him, grows huge and detached, an attribute of the cosmos, nebulous, shifting.

It is not surprising, then, that the reader of "The Lover's Tale" cannot feel that he has any secure knowledge about the protagonist; there is a pervasive Julianness but no Julian, no focused character to engage the reader's sympathy or interest. Indeed Julian is little but a pretext to investigate disembodiment and dementia. We have seen how Julian's body threatens to disintegrate from the sheer pressure of expression; but the loss of his mind is the true subject of the poem. In his delirium he imagines he sees a funeral cortege bearing the dead Camilla; and it seems to him as if his mind were at once

lord and slave, as if his imagination were at once abnormally potent
in that it can realize such detailed and picturesque fantasies, and
abnormally feeble in that it is helpless, at the mercy of its obses-
sions:

Alway the inaudible invisible thought,
Artificer and subject, lord and slave,
Shaped by the audible and visible,
Moulded the audible and visible;
All crispèd sounds of wave and leaf and wind,
Flattered the fancy of my fading brain;

(2.101–6)

Julian understands his mind as a kind of gross mechanism for
altering the harmless Arcadia in which he lives into a variety of
vivid, exacerbated images of his pain.

It is at this moment in the poem that Julian starts to change
from a psychiatrist with only one patient—himself—into an art
critic; and, similarly, the poem shows itself as a myth about the
enslaving qualities of the aesthetic image. He remembers a picture
that Camilla had drawn long ago, a picture of a vessel tossed in a
stormy sea; he savors the intimacy that he and Camilla felt in gazing
at this painting. So far it seems as if the soul defended itself from
suffering by becoming a student of satisfying images of melancholy, a connoisseur of imaginary funerals, an abstract spectator of
rich sad memories of bygone joy; every image of grief is a deflection, an assuaging of that grief. But Julian has felt a certain pressure
to participate in these images; for instance, when he hallucinates the
funeral procession he rushes up to the weeping Lionel to confess his
love for Camilla, then faints and falls and dies away at Lionel's
feet—as if Lionel were himself no more than a surrogate expression
for Julian's loud love, loud sorrow. In the episode of the painting,
however, Julian finds a more remarkable way of participating in his
dream: he sees the painted vessel beginning to heave on the painted
sea, and suddenly he feels that he and Camilla are foundering in the
painted whirlpool:

Aloud she shrieked;
My heart was cloven with pain; I wound my arms
About her: we whirled giddily; the wind

(2.196–205)

Sung; but I clasped her without fear: her weight
Shrank in my grasp, and over my dim eyes,
And parted lips which drank her breath, down-hung
The jaws of Death: I, groaning, from me flung
Her empty phantom: all the sway and whirl
Of the storm dropt to windless calm, and I
Down weltered through the dark ever and ever.

Just as Julian's body tends to diffuse into the surrounding landscape, so his mind cannot maintain aesthetic distance, cannot keep itself separate from what it contemplates. The picture, which had seemed a refuge from his present misery, a pleasing object for sentimental reflection, instead engulfs him; instead of being emblematic, mediatory—"The poesy of childhood; my lost love / Symbolled in storm" (2.181–82)—it is point-blank, immediate, irresistible. The fantasy exposes its purely fantastical nature, for Camilla is known to be merely an empty phantom, and yet Julian cannot extricate himself from this overtly unreal seascape, this condition of damnation.

This, then, is the pattern of action in Tennyson's early poetry: the protagonist tries to relieve himself of excessive emotion, emotion denied its usual outlet, by means of two strategies, both of which partake of Romantic sublimity: first, a systematic derangement of the cosmos, so that nature will bear the burden of the suffering; and second, a systematic disengagement from the vicarious images employed to suffer in one's stead. These strategies fail, for derangement exhausts and disengagement famishes; and the moment of collapse, when all the keen anguish, no longer mitigated by sublimity, falls on one's head, is the beginning of sanity, prosaic health, good government, the whole happy commonplace world. Tennyson was a member of the first generation of poets following the great elaboration of the literary postures of sublimity that took place during the Romantic period; his protagonists continually adopt the poses of Romantic inflation—I am all that I behold (that is, derangement), or, I transcend all that I behold (that is, disengagement)—but these devices are no longer an enhancement of human feeling but instead an escape from human feeling, a system of rhetoric rather than authentic self-revelation. Tennyson is, like his predecessors, fascinated by the state in which the mind is so entirely filled with its object that it cannot entertain any other—I quote again from Burke's description of the sublime—but he is suspicious of the literary conventions of this arrestedness, this ecstasy, conventions stiffened into something like parody. Tennyson must engage himself in deflating the false sublime; but this is not easy for a poet who does not always seem confident of his ability to distinguish the false sublime from the true.

Part One

―――∽◦∾―――

ART VS. NATURE

III

————— ❦ —————

The Prison of Mirrors

IN THE NEXT STAGE OF TENNYSON'S CAREER, his first maturity, his poetry becomes more self-regarding: the imagination, now more than a means by which a poem is produced, is often the subject of the poem. In fact there are two different imaginations at work, engaged in an uncomfortable competition: a faculty of mimesis that dotes upon the definite shapes of the sensible world, and a shivery, celestial faculty that creates images beyond the range of our usual eyesight, images either overelaborate or improperly constituted, not quite coherent. There is an imagination that is unobtrusive, tame, in easy conformity to nature—

(*Winter's Tale* 4.4.95–97)

> This is an art
> Which does mend Nature, change it rather, but
> The art itself is Nature.

—and there is an imagination that resists and deprecates, isolates itself from the natural. In this chapter we shall study Tennyson's criticism of this high imagination.

Some instinct in Tennyson, perhaps associated with his deep engagement with language itself, kept suggesting that the sublime imagination was hostile, not only, as we have seen, to integrity and sanity, but at last even to language and art. The artist who, like Julian in "The Lover's Tale," dreams of decomposing into the world of his dreams, will find his vocation as artist dubious; the imagination that, like Julian's, cannot keep itself distinct from the images it studies, will not long retain its vigor, its identity. The important sections of "The Lover's Tale" were written in 1827–28, when Tennyson was still in his teens; by the time of his first annus mirabilis, 1832–33, when much of his great poetry was written and much of his finest later work conceived, these anxieties could be given a clearer, more satisfying expression. "The Lady of Shalott"

(1832), "The Palace of Art" (1832), and "The Two Voices" (1833) are all indictments of high imagination. In these and many lesser poems Tennyson struggles to find some earthier, more humble and tenable function for the imagination as well; but his great theme is the display of sublimity in its most devastating, extraterrestrial aspects, a dazzle of image making designed to frighten us, and himself, so that we will hanker after some more reasonable, manageable, ethical, commonplace activity.

In "Armageddon" Tennyson conceived of his image-making power as a faculty somewhat extrinsic from himself—"I could have fallen down / Before my own strong soul and worshipped it" (2.49–50)—but by 1832, in "The Lady of Shalott," the imagination seems to have abstracted itself from every physical or moral aspect of the human and to be perishing in the rarefied air. The mechanical processes of Julian's mind in "The Lover's Tale," his breaking asunder of his forest life and refashioning it into a private artifice, have elaborated themselves into a cottage industry: the Lady of Shalott sits in her high room, weaving a tapestry depicting the images reflected on a mirror trained through a window upon the passing scene. Tennyson refers to the tapestry as her "web," and the word *web,* combined with the complicated optical apparatus, reminds us of the skein of eye threads, the pulsing retinal effects of "Armageddon"; here imagination and eye have swollen into their own vast obscure chamber, penetrable only by the tiny aperture of the pupil. A colorful pageant of images forms and reforms beneath her disinterested gaze, but when at last her bland vigilance is broken by the figure of Lancelot and the sexual longing he arouses, the whole system of estrangement and self-idolatry shatters; the web blows away, the mirror cracks, and she descends into the public world, urgent, fatal, and actual. She has no other function than to die picturesquely, for the imagination, rapt in its filmy impossibilities, seems incompetent and feeble when dragged down to earth; among its exuberant dizzy fantasies it was queen, but it grows insubstantial, wraithlike, as it tries to cope with flesh and blood.

Again the Lady of Shalott, like the speakers of "Armageddon" and "Perdidi Diem" and "Supposed Confessions," appears to be a

child. The poem is so full of mystery and high strangeness that it is
hard to be certain of this, but in "Lancelot and Elaine" (1858), in
which the same story is expanded into one of the *Idylls of the King,* it
is clear that Elaine is an infatuated adolescent who comes to grief
from a kind of implacable, even noble, silliness. In the later poem
Tennyson recapitulates many of the motifs of the "The Lady of
Shalott," though he often transforms them from the elements of
lofty mythopoeia into charming fatuities:

Elaine the fair, Elaine the loveable,
Elaine, the lily maid of Astolat,
High in her chamber up a tower to the east
Guarded the sacred shield of Lancelot;
Which first she placed where morning's earliest ray
Might strike it, and awake her with the gleam;
Then fearing rust or soilure fashioned for it
A case of silk, and braided thereupon
All the devices blazoned on the shield
In their own tinct, and added, of her wit,
A border fantasy of branch and flower,
And yellow-throated nestling in the nest.

(ll. 1–12)

The Lady of Shalott's mirror is now the shield of an unknown
Knight (Lancelot) from which the sunlight gleams, for Elaine views
sunrise, her whole world, through the medium of her fantastical
obsession; the Lady of Shalott's web has contracted to the embroi-
dered covering of the shield, an obvious emblem for Elaine's tendency to conceal, extenuate, or find surrogates, to prefer the image
of the thing to the thing itself.

In "The Lady of Shalott" allegory is irresistible; the soul of the
artist enacts a dream about the poverty of its transfigurations of the
real world. In "Lancelot and Elaine" this large drama has been
reduced to a tale of juvenile pathology. Yet in it certain features
recall, and in some ways extend and revise, the myth of 1832. For
instance, we are told that Lancelot is no longer young, his face
marred from many battles, his mood often melancholic from sin,
but Elaine has a different image of him:

> And all night long his face before her lived,
> As when a painter, poring on a face,
> Divinely through all hindrance finds the man
(ll. 329–35)   Behind it, and so paints him that his face,
> The shape and colour of a mind and life,
> Lives for his children, ever at its best
> And fullest.

This is how the imagination operates in its lower, unpretentious, reasonable, painterly mode: it uncovers the essential, most characteristic face beneath the blemishes of accident. It is true that Elaine is living in unreality—she imagines that Lancelot's moments of good cheer and tenderness are due to his affection for her and not to his courtly manner—but she is nevertheless developing an image in her head according to the correct rules of low art, the rules by which art seeks to interpret and perfect nature and human life, not to usurp them.

Yet many traces of the Lady of Shalott's narcissism, her involution in the refuge of art, remain. Elaine's stylized picture of Lancelot allows her to overlook much that she wishes to remain ignorant of; and after the catastrophe, when she no longer has any illusion about marrying Lancelot, she populates her empty room with Lancelot's image, an image that forms on every surface:

> So in her tower alone the maiden sat:
> His very shield was gone; only the case,
(ll. 982–86)   Her own poor work, her empty labour, left.
> But still she heard him, still his picture formed
> And grew between her and the pictured wall.

All reality has abandoned her, man and shield alike; clinging to her evacuated images, she craves only further emptiness, death. It seemed that the Lady of Shalott left her room out of a frustrated desire to immerse herself in the real, to participate in human life; but, in the *Idyll,* Elaine reaches out, in excited desolation, further and further into dreaminess and artifice. Without hope of realizing her fantasy, without hope of escaping from it, she seeks only to publicize her fantasy, to make herself an image as spectacular as those that beguile her imagination. She commands that her bier be floated down the river: "I go in state to court, to meet the Queen. /

There surely I shall speak for mine own self" (ll. 1117–18). Dead, translated into an image, Elaine will be eloquent. Eventually, Arthur orders Elaine's image, along with Lancelot's shield, to be carved on her tomb; but this final declension into art seems almost superfluous, so thoroughly has Elaine managed to convert her death into a theatrical celebration of herself, complete with a queen sprinkling diamonds in the wake of her funeral barge. The imagination, caught up in its glassy world, is unable to cause any direct alteration in the reality that lies beneath its images—Elaine can never, never embrace Lancelot—but it can provoke in the public at large a momentary sense of awe, a brief confusion of the imaginary and the actual, a sudden accession of myth or drama or meaningfulness that heightens, quickens, our usual world—Elaine cannot make Lancelot love her but she can invoke in him wonder. The act of image making is likely to destroy the image maker, but he will be venerated nonetheless.

Among the prominent motifs in the stories of the Lady of Shalott and Elaine are diamonds, mirrors, and a river—in short, glass and water. When Tennyson makes up stories about the operation of the high imagination, he usually turns to such images, with their complicated suggestions of Narcissus' pool, shimmering unrealities, confusing trompe-l'oeil effects. Indeed one can deduce from these image patterns a mythology about the evolution of high imagination from the poet's carefree and potent youth to his cramped, constricted old age.

According to Tennyson's mythology of art, the poet's imagination, when he is young, is like a river. In a juvenile poem called "The Poet's Mind" (1830), Tennyson addresses those who would violate the poet's sanctuary of images, the landscape of his reverie:

> Vex not thou the poet's mind;
>   For thou canst not fathom it.
>   Clear and bright it should be ever,
> Flowing like a crystal river;
> Bright as light, and clear as wind.

(ll. 3–7)

The poet's mind is a rapid stream reflecting a bright hurried kingdom of images. This metaphor recurs in a later poem, "Youth"

(1833), written near the end of Tennyson's great year, which begins with one of Tennyson's best descriptions of the vivifying, kinesthetic power of the poet's young imagination:

> Youth, lapsing through fair solitudes,
>   Poured by long glades and meadowy mounds,
> Crowned with soft shade her deepening floods
>   That washed her shores with blissful sounds:

(ll. 1–8)

> Her silver eddies in their play
>   Drove into lines and studs of light
> The image of the sun by day,
>   The image of the moon by night.

The impetuous rush of faculty grasps the natural world, makes it vibrant. The disbeliever in art is not the enemy of this flow; the enemy is, instead, mere growing old. The voice that once shook the stars becomes mellow, nostalgic. In a remarkable deleted stanza, the original end of the poem, Tennyson shows that the river of youth eventually stops dead, crystallizes into glass:

(Ricks, p. 578, ll. [5]–[8])

> I was like purple glass, that glows
>   Most rich and warm, but if more nigh
> You look through it, it only shows
>   A frosted land, a chilly sky.

Age stains, thickens, renders cold and empty, those images of nature that once purled so effortlessly. As the poet grows human, emotionally rich, complicated, mature, his art grows lax, opaque, dull. The imagination ought to be a transparent medium for the fluent generation of images; but slowly it thickens, turns inward on the poet, until he can see only a blur, or his own face mirrored, impeding, closing in.

I believe that this is the evolution of the myth of "The Lady of Shalott" and "The Palace of Art": as the poet ages, his imagination grows disjunct, static, morbid, the river turns into a mirror. In "The Lady of Shalott" the imagination seems puzzled, hesitant, disheveled, uncertain how to behave in this odd situation; the prisoner of glass wishes to escape without quite knowing what escape entails. Christopher Ricks has pointed out that one of Tennyson's sources is Spenser's *Faerie Queene* 3.2, which contains the mirror, the tower, and the glimpse; but it is also true that, in "Lancelot and Elaine," something of Shelley's use of the symbols of cave and tower can be seen. Yeats said that for Shelley the cave and the tower symbolized the self-enclosed mind and the outward-streaming mind (*Essays and Introductions*, p. 87); and in Tennyson we find that Elaine ascends from the sociable cave in which she nurses Lancelot and schemes to woo him to the private tower in which she invents her desolate fantasy. By descending from her high room to the river, the Lady of Shalott seems vaguely moved by the hope that the mirror will once again thaw into a river, that she may actually move toward, attain, the object of her contemplation; but the process of freezing, like the process of growing old itself, seems irreversible. The imagination that huddles glassily within its own confines, that delights in thin second-hand images of nature, can never hope to enjoy again the old intimacy and charm of the natural world. The mirror can break but it cannot melt.

We have seen that the sublime imagination is both a giddy joy and a source of terror; and this mythology of river and mirror is Tennyson's attempt to articulate how the imagination changes its tenor from mania to depression.

If the Lady of Shalott seems somewhat unsure of her role, a mere apprentice at solipsism, the Soul in "The Palace of Art" (1832) is secure, malevolent. Here the imagination stiffens into a blood-thirsty Babylonian queen, a Semiramis not satisfied until her private world is drained of all its juices, rendered stony and vitreous, an Acrasia who has abandoned even the semblance of nature. In a passage, most of which was deleted after the first publication in 1832—one could compile a choice little anthology out of Tennyson's rejections—the Soul is presented as a zoetrope, a toy that produces the illusion of motion when the spectator stares through the slits of a cylindrical contraption of whirling images reflected on a central spindle made of mirrors:

> So that my soul beholding in her pride
>   All these, from room to room did pass;
> And all things that she saw she multiplied,
>   A manyfacèd glass;

(Ricks, pp. 408–9, ll. [1]–[24])

And, being both the sower and the seed,
    Remaining in herself became
All that she saw, Madonna, Ganymede,
    Or the Asiatic dame—

Still changing, as a lighthouse in the night
    Changeth athwart the gleaming main,
From red to yellow, yellow to pale white,
    Then back to red again.

"From change to change four times within the womb
    The brain is moulded," she began,
"So through all phases of all thought I come
    Into the perfect man.

"All nature widens upward: evermore
    The simpler essence lower lies.
More complex is more perfect, owning more
    Discourse, more widely wise.

"I take possession of men's minds and deeds.
    I live in all things great and small.
I dwell apart, holding no forms of creeds,
    But contemplating all."

This device is an improvement over the simple camera obscura of "The Lady of Shalott." The mirror is not static, trained upon a single pastoral scene, but instead rotates with a feverish but illusory sense of motion, a mirror trying to pretend that it is a river; there is no longer even a peephole through which glimpses of an external world may enter, for all the windows in the Palace of Art are themselves stained-glass images, leaden and stifling. The Soul is at once detached, transcendentally aloof—"remaining in herself"— and a characterless film that identifies itself with every image in the Palace—the prism circles through every color in the spectrum and yet remains neutral glass. The Soul, then, simultaneously manifests both the sublimities noted earlier: it is engulfed by everything it beholds and yet remains above, indifferent. The imagination claims that it is the highest human faculty, that all animal passion, all intellectual conviction, attenuate, become anesthetized in the bright images of passion and conviction which the imagination provides, images that make a mural of the whole earth and sky. Art smothers nature and provides manipulable surrogates over which the Soul may swoon, make histrionic shows of its rapture or its disengagement, in which the Soul may dwell in a perpetual mock-sublime. Where there is no external source of validation, no means by which the true may be distinguished from the untrue, the imagination dwells in ever falser relationships to its own goals.

Of course passion and conviction are not conquered by this overweening imagination; they are only repressed, and at last take their vengeance upon the Soul that has tried to supersede them. The higher faculties may pretend that the lower faculties are negligible, but man's homely affections will not be pushed aside so easily. The representations are destroyed by the moods they represented, tried to overcome. It is instructive to study those pictures that Tennyson devised in verse to satisfy the Soul's "every mood / And change" (ll. 59–60):

> Or the maid-mother by a crucifix,
>   In tracts of pasture sunny-warm,
> Beneath branch-work of costly sardonyx
>   Sat smiling, babe in arm.
>
> Or in a clear-walled city on the sea,
>   Near gilded organ-pipes, her hair
> Wound with white roses, slept St Cecily;
>   An angel looked at her.
>
> Or thronging all one porch of Paradise
>   A group of Houris bowed to see
> The dying Islamite, with hands and eyes
>   That said, We wait for thee.
>
> Or mythic Uther's deeply-wounded son
>   In some fair space of sloping greens
> Lay, dozing in the vale of Avalon,
>   And watched by weeping queens.

(ll. 93–108)

Christianity is demoted to one of the several mythologies that articulate human nature and desire; it is, like the others, chiefly decorative, soothing, an illustration from a child's Bible. The subjects of these four pictures consist of a baby, an allegorical figment, and two dying men, as if strenuousness, rigor, sweaty effort had already been purged from human life. The pictures are emblems of the passage from life into art: the smiling Christ child seems half resolved into the encrusted jewels that surround him; St. Cecilia, whose song drew an angel down in Dryden's great ode, seems herself ready to be wafted back to heaven; the dying Islamite has abandoned his earthly struggles in favor of the soft, infinitely yielding, bloodless fruit of a sexual heaven; and Arthur sleeps, satiated from his wounds, while weeping queens express the emotion from which he is, blissfully, free. In these last two pictures a passive, unconscious, dying figure is surrounded by mythy creatures who indicate, frame, illuminate, call attention to his condition; the Islamite and Arthur are in a posture similar to the Soul's, for the Soul is herself an inert, moribund thing enveloped by pretty images that emote with theatrical gestures, images that do her emoting for her. Some of the pictures allude to more potent passions:

Or sweet Europa's mantle blew unclasped,
　　From off her shoulder backward borne:
(ll. 117–20)　From one hand drooped a crocus: one hand grasped
　　The mild bull's golden horn.

However, the Titianesque scene is slack, disemboweled, neutralized. The pictures, while pretending to be a complete anthology of human passions and intellectual excellence, manage to suggest that there is something futile, annulled, at the center of all this busy image making.

What is the imagination to do? Its very fecundity tends to lock it in the museum of its own images. The more conscious of its power it becomes, the more it becomes a depraved tyrant. It seems that Tennyson wants the imagination to be humbled, enfeebled, made a servant of the more engaging and responsible aspects of one's being. In a poem written not long after "The Palace of Art," "The Gardener's Daughter" (1833–34), the protagonist is a love-stricken painter conscious of the limitations of his skill—indeed

Tennyson's English Idyls are full of well-mannered, unassuming, loyal and considerate poets and painters who never take on themselves the burden of genius. When the protagonist sees a drawing of an attractive girl made by a fellow painter, he says, "half in earnest, half in jest," that the excellence of the drawing is due not to his friend but to Love, "A more ideal Artist he than all" (ll. 23, 25). Here is a man not likely to fall into the aesthetic heresy of "The Palace of Art." When the protagonist catches his first sight of the gardener's daughter, he sees her with a painterly gaze:

> One arm aloft—
> Gowned in pure white, that fitted to the shape—
> Holding the bush, to fix it back, she stood,
> A single stream of all her soft brown hair
> Poured on one side: the shadow of the flowers
> Stole all the golden gloss, and, wavering
> Lovingly lower, trembled on her waist—
> Ah, happy shade—and still went wavering down,
> But, ere it touched a foot, that might have danced
> The greensward into greener circles, dipt,
> And mixed with shadows of the common ground!

(ll. 124–34)

The movement of the verse is unusual: full of large breathless gestures, enjambed, rapid but convoluted, as if it imitated the hasty sketching, shading, scumbling of a pencil, or the eye's dartings and lingerings over a finished drawing. I take this as a model act (by Tennyson's standards) of mimesis, the low mode of image making that dignifies the commonplace; instead of the mannered, virtuosic, overgorgeous stuff in the Palace of Art, an art of bravura and presumptuousness, we have the subtle verse-image of a simple comely girl, a portrait in which the artist is enamored more with his subject than with himself, an unpretentious album leaf instead of the whole Louvre transferred to Xanadu.

And yet "The Palace of Art" is a much better poem than "The Gardener's Daughter." The imagination exercising its proper function lacks the tension of the imagination grown wild. In fact, the English Idyls, like "The Gardener's Daughter," attracted Tennyson's mild bourgeois reading public, while the next generation of

poets was drawn to his mythopoeic works. The rhetoric proper to
the Soul in "The Palace of Art"—"the sower and the seed" who
"became / All that she saw"—a rhetoric anticipated in "The Lover's
Tale" and in Blake's *Jerusalem* and analogous to that of Emerson's
"Brahma," the rhetoric of a Hindu god who is indifferently perceiver and perceived, actor and acted-upon—became the basis of
such late Victorian experiments in sublimity as Swinburne's "Hertha"
(1871):

> I am that which began;
>   Out of me the years roll;
> Out of me God and man;
>   I am equal and whole;
> God changes, and man, and the form of them bodily; I
>   am the soul. . . .

(ll. 1–5,
36–40)

> I the grain and the furrow,
>   The plow-cloven clod
> And the plowshare drawn thorough,
>   The germ and the sod,
> The deed and the doer, the seed and the sower, the dust
>   which is God.

The condition that Tennyson fears is exactly what Swinburne wants,
and what the aesthetic movement wants; indeed, it is almost fair to
say that Tennyson created the movement by denouncing it. Swinburne's "The Garden of Prosperine" is little more than "The Lotos-
Eaters," rendered deader, waxier, more involuted, more delectable.
The reader of literature feels a sense of satisfaction when he comes
to the second (more fevered and urgent) Tennyson, D. H. Lawrence, much of whose work is also a denunciation of the aesthetic
movement, to whom such ladies of Shalott as Hermione in *Women
in Love* and Yvette in *The Virgin and the Gipsy* are always the
greatest villains. In the "Nascent" section of his "Dreams Old and
Nascent" he rewrites "The Palace of Art":

> The world is a painted memory, where coloured shapes
>   Of old, spent lives linger blurred and warm;
> An endless tapestry the past has woven, drapes
>   The halls of my mind, compelling my life to conform.

(ll. 1–12)

I have lived delighted in the halls of the past
Where dead men's lives glow gently, and iron hurts
No more, and money stinks not, and death at last
Is only sad men taking off their shirts.

But now I think I have seen it all, and now
I feel thick walls of stone behind the arras.
I am shut in, a prisoner, I know not how.
And past lives hamper me, clog and embarrass.

Lawrence originally wrote "fresco" for "memory" in the first line.
We have the same anesthetizing, the same smothering in images, as
in Tennyson's poem; and in Lawrence's "New Heaven and Earth"
we have the same rhetorical pattern:

I was so weary of the world,
I was so sick of it,
everything was tainted with myself,
skies, trees, flowers, birds, water,
people, houses, streets, vehicles, machines,
nations, armies, war, peace-talking,
work, recreation, governing, anarchy,
it was all tainted with myself, I knew it all to start with
because it was all myself.

(ll. 13–26)

When I gathered flowers, I knew it was myself plucking
my own flowering.
When I went in a train, I knew it was myself travelling
by my own invention.
When I heard the cannon of the war, I listened with my
own ears to my own destruction.
When I saw the torn dead, I knew it was my own torn
dead body.
It was all me, I had done it all in my own flesh.

First Lawrence is stifled by history and art; then he is stifled by himself. He dismisses both of these sublime depravities, in "Dreams
Old and Nascent" by a vision of happy railway workers whose
pick-axes break through the close thick walls, in "New Heaven and
Earth" by the immediacy of his wife, a genuine Other whose distinct existence relieves him of the burden of constituting a world, of

seeing his own image reflected in a ubiquity of mirrors. It is pleasing to think that these two men, possessed by such a fierce but equivocal hatred of the heaven of art, may have defined its lineaments, its charms, more exactly than any of its proponents. It may also be that, for the last two centuries, the revulsion against the sublime has been a more fruitful theme than the discovery of it; having spent a long time striving toward the beatific vision, poets must struggle for a while to disengage themselves from it, to grow commonplace, sociable, persuasive, uxorious, to walk with sensible shoes.

The Soul in "The Palace of Art" deflates herself by inflating until she bursts. As she struts, preens, thumps her chest—what else could her speech be but self-celebration, since she is the sole entity in her world, a mirror strolling down halls of mirrors?—the contempt she feels for the men outside her Palace, mere swine, starts to turn into self-contempt. The Soul, abstracted from the body, has understood the body as something loathsome and corrupt, to be excluded at any cost—in a sense the Soul is a Circe who has cast a spell to diminish, to bestialize, every other aspect of the human. But the Soul is so rapt and involute that she cannot really credit the independent existence of anything at all; she can believe only in mirror images, projections, and so all her feelings—pride and scorn alike—logically redound to self-pride, self-scorn. If you are the only fully existent being in your cosmos, your ideas and emotions can have no object other than yourself. The strategy of anesthesia, of reducing life and nature to aesthetic delight, fails; and the Soul's attempts at further abstraction from herself grow more desperate, vertiginous:

> Deep dread and loathing of her solitude
> Fell on her, from which mood was born
> Scorn of herself; again, from out that mood
> Laughter at her self-scorn.

(ll. 229–32)

Empedocles, in Arnold's *Empedocles on Etna* (1852), will wonder if the human mind is incapable of being resolved into the vital immensity of the phenomenal world, wonder whether consciousness is itself not a kind of damnation. Empedocles, expanding a

passage from Byron (*Childe Harold's Pilgrimage* 3.33), sees himself
as a twirling mirror, just like the Soul in "The Palace of Art":

> The outspread world to span
> A cord the gods first slung,
> And then the soul of man
> There, like a mirror, hung,
> And bade the winds through space impel the gusty toy.

(1.2.77–86)

> Hither and thither spins
> The wind-borne, mirroring soul,
> A thousand glimpses wins,
> And never ·sees a whole;
> Looks once, and drives elsewhere, and leaves its last
>   employ.

In both *Empedocles on Etna* and "The Palace of Art," then, the
hero is a mirror that desires to stop being a mirror, a mirror that
wishes to shatter. The mind sickens at its own tenacity, integrity,
disengagement, its inability to lapse into the spontaneous energies
that surround it; the machine cannot stop, it cannot prevent itself
from flattening the world's richness to dead flickering images on
its silvery surfaces. Empedocles feels that intelligence is to some
degree extraterrestrial:

> To the elements it came from
> Everything will return—
> Our bodies to earth,
> Our blood to water,
> Heat to fire,
> Breath to air.
> They were well born, they will be well entombed—
> But mind? . . .

(2.331–38,
345–54)

> But mind, but thought—
> If these have been the master part of us—
> Where will *they* find their parent element?
> What will receive *them,* who will call *them* home?
> But we shall still be in them, and they in us,
> And we shall be the strangers of the world,

And they will be our lords, as they are now;
And keep us prisoners of our consciousness,
And never let us clasp and feel the All
But through their forms, and modes, and stifling veils.

Empedocles then leaps into the boiling volcano in a desperate attempt to disperse that vigilant immiscible phantom of himself that grinds the world to philosophy; Etna, he hopes, will be real and not an image. He commits suicide to make himself human. Tennyson's Soul also goes to the brink of death—the Palace, once an aesthetic refuge from the world that pretended to be coextensive with the world, is at last a "crumbling tomb" (l. 273), shrunk to coffin-size—but draws back, enters a cottage to mourn and pray; and there is some hope that a life of humility, devotion, and public service will make the Palace of Art habitable once again. Narcissus does not drown, but is compelled to leave his pool, to seek out things other than his own face when he dabbles in image making. The most august muse, the muse of the keenest elation, has shown herself to be a shrieking harpy, a despoiler of all the world's banquets; but so far Tennyson has been unable to find a successful replacement for her, a lively and witty lower muse.

Other poems of Tennyson's may suggest that that imagination cures itself of its self-infatuation by falling in love with something, or someone, else. The Soul in "The Palace of Art," if we take her not as an allegory but as a representation, is a rich dowager who, despairing of finding a suitable husband, comforts herself with the thought that in a life so luxurious a new man would be superfluous, an intrusion; indeed an alternate ending to the poem would have the Soul wither into Miss Havisham in *Great Expectations*. In "A Dream of Fair Women," written at the same time as "The Palace of Art," the poet, in a deleted simile at the beginning of the poem, ascends in a balloon—an agreeably mundane variant of the Soul's obnoxious world transcendence in "The Palace of Art"—into a dreamy contemplation of famous mythic and historical women. They reside in a flowery, tendriled, luminous Arcadia—Tennyson himself called it Turneresque—but there are disturbing features in this Elysium of beauty; among the women interrogated by the poet are two sacrificial victims, one suicide, one murdered woman, and one destroyer of men.

Cleopatra is perhaps the most pertinent of the crew:

> She, flashing forth a haughty smile, began:
>   "I governed men by change, and so I swayed
> All moods. 'Tis long since I have seen a man.
>   Once, like the moon, I made

(ll. 129–36)

> "The ever-shifting currents of the blood
>   According to my humour ebb and flow.
> I have no men to govern in this wood:
>   That makes my only woe."

These two stanzas are surprisingly similar to some of the speeches of the Soul in "The Palace of Art." Cleopatra's infinite variety has not grown stale, but, in the absence of any men, it exercises itself in vacuo; a Cleopatra charmed by her own fleeting moods, enchanted with her own glamour, deliberately provoking shifts in the ever shifting currents of her own blood, would be identical to the Palace's haughty Soul. There is, however, a disquieting feeling in the poem that her world-consuming love for Antony, instead of breaking her superb involution, instead of reconciling her to some public life, only managed to lock up Antony in the same destructive sublimity in which the Soul in "The Palace of Art" perishes—as if love pitched to a certain ferocity could make a mutual schizophrenia, a folie à deux. " 'We drank the Libyan Sun to sleep, and lit / Lamps which out-burned Canopus' " (ll. 145–46), says Cleopatra, describing a love that competes with the natural world, a refuge of passion equal to the refuge of art. The result of all their wild kisses is his death, followed by her suicide; this engrossment in love, this exclusion of the world, is no more tenable than the Soul's engrossment in images. Finally Cleopatra tears her robes apart to show the poet her naked breast, the asp's wound; she raises her eyes from the ground, and his eyes dazzle; from "Armageddon" on, the high visionary mode floods the poet's eyes with light.

It is as if Cleopatra briefly succeeded in doing what the Lady of Shalott could not manage to do, to seduce Lancelot into her high room, to keep him prisoner, to feed him with glass and mercury until the sick lovers grew absorbed into the same spectral fantasy. Tennyson had no particularly keen sense for the possibilities of this emotional drama—the horror of solitary involution, not of double involution, is an important theme in his work—but some of his Victorian successors did: Dante Rossetti, in the Willowwood sequence (1868) in his *The House of Life,* writes as follows:

49. WILLOWWOOD—I

I sat with Love upon a woodside well,
Leaning across the water, I and he;
Nor ever did he speak nor looked at me,
But touched his lute wherein was audible
The certain secret thing he had to tell.
Only our mirrored eyes met silently
In the low wave; and that sound came to be
The passionate voice I knew; and my tears fell.
And at their fall, his eyes beneath grew hers;
And with his foot and with his wing-feathers
He swept the spring that watered my heart's drouth.
Then the dark ripples spread to waving hair,
And as I stooped, her own lips rising there
Bubbled with brimming kisses at my mouth.

Narcissus stares into his pool, but, provoked by Love's ventriloquism, Love's image making, he sees an inchoate, hybrid image in which the poet and his dead beloved and Love itself all take shape without becoming discrete entities; the mirror is transparent, the transparency is mirrorlike.

In Rossetti's following sonnets the surrounding woodland is populated by a throng of "mournful forms, for each was she or I"—mute haunting phantoms evoked by the poet's memories of himself and his beloved, phantoms unable to find relief in oblivion, unable to find expression in a real embrace, for the poet's imaginary kiss tastes only of water, glass. Rossetti had drawn pictures of "St Cecily" and "King Arthur and the Weeping Queens" in "The Palace of Art" for Moxon's 1857 illustrated edition of Tennyson; and Willowwood is a kind of Palace, or Grove, of Art in which the only images are the teeming phantoms of the poet and his beloved, interlinked, obsessive, half realized by Love's blurry imagination. The image of the beloved, summoned to the surface in the first sonnet, sinks back into the pool in the last sonnet, grows still more vague and shimmery in Love's transfiguring light. The beloved seems to struggle to materialize, to lift herself from image to reality, but, being dead, she cannot, and must lapse. The poet seems to manifest no healthy state of mind.

D. H. Lawrence, in his essay mocking John Galsworthy, summarizes the plot of Galsworthy's story "The Apple Tree," in which a "young gentleman, in the throes of narcissistic love for his marvellous self, falls for [a little Welsh farm-girl] because she has fallen so utterly and abjectly for him." A grand passion ensues, and he marries her: "But to fill the cup of his vanity, the maid drowns herself. It is funny that maids only seem to do it for these narcissistic young gentlemen who, looking in the pool for their own image, desire the added satisfaction of seeing the face of drowned Ophelia there as well; saving them the necessity of taking the narcissus plunge in person. We have gone one better than the myth. Narcissus, in Mr. Galsworthy, doesn't drown himself. He asks Ophelia, or Megan, kindly to drown herself instead. And in this fiction she actually does. And he feels so *wonderful* about it!" (*Phoenix,* p. 546).

The poet of "Willowwood" seems vulnerable to Lawrence's reproach; the image he kisses in the water has only partially resolved into the drowned Ophelia—it is his own face adorned with a few feathery curls to simulate a woman's. The poet has, so to speak, allowed his beloved to commit his suicide in his stead, and he flatters himself, congratulates himself on the intensity of his feeling, on the pathetic qualities of Love's aria, on his skill at stage decoration. When Rossetti was forced to exhume from his wife's grave the uncopied manuscripts he had buried with her, he illustrated something of the lameness of the attempt to abolish the barriers between poetry writing and human relations, between images of women and genuine corpses; Tennyson's "The Palace of Art" may end abruptly and unsatisfyingly, but one feels that Tennyson, for all his flat exhortations, knew something about the nature of art, about art's power to impoverish as well as to sustain, that Rossetti did not.

In Tennyson's poetry the theme of the prison of mirrors reaches its final form in the Idyll "Merlin and Vivien" (1856). It is possible that Tennyson's study of Arthurian material in the early 1830s, when he wrote "The Lady of Shalott," "Sir Launcelot and Queen Guinevere," and "Sir Galahad," permits the hypothesis that the story of Merlin and Vivien influenced the shape of the myth of "The Palace of Art" (1832); I think it certain, in any case, that Tennyson recalled the earlier poem when working on the Idyll. In "The Palace of Art" the speaker of the poem builds a palace for his soul, invests it with every splendor, fills it with every gewgaw of delight. In "Merlin and Vivien" Merlin tells the story of a certain king whose realm was threatened by the excessive beauty of his queen; the young men sickened, the councillors stultified, the armies waned, the very beasts knelt before her in homage (ll. 568–77). He sent out a general summons to the world's wizards, to find some charm, which, wrought upon the queen, would keep her all to himself; eventually a wee bald man appeared, expert in shadows, who cast a spell upon the queen, the very spell that Vivien yearns to know:

> For Merlin once had told her of a charm,
> The which if any wrought on anyone
> With woven paces and with waving arms,
> The man so wrought on ever seemed to lie
> Closed in the four walls of a hollow tower,
> From which was no escape for evermore;
> And none could find that man for evermore,
> Nor could he see but him who wrought the charm
> Coming and going, and he lay as dead
> And lost to life and use and name and fame.

(ll. 203–12)

The speaker of "The Palace of Art" casts this spell upon his queen, upon his own soul, of whom he is so jealous that he wishes to whisk her away to a palace where no one will ever see her and she will see no one. Disconnected from all human contact, shut in a hollow cloud, the soul is thrown back on her own resources, fashions on her void the thin gaudy images that half-express her state, half-distract her from it. In her nutshell she is queen of infinite space; but—and this is made explicit in Merlin's narrative—she is actually a slave; the imagination is translated into a mere image. Merlin and Vivien are, in a sense, engaged in a competitive exercise of image-making power; each wishes to render the other imaginary, fictitious, useful—Merlin wishes to compel Vivien's sexual obedience, Vivien wishes to gain the power to destroy Camelot. If one takes the plot of "The Palace of Art" and changes the ending in such a manner that the Soul does not repent her wickedness but instead decides to leave her Palace, go on a rampage in the world of men—after which the speaker, the "I" of the opening stanzas, anxiously reappears on the scene to try to keep her locked in the Palace, while the Soul schemes to trick the speaker into teaching her how to build a better, bigger Palace, a Palace in which the whole human race scurries about her ministering to her whims, then one would have the plot of "Merlin and Vivien."

The Soul in "The Palace of Art" saw herself as a multiple mirror; and, similarly, Vivien is water. Near the beginning of the Idyll, when she sees the noble guilty couple Lancelot and Guinevere riding to the hunt, Vivien delivers a quasi-Elizabethan soliloquy:

> "Ah little rat that borest in the dyke
> Thy hole by night to let the boundless deep
> Down upon far-off cities while they dance—
> (ll. 110–16) Or dream—of thee they dreamed not—nor of me
> These—ay, but each of either: ride, and dream
> The mortal dream that never yet was mine—
> Ride, ride and dream until ye wake—to me!"

Vivien is the rat, but by another analysis she is the ocean that is pressing on the walls of Camelot, the disenchantress who will arouse the court from its dream of glory. Later, when Vivien abases herself before Merlin and offers him a kiss, Tennyson uses a much-admired and long-gestated simile to describe Merlin's state of mind.

>   he was mute:
> (ll. 227–31) So dark a forethought rolled about his brain,

> As on a dull day in an Ocean cave
> The blind wave feeling round his long sea-hall
> In silence.

Merlin's skull is a hollow cave, and a slow tentacular trickle of Vivien is beginning to invade it, to break it down. Soon Merlin forefeels that the tidal pressure is increasing, on himself and on Camelot:

> "O did ye never lie upon the shore,
> And watch the curled white of the coming wave
> Glassed in the slippery sand before it breaks?
> Even such a wave, but not so pleasurable,
> Dark in the glass of some presageful mood,
> Had I for three days seen, ready to fall.
> And then I rose and fled from Arthur's court
> To break the mood. You followed me unasked;
> And when I looked, and saw you following still,
> My mind involved yourself the nearest thing
> In that mind-mist: for shall I tell you truth?
> You seemed that wave about to break upon me
> And sweep me from my hold upon the world,
> My use and name and fame."

(ll. 289–302)

Long before Merlin succumbs to Vivien's enticements, she is constructing a kind of tank around Merlin, an aquarium in which he is to be the sole specimen. She seizes control of the similes by which Merlin understands his condition before she seizes the man himself; she is the superior magician, the superior image maker, because she can govern the internal emblems, the interpretation of language. In a contest of semblances the dissembler always has the advantage. Merlin is either mute, or not eager to speak, or given to sententiousness:

> he spoke and said,
> Not looking at her, "Who are wise in love
> Love most, say least," and Vivien answered quick,
> "I saw the little elf-god eyeless once

(ll. 244–49)

In Arthur's arras hall at Camelot:
But neither eyes nor tongue—O stupid child!"

By the end Merlin himself will be as eyeless, tongueless, as Vivien's image of Cupid. If Merlin finds it difficult to sustain their argument, Vivien is fluent, all too ready to be the tongue that Merlin lacks, as is clear from her response to Merlin's presentiment that she is the wave about to sweep over him:

(ll. 315–22)

> "The people call you prophet: let it be:
> But not of those that can expound themselves.
> Take Vivien for expounder; she will call
> That three-days-long presageful gloom of yours
> No presage, but the same mistrustful mood
> That makes you seem less noble than yourself,
> Whenever I have asked this very boon,
> Now asked again."

Both Merlin and Vivien are imaginative, and to a great degree share the same images, images of flies, misty stars, breaking waves; but Merlin is unsure about his correct interpretation of their meanings, while Vivien is convincing, confident of her false interpretations. By mastering the meanings of images, Vivien directs the outcome of events, and soon, far from being reduced to another of the buxom captives of Merlin's zoo (l. 540), she reduces him to unbeing, traps him in helpless imagelessness. Vivien is, like the Soul in "The Palace of Art," a muse elevated beyond the level of oxygen, a muse who sentences her follower to a kind of living death. She is proof that the imagination can attain a height at which, paradoxically, it is incapable of making images. The prison without walls in which Merlin is locked forever is simply a Palace of Art from which all pictures have been carted away.

IV

The Decay of Symbols

So FAR IT HAS SEEMED that the high imagination and the low imagination have no common ground at all; that images must be either low representations or high blurs, mimetic or sublime. There is, however, a mode of art that might connect them: the symbolic mode. A symbol is a common thing that bears a huge electrical charge; an object distended with meaning beyond its usual capacity to hold. Therefore it is possible that a symbol might reconcile the high and the low imaginations, might provide a model for the ideal poetic act in which the celestial and the earthly muses join hands and dance. As we shall see, alas, Tennyson is rarely able to sustain the requisite focus, and the symbolic mode fractures into a headache of double vision.

Idylls of the King offers several fine test cases for the adequacy of the symbolic mode. We have already seen, in "Merlin and Vivien," how imagination can be used for purely evil ends. There, images are the province of the watery Vivien, on whose shifting surfaces they form and disperse; and as *Idylls* comes to an end it seems that image making, emblem deploying, is increasingly corrupt. By the end of the last Idyll, "The Passing of Arthur," it seems that the vigor of myth and symbol is at last restored—the arm reaches out of the lake to grasp the sword Excalibur—but up to that point there has been a steady degradation of the high pageant of sharply incised images into complexities and dubieties of every sort. Myth has threatened to turn into commonplace history, type into society, noble discourse into gossip. With every ramification, every elaboration of Arthur's court, a certain intensity of meaning is lost. In Tennyson's sketch for a five-act drama about Arthur, one of his foreconceits of the *Idylls,* Modred represents "the sceptical understanding," scoffs at the existence of supernatural beings (Ricks, pp. 1461–62); and, although Tennyson has almost nothing to say about Modred in the *Idylls* as we have it—Modred does little but eavesdrop until he foments the great revolt that destroys Camelot—the spirit of rationalism is the hidden villain of the entire sequence. The efficacy of symbols is everywhere menaced, and with it the efficacy of Arthur, and of poetry itself.

Much of Tennyson's treatment of symbols is related to, and perhaps influenced by, Carlyle's chapter "Symbols" in *Sartor Resartus*. There Teufelsdröckh, a windy gleeful disreputable philosopher so arresting that the reader is forced to take his facetiousness very seriously indeed, develops the theory that " 'in a Symbol there is a concealment and yet revelation: here therefore, by Silence and by Speech acting together, comes a double significance' " (ed. W. H. Hudson, p. 165). He believes that the highest and fullest meanings of the universe are concealed, not expressible in rational discourse; but that, by means of the amphibious nature of the symbol, the imagination can apprehend what reason cannot— " 'not our Logical, Mensurative faculty, but our Imaginative one is King over us' " (p. 166). Though Teufelsdröckh distinguishes intrinsic from extrinsic symbols—thereby anticipating a question that will vex Yeats, Ezra Pound, and other symbol makers of the twentieth century—he does not think that extrinsic symbols are less potent—even " 'the Cross itself, had no meaning save an accidental extrinsic one' " (p. 168). Though we dwell in symbols, and everywhere touch and handle and adore symbols, and are ourselves symbols, nothing can stay symbolic forever; even the most effective symbol eventually loses its glamor, becomes " 'smaller and smaller, like a receding Star' " (p. 169), and is replaced by other acts of fantasy, our " 'organ of the God-like' " (p. 164). Symbols, then, constituting our lives, must germinate and wax and decay like living things.

This intimate feeling for this organic quality of symbols, for their ability to refresh and enrich discourse before they lose their potency, often appears in Tennyson's later poems. For instance, "Sir John Oldcastle, Lord Cobham" (1880) is a dramatic monologue spoken by a follower of Wycliffe, persecuted under Henry V; the icon-venerating nature of unreformed Catholicism repels him:

Here is the copse, the fountain and—a Cross!
To thee, dead wood, I bow not head nor knees.
Rather to thee, green boscage, work of God,
Black holly, and white-flowered wayfaring-tree!
Rather to thee, thou living water, drawn
By this good Wiclif mountain down from heaven,
And speaking clearly in thy native tongue—
(ll. 120–34)   No Latin—He that thirsteth, come and drink!
          Eh! how I angered Arundel asking me
To worship Holy Cross! I spread mine arms,
God's work, I said, a cross of flesh and blood
And holier. That was heresy. (My good friend
By this time should be with me.) "Images?"
"Bury them as God's truer images
Are daily buried." "Heresy."

To Oldcastle, the crucifix is an example of exactly that sort of superannuated symbol Carlyle complained of; Oldcastle feels that the image of Christ is more vibrant, more perspicuous in Oldcastle's own body, in a living tree, in a living spring, than in the dry joined sticks. In the case of the crucifix, the symbol is too far removed from what it purports to symbolize.

The Protestant Oldcastle is also sensitive to the opposite heresy, the doctrine of transubstantiation, the claim that the symbol is magically identical to the thing symbolized:

               "Bread—
Bread left after the blessing?" how they stared,
That was their main test-question—glared at me!
(ll. 146–52)   "He veiled Himself in flesh, and now He veils
His flesh in bread, body and bread together."
Then rose the howl of all the cassocked wolves,
"No bread, no bread. God's body!"

In the case of the Eucharist, the symbolic role of the bread is precisely analogous to the symbolic role of Christ, but the bread is still a symbol, nothing more than a symbol. The bread is made of flour and water, not of actual flesh, but its efficacy is not impaired. Oldcastle thus makes a precise statement about the relation of a

symbol to what it symbolizes, for he refuses either to permit the
thing and its referent to drift too far apart and grow irrelevant, or to
permit them to become confused, identical; and if Tennyson could
deploy poetic symbols as accurately as Oldcastle can conceive
religious symbols, many of his difficulties would be solved.

In the later *Idylls,* Tennyson meditates a good deal about the
symbolical quality of images and the various diseases that frustrate
the proper operations of symbols. The last written of the *Idylls,*
"Balin and Balan" (1872–74), an expansion of a passage deleted
from an early version of "Merlin and Vivien," is Tennyson's most
thoughtful investigation of this theme. Arthur has dispatched some
knights to exact just tribute from the reluctant King Pellam, but one
of their number has been killed, according to hearsay, by a Fiend of
the woods, the ghost of a black magician, doubtless, as Hallam
Tennyson notes, symbolic of slander (ll. 126–28). When Arthur
hears of this outrage, he assigns Balan to hunt down and slay the
demon. Now it so happens that Balan's brother Balin, while an
amiable and hearty fellow most of the time, is given to fits of black
rage, especially when he thinks people are slandering him (l. 56),
fits in which he may injure himself or others. It is clear, therefore,
that Balan has embarked on a quest to murder an image, a half-
defined, not strongly realized emblem of his brother's spasms of
destructiveness. Indeed the brothers are so intimate, so consonant,
so assonant, that they may be regarded as one entity, searching
among hazy states of being for self-control. While Balan is engaged
in his futile hunt—it is one of the general rules of psychomachy that
the external beast will never appear until the internal one is stimu-
lated—Balin stays behind at Camelot; he conceives the idea that his
behavior would be improved, his mind made gentle, if he could
only have some token of gentle Queen Guinevere to pacify him, to
cure him of violence. He decides to ask Arthur for a boon:

> "Some goodly cognizance of Guinevere,
> In lieu of this rough beast upon my shield,
> Langued gules, and toothed with grinning savagery."

(ll. 191–
204)

> And Arthur, when Sir Balin sought him, said
> "What wilt thou bear?" Balin was bold, and asked

To bear her own crown-royal upon shield,
Whereat she smiled and turned her to the King,
Who answered "Thou shalt put the crown to use.
The crown is but the shadow of the King,
And this a shadow's shadow, let him have it,
So this will help him of his violences!"
"No shadow" said Sir Balin "O my Queen,
But light to me! no shadow, O my King,
But golden earnest of a gentler life!"

This is how a symbol should operate, if the high and the low imaginations are to attain the proper connection; this symbol is a copy of a copy, but, far from suffering from any Platonic deficiency, it is a viable link in a well-established chain; it is the agency of transmission of virtue from its heavenly referent down to Sir Balin the Savage; it exerts control, a shaping force, by means of a shapeliness, an economy of concealed things made manifest by images. It works, however, only as long as Balin does not look too closely at the mediating image. As Balin lingers at the court, he cannot help observing the conduct of Lancelot and Guinevere: he overhears Lancelot tell the queen about his dreams of lilies, saints, holy chastity, overhears Guinevere reply that she prefers "this garden rose / Deep-hued and many-folded" (ll. 264–65) to any talk of lilies. Balin, though a rough knight, is not so poor an art critic that he does not wonder whether Guinevere is using this little symbolical flower drama to try to seduce Lancelot. He rushes away from Camelot down the same road that Balan took, runs into a tree as he falls into his old vain rage. As long as Guinevere was an abstract type, a mere personification of gentleness, the picture of her crown had power to tranquilize; as she evolves into a complicated woman, as she grows real, grows interesting, the image grows impotent. It is not only her adultery that vitiates her emblem, for sin as well as virtue has a kind of magic proper to it; it is her complexity that undoes it, for a symbol can be symbolic of only one thing at once. As long as Guinevere was concealed, mute, the image of her crown could speak; when she starts to talk, starts to reveal her prosaic self, the image grows mute. Thus it is seen that Carlyle was right: what is concealed is what is expressive, gripping.

Balin's headlong flight reaches Pellam's castle, where Pellam's vile son, the hissing Sir Garlon, teases and teases Balin with rumors of Guinevere's adultery, mocks him for wearing Guinevere's "crown-scandalous" (l. 384) on his shield, until Balin's temper breaks and he smites Garlon. Pellam's knights raise hue and cry, and give chase to Balin, who escapes in Pellam's chapel, where he finds a long lance, a useful pole for vaulting out of the castle. The lance, as it happens, once belonged to Joseph of Arimathea, and has a red point because a Roman soldier stuck it in Christ's side. Therefore the lance, like the bread of the Eucharist, is so charged with significance, so intensely symbolical, that it can almost provoke a breakdown of the wall that separates the celestial from the earthly. Pellam is the Klingsor of Tennyson's Grail legend, the wizard-custodian of the Spear, much less ferocious, insane, formidable, than Wagner's sorcerer; Pellam is instead almost donnish, slack, nerveless, histrionically ascetic, as reported to Arthur by his embassage:

> "Sir King" they brought report "we hardly found,
> So bushed about it is with gloom, the hall
> Of him to whom ye sent us, Pellam, once
> A Christless foe of thine as ever dashed
> Horse against horse; but seeing that thy realm
> Hath prospered in the name of Christ, the King
> Took, as in rival heat, to holy things;
> And finds himself descended from the Saint
> Arimathaean Joseph; him who first
> Brought the great faith to Britain over seas;
> He boasts his life as purer than thine own;
> Eats scarce enow to keep his pulse abeat;
> Hath pushed aside his faithful wife, nor lets
> Or dame or damsel enter at his gates
> Lest he should be polluted. This gray King
> Showed us a shrine wherein were wonders—yea—
> Rich arks with priceless bones of martyrdom,
> Thorns of the crown and shivers of the cross,
> And therewithal (for thus he told us) brought
> By holy Joseph hither, that same spear

(ll. 91–116)

Wherewith the Roman pierced the side of Christ.
He much amazed us; after, when we sought
The tribute, answered 'I have quite foregone
All matters of this world: Garlon, mine heir,
Of him demand it,' which this Garlon gave
With much ado, railing at thine and thee."

Pellam has repudiated wife and social responsibility to erect that familiar place, the Palace of Art, now decorated with the relics of an unsavory Christianity, a palace just as choking, involved, claustral as any of its predecessors. Again, organic life is merely pollution. Pellam's palace is the repository of an amazing array of symbols; the collection, if it contained the Grail as well, would corner the market of important Christian emblems. Yet something is wrong with this heap of all-too-crucial symbols. By being the objects of connoisseurship, by being locked in a shadowy castle, the symbols have suffered a certain attenuation, grown magnificent and empty; they have shriveled into objets d'art, toys in Pellam's fantasy of solitary sainthood. When Balin, ignorant of his sacrilege, presumes to handle the priceless lance, dares to use it to vault away from his pursuers, Pellam makes a feeble cry, "Stay, stay him! he defileth heavenly things / With earthly uses" (ll. 415–16). Of course, heavenly things ought to have earthly uses; it may be that the lance is suited to other, better earthly uses than the one to which Balin puts it, but if it lacks all earthly use it is nothing. Balin, without knowing it, is making an oblique attempt to resuscitate a dead symbol, a symbol that has withered into a vain fantastical private image. Similarly, the images on the tapestries, paintings, stained-glass windows in "The Palace of Art" were all arrested and emaciated symbols, not superannuated but only dormant, perverted, capable of being turned again toward public life, made efficacious once again, if only the Soul could escape from its voluntary imprisonment.

Having half-profaned, half-revivified the lance of Joseph of Arimathea, Balin seems to wish to rid himself of symbols altogether; as soon as he has made good his escape, he hangs his crown-bearing shield high on a branch, for his shield, whether by his own rage or by Guinevere's adultery, is now a hopelessly compromised symbol. He has lost whatever protection such a token could afford; and there immediately rides onto the scene the witch Vivien, singing a hymn to the sun:

(ll. 442–5)

> "The fire of Heaven is on the dusty ways.
> The wayside blossoms open to the blaze.
> The whole wood-world is one full peal of praise.
> The fire of Heaven is not the flame of Hell."

I wonder whether Joyce, half-remembering the rhymes in this stanza when he wrote Stephen Dedalus's villanelle in *A Portrait of the Artist as a Young Man,* did not associate the temptress of the villanelle, who made the angels fall, with Tennyson's Vivien.

We have seen in Pellam one sort of malfeasance with symbols, the attempt to disembody them, abstract them from every earthly meaning; Vivien's heresy is exactly opposite, for she equates the material sun, the blazing ball of gas, with the true God that is beyond apprehension. As in "Sir John Oldcastle, Lord Cobham," symbols either drift into irrelevance or pretend that they are not analogies but identities. Sun worship is one of Tennyson's most curious themes, for the practice seems to have attracted and repelled him. (A Christian poet, perhaps, can never be quite happy as a symbolist; for the symbolic mode always has a tinge of the idolatrous.) In "Balin and Balan" sun worship is clearly evil, as it is in "The Holy Grail" when a horde of Druid sun worshipers capture and imprison Sir Bors; on the other hand King Arthur is persistently compared to the sun, and Akbar, in "Akbar's Dream" (1892), who seems to be one of the most reliable of Tennyson's later spokesmen, exclaims,

(ll. 98–105)

> Let the Sun,
> Who heats our earth to yield us grain and fruit,
> And laughs upon thy field as well as mine,
> And warms the blood of Shiah and Sunnee,
> Symbol the Eternal! Yea and may not kings
> Express Him also by their warmth of love
> For all they rule—by equal law for all?
> By deeds a light to men?

Vivien's hymn to the sun seems a foreparody of Akbar's:

> Shadow-maker, shadow-slayer, arrowing light from
>   clime to clime,
> Hear thy myriad laureates hail thee monarch in their
>   woodland rhyme.
> Warble bird, and open flower, and, men, below the
>   dome of azure
> Kneel adoring Him the Timeless in the flame that
>   measures Time!

(ll. 198–201)

Akbar differs from Vivien in that he is careful to use the language of analogy; the sun is an unusually satisfying symbol, a symbol that shares many of the attributes of the thing it symbolizes, but it still remains a symbol.

The niceness of Akbar's similitudes reminds us what a delicate process symbol making is; the entry into "Balin and Balan" of Vivien, whose magic is at once subtle and coarse, reminds us what dangerous results the improper use of symbols may lead to. But there are many proper uses of symbols as well. The Merlin of "The Coming of Arthur" (1869) uses his powers of invention to certify the dubious Arthur as the legitimate heir of King Uther; Merlin's fable of the naked babe washed to shore by a great wave, the newborn Arthur clothed in fire, serves an important public function, the discovery of succession to the monarchy. An image has been converted into a symbol; in a sense every image yearns to become invested with potency, to be symbolic, to achieve some result in the public world. In "Merlin and Vivien" Merlin begins with the hope of exercising symbolic magic, of seducing Vivien; but the image of Vivien, instead of realizing itself in some satisfying embrace, dances away from his grasp, teases him, grows obsessive, unreal, ubiquitous, until at last he is impotent, blind, dead to all the world. Vivien is a materialist, a rationalist like the Modred of Tennyson's early notes, an antimagician in that she schemes to lock up all the healing sacramental energies of Merlin's symbols in Merlin's brain, to deprive the sinful Knights of the Round Table of what would make them other than the swine she scorns. For Merlin, for Pellam, for the Soul in "The Palace of Art," all playing with images is sinister as long as the images remain unsymbolical, useless, a slow rotation of chimeras. Symbols are perilous when- ever they are coveted, neutralized, rendered sterile and vain. Things must have meanings, and meanings must coagulate into things, if good art and sanity are to be achieved.

At the end of "Balin and Balan"—the plot is mostly original, not borrowed from Malory—there is a systematic destruction of the symbolicalness of symbols. Vivien finally convinces Balin of Guinevere's adultery; Balin retrieves the emblematic shield, throws it on the ground, defaces it with his foot, casts it into the weeds, curses "the tale, / The told-of, and the teller" (ll. 533–34). Balan, still prowling through the forest, hears Balin's unintelligible curs- ing and thinks that he has at last found the demon of the woods. The two brothers, unrecognizable, charge, and slay each other. Balin kills Balan with the sacred lance, the lance once too far removed from the world, now too much enmired in foulness; and the broth- ers too late recognize each other and reconcile themselves to their fate:

> "Goodnight, true brother here! goodmorrow there!
> We two were born together, and we die
(ll. 616–20)   Together by one doom:" and while he spoke
> Closed his death-drowsing eyes, and slept the sleep
> With Balin, either locked in either's arm.

It is oddly similar to that passage in "The Lover's Tale" in which Julian remembers his childhood intimacy with Camilla and hopes to perfect it in marriage; both suggest narcissistic involution, a world collapsed into a deathly embrace. One of the lessons of the *Idylls of the King* is that, in the absence of symbols, the whole social order lapses, all distinction and degree vanish. Without Gleam and Grail, without inspiration, no earthly institution can survive; and there is every reason to believe that Tennyson, in such poems as the "Ode on the Death of the Duke of Wellington," tried to exercise the poet's symbol-making power in order to shore up the British Empire. *Idylls* is cautionary: as belief in the supernatural efficacy of symbols fades, each man drifts into anomie, private fantasy, or deranging obsession; Merlin retreats into his prison without walls,

Pelleas into his mock Camelot of thugs, Guinevere into her cloister, groveling at the feet of the Arthur whom she has ruined.

Arthur has little to do in the *Idylls* in which he is the central character. Tennyson keeps him off-stage for most of the action, knowing, as Spenser knew about Gloriana and Milton about God, that such characters are likely to disappoint. His major function is to be the guarantor of symbols. Himself denoting nothing very specific—religious faith, according to the early notes, or kingliness, or the unfallen soul—Arthur appoints and defines, delegates meaningfulness at his discretion. Arthur is a hypothetical apex where meanings converge, like Shelley's Mont Blanc or Yeats's Rose, a symbol of the symbolicality of symbols. Tennyson took some pains to insure that the reader would find him human—he added the line "Ideal manhood closed in real man" to the Epilogue to the *Idylls*— but Arthur can only grow unattractive, priggish, if we try to assign a psychology to him; he is best left a governing figment. John D. Rosenberg (*The Fall of Camelot,* p. 131) has briefly called attention to the relation of Arthur to the God of *Paradise Lost,* and the comparison is indeed suggestive. Milton, by leaving his God psychologyless, was wiser than Tennyson: in his *Christian Doctrine* Milton inveighs against what he calls anthropopathy, the ascription of human feelings to God, and does as much as he can in Book 3 of *Paradise Lost* to render his God chill and monumental; God makes it explicit that all that is discursive, dramatic, in the story of the Fall is only a majestic pretense in his timeless, all-foreknowing mind, a charade to enlighten feeble-brained mankind. Tennyson's inability to effect a satisfactory fusion of ideal manhood and real man is suggestive of his larger failure to make the symbolic mode credible; the mere allegation that low thing and high significance are one will not persuade, unless the poet can realize it in the poem.

Tennyson's Arthur can be tricked, even injured; yet when he enters the scene he is usually accompanied by nimbuses and shudderings, the full apparatus of divine awe:

(ll. 95–99)
> When Arthur reached a field-of-battle bright
> With pitched pavilions of his foe, the world
> Was all so clear about him, that he saw

> The smallest rock far on the faintest hill,
> And even in high day the morning star.

This passage, from "The Coming of Arthur" (1869), shows how Tennyson, even late in life, could quarry the themes of his early visionary poetry: it is exactly parallel to the passage in "Armageddon" in which the angel unclogs the poet's eyes and shows him the moon's white cities, and the smallest grain that dapples the dark earth. As Arthur proves himself on the field of battle, lightnings and thunders pass over him, dazing all eyes, and the enemy kings shrink before him:

> Then, before a voice
> As dreadful as the shout of one who sees
> To one who sins, and deems himself alone
> And all the world asleep, they swerved and brake
> Flying, and Arthur called to stay the brands
> That hacked among the flyers, "Ho! they yield!"
> So like a painted battle the war stood
> Silenced, the living quiet as the dead,
> And in the heart of Arthur joy was lord.

(ll. 115–23)

Arthur is the eye of God, for this seemingly ordinary quarrel among rival warlords has suddenly grown eschatological, a type of Judgment Day; it seems that Arthur need scarcely lift his sword, for the sheer pressure of his gaze paralyzes his opponents, freezes the battle into a pictorial tableau. The only power Arthur requires is vision; and he is the human sublime. Therefore he cannot be the true subject of Tennyson's poem; he is too concentrated, too significant, too abstract and unfigured, threatens to render trivial all the things surrounding him, as we see near the end of "The Coming of Arthur." King Leodogran, the father of Guinevere, is unsure whether to allow Arthur to marry his daughter; he cannot decide until he dreams of a phantom king, sometimes looming, sometimes invisible, in the smoke of a burning mountainside on which a confused rabble fought and yelled, denying Arthur's kingship,

Till with a wink his dream was changed, the haze
Descended, and the solid earth became
(ll. 440–43)
As nothing, but the King stood out in heaven,
Crowned.

Shadow and substance reverse themselves; Arthur, outrageously freighted with meaning, makes tenuous all the world around him.

This revelation, that what has mass and shape, substance, is less real than our intuitions of the divine, is the basic doctrine of Tennyson's Higher Pantheism, of Arthur's speech at the end of "The Holy Grail," even of the little wizard who taught Merlin the spell of prison-without-walls. It is a doctrine which suggests that everything, properly understood, is a symbol, as we can see directly in "The Higher Pantheism" (1867):

The sun, the moon, the stars, the seas, the hills and the
    plains—
Are not these, O Soul, the Vision of Him who reigns?

Is not the Vision He? though He be not that which He
(ll. 1–6)   seems?
Dreams are true while they last, and do we not live in
    dreams?

Earth, these solid stars, this weight of body and limb,
Are they not sign and symbol of thy division from Him?

"The Higher Pantheism" is an easy poem to ridicule—Swinburne did so magnificently in "The Higher Pantheism in a Nutshell," although I am not sure why Swinburne's own "Hertha" would not be subject to the same derision—but Higher Pantheism may be a doctrine more worthy of attention than it first appears. Carlyle taught that a symbol expresses something concealed; Tennyson here teaches that a symbol conceals what it expresses. Sun, moon, sea, earth, the poet's own body, all reveal God, yet these very vehicles of revelation estrange us from what they reveal. Clearly the symbolic mode has drifted somewhat out of alignment, for Higher Pantheism is insufficiently respectful of material realization; the celestial muse has partly vanquished the earthly, wrapped herself in dark shadows. But the Higher Pantheism does not suggest that God can be apprehended without reference to his creation; we can approach him only through the symbols that half-embody and half-obscure him.

By 1867 Tennyson had long abandoned the Romantic quest to display in his poems the divine in itself, absolute and uncontaminated with the common matter of life; and so in such mature works as the *Idylls of the King* we inspect the gates of Camelot, the knights of the Round Table, the suburbs and the countryside, all that Arthur controls or erects, but rarely Arthur himself, who appears only often enough to make us feel that he is not entirely obscured by those entities that manifest him. The knights are fallible, foibled men, distinct and sometimes quarrelsome, but as Bellicent tells Leodogran,

> when he spake and cheered his Table Round
> With large, divine, and comfortable words,
> (ll. 266–70) Beyond my tongue to tell thee—I beheld
> From eye to eye through all their Order flash
> A momentary likeness of the King.

Often the knights are individual, vicious, but at times the eyes of Arthur can be seen playing in their own eyes. Arthur's knights are his symbols, symbols that may be obscure, even treasonous, but nonetheless his symbols, as long as the viability of symbols can be sustained. As Tennyson says in "The Two Voices," every cloud that veils love, itself is love.

Despite Tennyson's claim that Arthur is human, no one in the *Idylls,* except perhaps the debunking Vivien, can really believe it, certainly not his own queen:

> "Arthur, my lord, Arthur, the faultless King,
> That passionate perfection, my good lord—
> But who can gaze upon the Sun in heaven?
> ("Lancelot and Elaine," He never spake word of reproach to me,
> ll. 121–35) He never had a glimpse of mine untruth,
> He cares not for me: only here today
> There gleamed a vague suspicion in his eyes:
> Some meddling rogue has tampered with him—else

Rapt in this fancy of his Table Round,
And swearing men to vows impossible,
To make them like himself: but, friend, to me
He is all fault who hath no fault at all:
For who loves me must have a touch of earth;
The low sun makes the colour: I am yours,
Not Arthur's, as ye know, save by the bond."

Arthur is ideal, insipid, mere high noon; Guinevere prefers someone more colorful, individual, shaded, endearing—Lancelot,
however noble he may be, is stamped, scarred, human. John D.
Rosenberg (*The Fall of Camelot,* p. 139) claims that "there are no
individual characters in the *Idylls,* only juxtaposed relationships in
which diametrically opposite characters often share the same sym-
bolism"; but I believe that the lower strata of personages are in
continual danger of falling out of the high meaningfulness of King
Arthur, King Allegory, down into common characterhood. It is as
if Arthur's relation to his knights were that of white light to the
various bands of color in the rainbow; each is a faulty, somewhat
deformed expression of some aspect of his piercing integrity.
Again, Arthur is a point of convergence, where Lancelot's might,
Percivale's sacred zeal, Gareth's innocent valor, perhaps even Tristram's sexual passion, Gawain's oily courtesy, Kay's rough effi-
ciency, all meet, no matter how perverse or profane the particular
knight's use of his gift may be. In a sense, each knight is human to
the degree that he fails to be Arthur.

Arthur moves through the *Idylls,* then, in an unusual state of
intimate unrelatedness to the other characters, in a slightly different
dimension, skewed upward and outward from the rest of the
action, ubiquitous and ignorant. In some of his early visionary
poems Tennyson was preoccupied with the idea of a single image,
unapproachable and monumental, at the core of the phenomenal
universe:

Always there stood before him, night and day,
(ll. 11–24)   Of wayward varycolored circumstance
The imperishable presences serene

Colossal, without form, or sense, or sound,
Dim shadows but unwaning presences
Fourfacèd to four corners of the sky:
And yet again, three shadows, fronting one,
One forward, one respectant, three but one;
And yet again, again and evermore,
For the two first were not, but only seemed,
One shadow in the midst of a great light,
One reflex from eternity on time,
One mighty countenance of perfect calm,
Awful with most invariable eyes.

This passage from "The Mystic" (1830) presents a sort of Easter Island statue, a single central icon so multiplied by temporal sequence that its apparitions populate, constitute a cosmos. The narrower circle is "a region of white flame," the broader circle is "wayward varycolored circumstance"; eternity breaks itself into time as a prism breaks sunlight into colors. Behind both "The Mystic" and Guinevere's description of Arthur may lie Shelley's image of the dome of many-colored glass, but Tennyson does not quite share Shelley's nostalgia for white light, for the abode where the eternal are, indeed finds his true theme in the homely profusion of appearances and the faint traces of sublimity which linger in them. If one values only being, only eternity, then the abundance of the phenomenal world is illusion, decorative imagery; and the mystic, when he turns his gaze away from the deep truth, will find himself, like the Soul in "The Palace of Art," in a prison of mirrors.

By upholding his political responsibilities, Arthur keeps himself sane and shapely; he is a sun that remembers to illuminate a world, that refuses to turn inward and admire its own incomparable brightness. Yet Arthur has trouble maintaining a fixed form, is threatened by the shapelessness characteristic of all sublime beings. Burke in his *Philosophical Enquiry* quotes with approval Milton's description of Death in *Paradise Lost:*

                                   The other shape,
(2.666–68)   If shape it might be call'd that shape had none
                    Distinguishable in member, joint, or limb.

Burke remarks that here all is "uncertain, confused, terrible and sublime to the last degree" (2.3). The twentieth century has been particularly copious in artists expert in the emotions of shapelessness; but the nineteenth century has its share as well.

Tennyson presented Arthur in "The Coming of Arthur" as someone sublime in a sunny, dazzling, too intense manner; but by the end of "Guinevere" Arthur's style of sublimity has been considerably altered, darkened, until Arthur starts to seem a bit like Milton's Death:

> and more and more
> The moony vapour rolling round the King,
> Who seemed the phantom of a Giant in it,
> Enwound him fold by fold, and made him gray
> And grayer, till himself became as mist
> Before her, moving ghostlike to his doom.

(ll. 596–601)

He is again the cloudy phantom that he was at the beginning of Leodogran's dream; for a while he could congeal, exert his heavenly authority by means of his careful apparatus of symbols, but at the end he disperses, grows nebulous, vanishes in a boat with three weeping queens, descends into the vague evocative picture that decorates one wall in the Palace of Art.

In the Epilogue, Tennyson begs Queen Victoria to

> accept this old imperfect tale,
> New-old, and shadowing Sense at war with Soul,
> Ideal manhood closed in real man,
> Rather than that gray king, whose name, a ghost,
> Streams like a cloud, man-shaped, from mountain peak,
> And cleaves to cairn and cromlech still.

(ll. 36–41)

Because Arthurian place-names give piquancy to much of Cornwall and other regions of England, Tennyson imagines an Arthur distended into a vast countryside, an Arthur whose disintegration imperils the neat allegory of the *Idylls;* I am not sure that Tennyson understood to what extent the theme of his whole sequence was the very attenuation of significance, of power, which is properly imagined in these huge hazy ghosts. Tennyson half-accepts, half-rejects, a vision of Arthur who can persist in modern times only as a weak specter, so big and thin that the stars shine through him; but this is the usual fate in Tennyson's poems of lofty beings that cannot maintain their grasp on the world of experience. Here is "The Idealist" of 1829:

> A mighty matter I rehearse,
> A mighty matter undescried;
> Come listen all who can.
> I am the spirit of a man,
> I weave the universe,
> And indivisible divide,
> Creating all I hear and see.
> All souls are centres: I am one,
> I am the earth, the stars, the sun,
> I am the clouds, the sea.
> I am the citadels and palaces
> Of all great cities: I am Rome,
> Tadmor, and Cairo: I am Place
> And Time, yet is my home
> Eternity: (let no man think it odd,
>   For I am these,
> And every other birth of every other race;)
> I am all things save souls of fellow men and very God!

We may almost believe that Arthur is "Ideal manhood closed in real man"; but we cannot begin to imagine the idealist as a finite human being, brushing ancient cities off his waistcoat, cradling the Atlantic in the palm of his hand. He is too large. The Soul in "The Palace of Art," as we have seen, suffers from the same inflation, the same inchoateness, the same overinclusiveness, the same bewilderment, as she becomes all that she sees, as she feels inside her own complex self all the lower generations of being; indeed in one deleted stanza she studies the night sky with a telescope, gazes at

> Regions of lucid matter taking forms,
>   Brushes of fire, hazy gleams,
> Clusters and beds of worlds, and bee-like swarms
>   Of suns, and starry streams.

(Ricks, p. 412)

Tennyson showed much interest in the scientific hypothesis that stars congealed out of great clouds of gas, and here the Soul seems fascinated by a heavenly shapelessness analogous to her earthly incoherence, her lazy and jejune, purely ornamental potentialities. The Soul's ontological vertigo is meant to show the reader the impossibility of sustaining a sublime identification of oneself with one's world; but Arthur's dispersal may have a slightly different meaning. As a ghost haunting cairn and cromlech, saturating England with his presence, Arthur seems a tutelary spirit, a genius loci good for any locus, a household god good for any household. He impregnates the land with meaning, and seems to linger as a vague benign presence enabling the formation of heroic symbols even in the England of the Duke of Wellington and the present day.

In "Merlin and the Gleam" (1889), which seems to me a kind of pendant to the whole of the *Idylls,* embedding the myth of Arthur into the large myth of Tennyson's career as a poet, the Gleam, the light of imagination, is in the poet's youth concentrated in Romantical places, in desolate hollows, elfin woodlands, dragonish cataracts, but as the poet ages the Gleam grows steadier and broader until it illuminates field laborers and garrulous children as well as Arthurian pageantry; no longer an uncertain flicker or ignis fatuus, the Gleam becomes a calm glow, in which hamlet and cemetery are alike visible, images accepted without terror. The dispersed Arthur of the Epilogue to the *Idylls* is a kind of Gleam. It is almost as if Arthur had changed from a celestial presence to a low earthly muse, helping the poet to imagine England in its most rustic and humbly picturesque details.

And yet there is in the *Idylls* a fringe of the miraculous, the Romantically preposterous, as if a spirit of unearthly playfulness hovered at the edges of the tales. One of the strangest passages in the *Idylls* occurs in "Guinevere," when a little novice explains to Guinevere, cloistered and incognita, the marvels of Camelot before Guinevere's sin spoiled the kingdom:

> "Yea, but I know: the land was full of signs
(ll. 230–57)   And wonders ere the coming of the Queen.
> So said my father, and himself was knight

Of the great Table—at the founding of it;
And rode thereto from Lyonnesse, and he said
That as he rode, an hour or maybe twain
After the sunset, down the coast, he heard
Strange music, and he paused, and turning—there,
All down the lonely coast of Lyonnesse,
Each with a beacon-star upon his head,
And with a wild sea-light about his feet,
He saw them—headland after headland flame
Far on into the rich heart of the west:
And in the light the white mermaiden swam,
And strong man-breasted things stood from the sea,
And sent a deep sea-voice through all the land,
To which the little elves of chasm and cleft
Made answer, sounding like a distant horn.
So said my father—yea, and furthermore,
Next morning, while he past the dim-lit woods,
Himself beheld three spirits mad with joy
Come dashing down on a tall wayside flower,
That shook beneath them, as the thistle shakes
When three gray linnets wrangle for the seed:
And still at evenings on before his horse
The flickering fairy-cycle wheeled and broke
Flying, and linked again, and wheeled and broke
Flying, for all the land was full of life."

Many of these images are drawn from Tennyson's early visionary
poems—the mermen remind us of the "The Merman" (1830), and
"headland after headland flame" seems related to the range of high
pillars in "The Coach of Death" (1823) "That darken with excess of
heat / And run from sky to sky" (ll. 171–72). This rehearsal of
wonders is of course a tale told by an excitable child, but nevertheless it seems to pertain to a place different from the one we are
accustomed to: we are used to a certain delirium or magical awe, for
example in "The Holy Grail," but not to this delicate animism, this
panpsychism, this attribution of a little spirit to every wave and
flower. One of the high muses in Tennyson's work—though cer-

tainly not the very most celestial—seems to be a muse who relishes marvels, Romantic unrealities.

As we have seen, symbols possess transcendental efficacy, but this efficacy is not miraculous; it is the usual case that, if a knight calls himself Death, and decorates his night-black armor with skeleton and skull, and claims supernatural strength, he will turn out to be a hoax, a little lad dressed up to frighten the gullible ("Gareth and Lynette," l. 1373). Yet in the novice's speech the world continually resolves itself into miracle; it is as if we got a glimpse of some alternative constitution of the whole Arthurian mythology, of Tennyson's imaginative prehistory to the *Idylls*. If the novice is right, Guinevere's adultery is an act of disenchantment, for Guinevere has helped to depopulate the island of fairies; the novice's speech is parallel to Prospero's address to the elves of his island at the end of *The Tempest,* and indeed Arthur himself will vanish at the end of "Guinevere" and leave scarcely a rack behind. The relocation of the Gleam in "Merlin and the Gleam" from fairy-haunted forests and chasms to the complexities of English village life is similar to the decline of Camelot from the gauzy midsummer night's dream of the novice to the realpolitik of Modred and Pelleas.

And yet the imagination's strength seems to lie precisely in its ability to treat the disenchanted, the unsublime. In the *Idylls,* as in so many other places in Tennyson's work, there is a steady heightening of the value of the earthly muse; and there is a hope that earthly things can be endowed with heavenly reverberations, can be made symbolic. As Arthur grows ethereal, wispy, unreal, as the barbarians take over his kingdom, his presence still imbues the desecrated land with a remnant of sanctity. Much of Victorian poetry, like Victorian astronomy, is preoccupied with the coagulation of large vaguenesses into well-defined shapes, things capable of measure, assessment; but every fixed form must be shown to allude to its origin, to nebulous states of feeling, unsettled, clinging, never wholly resolved. It is far from certain that Tennyson has managed to produce effective symbols in the *Idylls;* his vectors of significance are often undirected, impossible to follow; but the reader always feels the poet's groping toward the symbolic mode.

One of the most vexing problems in the *Idylls* is human

identity. The sublime man, whether Tennyson's idealist or Keats's Shakespeare, has no identity at all; and the line between negative capability and complete incapacity in thin indeed. Arthur's little flashes of humanity—he even shows a certain sense of humor when he accepts an anonymous challenge at the beginning of "Balin and Balan"—do not compromise his celestial nature, but neither do they establish him as a particularly coherent or credible man. If one asks, What does Arthur do? the answers spring readily to mind; if one asks, Who is Arthur? the brow furrows, the shoulders shrug. Tennyson uses a simple device to distinguish Arthur's predilection from Lancelot's: Lancelot is better at jousting, Arthur at fighting the heathen. But the reader does not need frequent reminders that Arthur does not have a playful temperament. As for the rest, he is benign and unsparing, forbearing and implacable, all good things, even contradictory good things. From a novelist's point of view, Arthur is an angelic mess.

Just as Arthur and his knights are necessary complements—without the knights, Arthur is merely an intense inane, and without Arthur the knights are only desultory fragments, types of various passions and obtusenesses—so it is true that, throughout his career, Tennyson's characters are usually counterpointed against some vision of human sublimity. Tennyson knows that excessive magnanimity is madness, that the too inclusive man is no one at all—it is a theorem he proves over and over—but he seems to fear that without some allusion to the abyss, without some background of divine repleteness, any specific character will be unresonant, puny, a caricature. In the following chapters we shall look more closely at Tennyson's processes of defining character and identity, and we shall see how hard it is to find the right balance between the gingerbread man and the god.

Part Two

———— ∞ ————

PERSONAE

V

The Determinacy of the Song,
the Indeterminacy of the Singer

I BELIEVE THAT THE DIFFICULTY in forming poetical personae has been
one of the crucial issues in the poetry of recent centuries. To show
why persona formation was such an exasperation to Tennyson, I
will offer a brief outline of the literary history of personae.

   In poetry written before 1750, the formation of personae was
no laborious matter; the poet rummaged among the traditional
lyric masks, lover or saint, sage or sensualist, according to Yeats's
enumeration, until he found the one appropriate to his purposes. In
general, before 1750 what the poet said was considered more significant than the fact that it was he, and not another man, who said it.
Indeed a poet would prove his genius by choosing a great theme,
such as the Fall of Man, rather than by attempting to exalt his
private life, his divorce and political quarrels, to epic magnitude. In
the great poets it is easy to see how the personae begin to become
self-interested, detachable from the text; Chaucer is beguiled with
his role as the least prepossessing, most downcast and aloof pilgrim
on the road to Canterbury; Spenser writes in the eightieth of the
Amoretti about a situation that pertains to him and him alone of all
men on earth, the difficulty of being a lovesick man writing *The
Faerie Queene;* and Pope puts an unprecedented amount of effort
into defining an image of Pope so memorable that it will last as long
as the language. But although Pope seems consciously to strive for
self-definition, his method is to refine an existing persona—that of
Horace or Juvenal—to carve the cheeks of this traditional mask
until the face is suitably gaunt, lipless, affectedly malicious. With
the development of Romantic poetry, this ease of adopting personae seems to have become impossible; Blake, Wordsworth,
Coleridge did not always use their heaviest megaphones, but their

attempt to speak with the voice of the human race at large, or the voice of mind or sensibility disconnected from the lower self, seems to have allowed certain corners of the poet's workshop to fall into neglect, seems to have ruined certain old conventional intimacies between poet and audience. It is as if masks were lost in Romantical infinitude, and poets had to learn the art of mask making all over again, without any instruction.

The tendency of Romantic poetry is to magnify mankind in the most literal manner possible: to use the word *human* in such outrageously extended fashion that every nonhuman thing begins to acquire a face, assume a volition, grow bloodthirsty or sympathetic, debonair; and then to train this vast vague human sentience to speak in the poet's own voice. This sophisticated hylozoism seeks to erase most of the boundaries between the human body and the inanimate world. Blake struggles to achieve a vision of one man who sums up in himself all men, whose perceptual nerves entertain themselves by ramifying into a phenomenal world, in whose discourse "every Word & Every Character / Was Human" (*Jerusalem* 98:35–36). In Wordsworth's poem "Resolution and Independence," he employs a simile comparing his leech-gatherer to a stone so oddly perched that "it seems a thing endued with sense" (l. 61), a sea beast sunning itself—a double simile which confuses animate and inanimate by comparing a man to a stone, and then that stone to an animal. In his 1815 Preface, Wordsworth explains that in this simile he has exemplified "the modifying powers of the Imagination" by divesting sea beast and leech-gatherer of some of their life and endowing the stone with that quantity of life removed from the living; thus the eye of imagination seeks to discover a uniformly reasonable, equably human field, like those Persian illustrations in which rocks and streams and meadows all shine forth with a mild iridescence of tiny grinning or scowling faces, temporarily stunned into a world. As his own description of his simile shows, Wordsworth was conscious, as Blake was not, of the inevitable corollary of the expansion to world size of the human sentience: as the whole of nature starts to assume a human aspect, any particular man will recede, become effaced, deadened; the petrification of the noble leech-gatherer is a sign of the general resorption of every person beheld by the poet into the immensely strong, vaguely numb corpus of the world. The personages of Wordsworth's earlier poems, if they are not already dead, rolled round in earth's diurnal course, are for the most part picturesque, fleeting entities, tutelary spirits, drones, specialized organs cooperant to the good of the polyp colony to which they have resigned themselves.

His Victorian successors disliked the sober, rational, blandly magniloquent, grandly commonplace, milky, self-absorbed, locally anesthetized, ovine tone of Wordsworth's poetry, the sound of a voice talking to itself as if to some hard-of-hearing companion— Arthur Hallam, in his great essay on Tennyson, complained of the ungenial climate of Wordsworth's region of Parnassus. But the persona adopted by a poet, just like the personages described in his poems, will necessarily become deformed by the stresses of over-humanization. The poet who aspires to imitate the impulsive voice that he hears instructing him in forest and mountain will find that his own speaking voice grows depersonalized in direct proportion to the extent that he succeeds in personifying the external world.

At the end of the high Romantic movement we can see in many places a movement toward narrower, better-behaved personae; in the matter of personae, as in many other poetic matters, the earthly muse begins to seem more comfortable, more beguiling, than the heavenly. In *Don Juan,* in the "Letter to Maria Gisborne," perhaps in *The Fall of Hyperion,* Byron, Shelley, and Keats move with some success toward the adoption of a well-delineated, humane persona; but Tennyson was the first great poet for whom the discovery of a proper speaking voice was of paramount importance, the first of a long line of Victorian and modern poets who labor the whole length of their careers to create a mask, as if the mere achievement of a voice superseded anything that that voice might say.

Of course it is a labor of contraction. Tennyson, at the beginning of his career, sounded all the organ pipes at once; later he learned to select a few tones, to modulate, to make leaner and more agile noises. However, he gave himself this good advice before he was capable of obeying it; in "The Palace of Art" (1832) the poet in effect tells himself that sublime orotundity is harmful to his vocal chords, without knowing exactly what sort of alternative is open to him. After 1830 or so Tennyson starts to put much of his effort into poems written in the first person, poems in which a character arrested by some emotional crisis explains the circumstances that led to his present state. Many of these characters, such as Œnone or Ulysses, are notably dissimilar to Alfred Tennyson; but I believe that all of them are parts of a long and difficult elucidation of self. I have said that Tennyson was preoccupied with his own namelessness; and I believe that in his series of dramatic monologues he tried to approximate a description of his own nameless self by adding up a long sequence of names, as if every new term modified the whole, offered a fuller allusion to that unspeakable being Alfred Tennyson, as if a bundle of finite personae—an oboe, a horn, a violin, and so forth—could hint at a sublime diapason of identity.

In nineteenth-century England, selfhood was considered, at least in some quarters, mysterious and shifting, probably unknowable. Hazlitt, in his essay "On the Knowledge of Character" (1821), insists that a man's words and actions are likely to give us a false image of him, although his looks may give him away; our first impressions of character may be correct, but our immediate knowledge is quickly smothered in conscious or unconscious prevarication. In order to prove that there is no such thing as, for example, a man who originally appears to be a blockhead but who reveals himself to be a genius after long acquaintance, Hazlitt tells the following story:

You say, there is Mr ——, undoubtedly a person of great genius: yet, except when excited by something extraordinary, he seems half dead. He has wit at will, yet wants life and spirit. He is (Selected *capable of the most generous acts, yet meanness seems to cling to* Writings, ed. *every motion. He looks like a poor creature—and in truth he is* Ronald *one! The first impression he gives you of him answers nearly to the* Blythe, *feeling he has of his personal identity; and this image of himself,* p. 100) *rising from his thoughts, and shrouding his faculties, is that which sits with him in the house, walks out with him into the street, and haunts his bed-side.*

I find this a resonant parable: self-image impedes a man, frustrates his faculties, is fatal, is a kind of shroud. The opposite of Mr. —— is the man of whom Hazlitt approves, the man who, while not ignorant of his limits, does not look too closely into himself, the un-self-preoccupied man; Hazlitt believes that analysis of oneself is futile, for "we are parties too much concerned to return a fair verdict" (p. 115).

Tennyson's sequence of dramatic monologues accords well with Hazlitt's conception of human identity: identity is dark, precarious, concealed, seized only in fitful intuitions; any secure, stable self-knowledge is likely to be a delusion. Introspection yields a bewildering series of related but discontinuous images; out of this welter one improvises an identity. This is how I reconstruct the genesis of many of Tennyson's dramatic monologues: Tennyson was haunted by certain images, consisting of detailed depictions or colored visual fields, images which seemed to him so significant that they were affiliated with his deepest feeling of self; he then tried to construct a narrative and psychological context for these images, a character who might plausibly behold them—that is, Tennyson took his image and imagined an imaginer. This method of auto-biography is ideally suited to avoid the pitfall of Hazlitt's Mr. ———, for the poet remains free of the stifling burden of a historical, accretive, declared self, free to state his significant, revelatory images through objective, plastic, experimental personae. Tennyson's contemporaries evidently did not examine too closely the degree of definition in the mythological personae; perhaps captivated by the rhetorical unity of each poem, the consistency of diction and speech pattern, they assumed that the underlying character was similarly unified, specific. But it is not so; indeed Tennyson in each monologue shows some manifestations of the plasticity, the irresolution, the blurriness of his speaker; each speaker has a shape of sorts, but continually appeals to some supervening shapelessness and obscurity. If the character attained full self-definition he would lack the psychological reverberation, the intimacy with his unclarifiable author, that made him appealing to Tennyson.

We know that we are reading a dramatic monologue—the term seems convenient, even though, as Dwight Culler notes, Tennyson would not have used it—of this kind when the speaker's energy in attempting to specify himself seems out of proportion to the difficulty of the task. In Dante's *Inferno* the denizens of hell, much distorted by their punishments, by the very sins that define them, swiftly rehearse the significant events of their lives, as if they could reconstitute their lost selves by reminiscence; the one sin they are all guilty of is pride, pride that leads them to expose what they should have effaced; even Guido, wishing to be forgotten by the living, cannot resist the compulsion to explicate himself to Dante, to remember the shape hidden in his shapeless flame. But Tennyson's mythological characters, equally compelled, equally eager to account for themselves, wander and waver and drift, make many fine inconclusive speeches which touch upon matters that must not be spoken of, speeches that distract our attention from some central indistinctness in them.

The first of these baroque, helpless, excessively lavish personae is Œnone. Tennyson admitted that the germ of "Œnone" (1830–32) was landscape, the Pyrenean scenery he had visited with Arthur Hallam in 1830, now transposed to the vicinity of Troy:

> There lies a vale in Ida, lovelier
> Than all the valleys of Ionian hills.
> The swimming vapour slopes athwart the glen,
> Puts forth an arm, and creeps from pine to pine,
> And loiters, slowly drawn. On either hand
> The lawns and meadow-ledges midway down
> Hang rich in flowers, and far below them roars
> The long brook falling through the cloven ravine
> In cataract after cataract to the sea.

(ll. 1–9)

After this brief stage setting, Œnone begins her monologue. What sort of being would be the proper resident of such a place? An intelligence as nebulous, hesitant, clingy, and billowing as the vapor; a passion as intricately droopy as the cataracts. In a sense this image manufactures a psychology appropriate to it, becomes the true subject of the poem; Tennyson's complicated local responses aggregate themselves into a pseudoperson who is then asked to explain herself but cannot, since she is articulate and lively without being real. Again and again, she talks about clouds: she remembers that Troy was once "A cloud that gathered shape" (l. 41), that over Hera's peacock flowed a golden cloud "slowly dropping fragrant

dew" (l. 104), that her "quick-falling dew / Of fruitful kisses" once
fell on Paris "thick as Autumn rains" (ll. 200–201). She is a cloudy
and watery woman, this daughter of a river-god, a figment of
geography who has been given a voice. Œnone and the events of
her life saturate the countryside; indeed she is herself humidity. Her
lament is formal, inexorable, given structure by a stately refrain,
and it seems as if she were, like Troy, trying to coalesce into shape.
The poem is in this sense a magic spell Œnone utters to give herself a
definition, a precision comparable to that of the rhetoric she employs.

This kind of spell can be observed more clearly in a slightly
earlier poem, "Ilion, Ilion" (1830):

> Ilion, Ilion, dreamy Ilion, pillared Ilion, holy Ilion,
> City of Ilion when wilt thou be melody born?
> Blue Scamander, yellowing Simois from the heart of piny
>   Ida
> Everwhirling from the molten snows upon the
>   mountainthrone,
> Roll Scamander, ripple Simois, ever onward to a melody
> Manycircled, overflowing thorough and thorough the
>   flowery level of unbuilt Ilion,
> City of Ilion, pillared Ilion, shadowy Ilion, holy Ilion,
>   To a music merrily flowing, merrily echoing
>   When wilt thou be melody born?

(ll. 1–9)

Troy was reputed to have been sung into being by Apollo; although
"Ilion, Ilion" is only an apostrophe to an unbuilt, imaginary city,
the metrical force seems to be trying to approximate that of the
divine song that gave entity to Troy. Similarly, Œnone tries to sing
herself into being. She vainly urges Paris to give the apple to
Athena, and doubtless she approves of Athena's motto: " 'Self-
reverence, self-knowledge, self-control, / These three alone lead
life to sovereign power' " (ll. 142–43). Yet neither Paris nor she is
capable of this wisdom; she pretends to desire self-control, clarity
of being, emphatic shape, she pretends to be of Athena's party, but
the images of greatest intensity in the poem suggest an altogether
different direction:

"It was the deep midnoon: one silvery cloud
Had lost his way between the piney sides
Of this long glen. Then to the bower they came,
Naked they came to that smooth-swarded bower,
And at their feet the crocus brake like fire,
(ll. 90–100)   Violet, amaracus, and asphodel,
Lotos and lilies: and a wind arose,
And overhead the wandering ivy and vine,
This way and that, in many a wild festoon
Ran riot, garlanding the gnarlèd boughs
With bunch and berry and flower through and through."

If one ponders on a pretty landscape in the Pyrenees, one may imagine it populated with a handsome shepherd and a beautiful shepherdess, rural swain and rural nymph; or one may imagine it embellished, improved, made spectacular, sublime. As a character in Ovid, Œnone embodies the desire for the first vision, pastoral tranquility, domestic bliss with Paris without gods, without war; but as a persona in Tennyson she embodies both that and the opposing desire, a tendency to scatter, diffuse, become a cloudy vehicle for epiphany. Through Œnone the poet can imagine divine apparition, flowers suddenly springing up under the feet of the goddesses, ivy and vine crisscrossing through the air, images multiplying in such profusion that all shape threatens to vanish in this abundance of shapes. Sleeping in the landscape are powers that may overwhelm all human construction. By the end of the poem Œnone seems about to scorch the land with fire:

"I will not die alone, for fiery thoughts
Do shape themselves within me, more and more,
Whereof I catch the issue, as I hear
Dead sounds at night come from the inmost hills,
(ll. 242–49,   Like footsteps upon wool. I dimly see
257–64)   My far-off doubtful purpose, as a mother
Conjectures of the features of her child
Ere it is born. . . .
                    I will rise and go
Down into Troy, and ere the stars come forth

> Talk with the wild Cassandra, for she says
> A fire dances before her, and a sound
> Rings ever in her ears of armèd men.
> What this may be I know not, but I know
> That, wheresoe'er I am by night and day,
> All earth and air seem only burning fire."

At first she was vapor and waterfall, a picture postcard; now she is a volcano. Her dream of becoming discrete, stable, human has been destroyed by Paris's faithlessness; and she abandons all claim to definite shape, deliberately grows vague, incoherent, the python of doom. The distinct images of the opening have yielded to an imageless apocalypse; and Œnone has grown furious, implacable, a god. What Apollo's song has built, her song will unbuild. Tennyson seems more adept at making his poems emotionally expressive when he depicts the destruction of images than when he depicts their construction; here rage is given a satisfying outlet in a great undoing.

Cloud, fire, dazzle, the Spirit of Prophecy, numen and lumen, all are reworkings of the sublimities of "Armageddon"; "Œnone" is a far more controlled and rigorous poem, but it derives its peculiar power from the fact that these elemental excesses are only half congealed into a finite persona. One of the signs that Tennyson could not manage fully to state Œnone within the limits of her poem is that she lived on in Tennyson's imagination, unresolved, ruined, until she reappeared, almost fifty years later, in one of Tennyson's last poems, "The Death of Œnone" (1889–90). Far from being a monologuist, she is now almost mute; but her mind is still the expression of a landscape:

> Œnone sat within the cave from out
> Whose ivy-matted mouth she used to gaze
> Down at the Troad; but the goodly view
> Was now one blank, and all the serpent vines
>
> (ll. 1–9) Which on the touch of heavenly feet had risen,
> And gliding through the branches overbowered
> The naked Three, were withered long ago,
> And through the sunless winter morning-mist
> In silence wept upon the flowerless earth.

The vatic fire at the end of "Œnone" is spent, and what has succeeded it is a still greater imagelessness; once again Œnone is misty,
drippy, but now fruitless, insipid, lacking any cohesion or viscosity.
The abundance of images in "Œnone" has withered into a little
flotsam, idle and lacking any symbolic potency; and Paris himself is
no longer beautiful, but poisoned, "Lame, crookèd, reeling, livid"
(l. 27), appearing in Œnone's imagination as "ghastlier than the
Gorgon head, a face,— / *His* face deformed by lurid blotch and
blain" (ll. 71–72). The Gorgon analogy suggests that Paris's deformity has deformed her; and indeed both have become shriveled,
evacuated, ghostly—Paris is "the wraith of his dead self" (l. 28),
and Œnone's white fog vanishes "like a ghost" (l. 67). Paris begs
Œnone to heal him, but she will not forgive his treachery; both
seem to cling to their former identities, yet by the end of the poem it
is clear that these half-dissolved figments, these revenants of a long-
extinct passion, crave only further dissolution. Œnone leaps into
the pyre that the shepherds have made for Paris, as the flames she
once foresaw kindled for the city of Troy consume her as well, and
the lovers attain mutual effacement, nonentity. The passage from
cloud to fire is the same as that of the earlier poem; but in "The
Death of Œnone" all is simple and spectral, classical, the sun burning away the mist without great ado.

The young Tennyson of "Armageddon" invented a deranged
landscape in which every detail was mysteriously expressive, correlative to the poet's sensibility; a few years later, in "Œnone,"
Tennyson does the exact opposite, invents a sensibility mysteriously expressive of a landscape. In many later poems we also hear
a speaking landscape. In a series of poems written in 1837–38, the
matters treated so earnestly in "Œnone" are turned into burlesque
and parody, as if the river-nymph had streaks of levity in her that
required expression before her final dismissal in 1890. The device of
the landscape-turned-human returns in strange guise in "The Talking Oak" (1837 or 1838): the narrator pines away for his Olivia
beneath an oak into which he once carved her name; the oak, having
"plagiarized a heart" (l. 19), tries to console him in a long monologue, an impulse from a vernal wood. The tree is capable of
imaginative participation in the narrator's life: the oak makes a nice

oaky simile in comparing Olivia's grasp around his trunk to the
fragile pressure of woodbine, and he half-blames Olivia for infan-
ticide when he recounts how she decapitated an acorn; but the most
remarkable stanza was deleted:

"The woodpecker is kindly bred,
    Has often tapt and clung,
And hammered with his garnet head,
    And kist me with his tongue."

(Ricks,
p. 680)

The attribution of quasi-sexual behavior to a tree brings us close to a
mythological world where men only enact the deeper passions of
landscape; and, at the end of the poem, the narrator swears that for
his marriage day he will dress Olivia as the dryad of the talking oak
(l. 286).

But the modern English climate is not congenial to dryads, and
the whole poem is pleasant silliness, "an experiment," as Tennyson
said, "meant to test the degree in which it was in my power as a poet
to humanise external nature" (Ricks, p. 675). Sometimes in "The
Talking Oak" Tennyson apes the themes of sublimity:

"For ah! my friend, the days were brief
    Whereof the poets talk,
When that, which breathes within the leaf,
    Could slip its bark and walk."

(ll. 185–88)

This is similar to a passage in a contemporaneous poem, "Amphion," in which the poet wishes he could use his poetical gift to
clear out his overgrown garden:

O had I lived when song was great
    In days of old Amphion
And ta'en my fiddle to the gate,
    Nor cared for seed or scion!
And had I lived when song was great,
    And legs of trees were limber,
And ta'en my fiddle to the gate,
    And fiddled in the timber!

(ll. 9–16)

Here the celestial muse is asked, so to speak, to bind up her hair in a
scarf, put on old clothes, and help with the yardwork. Tennyson is

full of dreams of exotic vegetation which he might transplant into his garden:

> But these, though fed with careful dirt,
>   Are neither green nor sappy;
> Half-conscious of the garden-squirt,
>   The spindlings look unhappy.
> Better to me the meanest weed
>   That blows upon its mountain,
> The vilest herb that runs to seed
>   Beside its native fountain.

(ll. 89–96)

The echo of Wordsworth's "Immortality Ode" is unmistakable, and the poem, like Wordsworth's, is about the contraction of glory, a recentering of energy on small significant things. The genre of "Amphion" is that of Gray's "The Progress of Poesy," and according to Tennyson, as to Gray, its progress is to some extent a regression, a paring-down of sublime aspiration to something less presumptuous, more secure. "Amphion," like "The Palace of Art," is a repudiation of a certain attitude to poetry writing; the world of "Œnone," where Apollo as well as Amphion could sing cities into being, where trees could hoist themselves on their roots and stroll about, where vines could interlace the sky, is hereby abandoned in favor of a hardy British garden. Tennyson did not cease writing poems on classical subjects after 1838, but he usually tried to frame, qualify, or otherwise apologize for his antiquarianism. Yet, despite his ridicule, his travesty, he never managed to suppress entirely the desire to be Amphion or Orpheus; a fully earthly muse, content with weeding a small suburban plot, is never quite to his taste. If some semblance of sublime vision can be induced by alcohol, the poet will not hesitate to get drunk, as in "Will Waterproof's Lyrical Monologue" (1837). Will Waterproof is the high visionary poet in his coarsest, most joking guise; when the waiter brings him his stout Will invests the waiter's hands with a halo, and invents a myth about a giant Cock that dropped the waiter, a new Ganymede, into the tavern:

(ll. 133–44)

> He stooped and clutched him, fair and good,
>   Flew over roof and casement:

His brothers of the weather stood
    Stock-still for sheer amazement.

But he, by farmstead, thorpe and spire,
    And followed with acclaims,
A sign to many a staring shire
    Came crowing over Thames.
Right down by smoky Paul's they bore,
    Till, where the street grows straiter,
One fixed for ever at the door,
    And one became head-waiter.

The Cock has suffered the ignominy of becoming a mere image, painted on the door of the Cock Tavern, Fleet Street; but in the inebriated imagination it is given weight and dimension, the power of flight, is summoned to minister to the poet's need for stout. In the labile world of myth, images and the things they are images of grow easily interchangeable, and in a lyrical monologue all must obey the force of the lyre. These are the sorts of rapid and unpredictable metamorphoses that make it difficult to state a coherent image of the poet or the world he inhabits. All sublimity is, in a sense, the postulation of a drunken cosmos.

One of the reasons why Tennyson's characters are so often shapeless, soft-edged, is that they are self-hypnotized, or self-destructive, or dwell in a state of narcosis. In "Ilion, Ilion" and "Œnone" Tennyson stresses the dissolving power of song; in "The Lotos-Eaters" (1830–32), the hazy chorus keeps itself lulled in its dreamy, saturated landscape, a world without emphasis, by means of its perpetual chant. I have referred to "Œnone" as a dramatic monologue—although some might object to the use of this term for such a ritualized, static, incantatory poem—because it resembles those poems which everyone would call dramatic monologues. "St Simeon Stylites" (1832) seems to differ from "Œnone" in every aspect of tone, diction, character, and plot; yet both are investigations of the uses of language in defining the limits of personality, a personality that threatens to dissolve into an ecstasy.

We have seen that one of Tennyson's favorite motifs from Greek mythology is the singer who can shape a world to his liking;

that is, the myth of Orpheus. Simeon Stylites is the anti-Orpheus, incapable of song, whose ugly croaks are the agency of his self-dismemberment, a perverse Orpheus who orders his own *sparagma*. Instead of the song that informs a landscape, we have speech that excoriates the speaker's flesh; the magic is turned inward, and becomes bilious, black. Like Merlin he traps himself in a prison without walls. His speech is essentially deconstructive in nature, a parody of the mystic's entry into the sublime.

Simeon Stylites also reminds us of some of Tennyson's earliest visionaries, such as the poet of "Armageddon," in that he tries to induce celestial visions of angels, of Christ, of paradise:

> While I spake then, a sting of shrewdest pain
> Ran shrivelling through me, and a cloudlike change,
> In passing, with a grosser film made thick
> These heavy, horny eyes. The end! the end!
> Surely the end! What's here? a shape, a shade,
> A flash of light. Is that the angel there
> That holds a crown? Come, blessèd brother, come.

(ll. 195–201)

Alas, unlike the angel of "Armageddon," this angel does not unclog the visionary's eyes, only makes them all the more bleary. Simeon's error is that he wishes to make a public spectacle of his rapture; he imagines that he will turn into an icon of himself, an image of ecstasy like Bernini's St. Theresa, but instead he only excites a kind of awe-stricken derision in those who behold him. Œnone, as water, as fire, possessed, despite her gentleness, a spontaneous elemental force; Simeon is an estranged calculating thing battered by the elements, oddly like the Soul at the end of "The Palace of Art." Lunatic from self-detachment, from hatred of the flesh, he is masochism's lord, a genius of disease:

> all my beard
> Was tagged with icy fringes in the moon,
> I drowned the whoopings of the owl with sound
> Of pious hymns and psalms, and sometimes saw
> An angel stand and watch me, as I sang.
> Now am I feeble grown; my end draws nigh . . . .

(ll. 30–35, 45–53)

O Jesus, if thou wilt not save my soul,
Who may be saved? who is it may be saved?
Who may be made a saint, if I fail here?
Show me the man hath suffered more than I.
For did not all thy martyrs die one death?
For either they were stoned, or crucified,
Or burned in fire, or boiled in oil, or sawn
In twain beneath the ribs; but I die here
Today, and whole years long, a life of death.

On his high pillar he ostentatiously excludes the world while invit-
ing it to attend to him, grows rapt and involuted in his fantasies of
self-aggrandisement, fascinated by his own decay. Late in life Tennyson wrote a poem called "Happy" (1888), a monologue by a
woman who chose to contract leprosy by marrying a crusader in
order to ease his wretched life. "St Simeon Stylites" is the demonic
parody of this freely chosen selfless suffering, for Simeon chooses
to make of his emaciation a theatrical spectacle. It is possible that
Tennyson is here indicting confessional poetry, such as "Supposed
Confessions of a Second-Rate Sensitive Mind," poetry in which the
poet exposes his squalor as an object of admiration—it is Tennyson's habit to express his deepest fears and hopes by means of his
most outrageously oblique, un-Tennysonian characters.

Œnone made a verbal artifact of her life and then cast it away,
lost herself in a dream; Simeon labors to annihilate himself, to
exuberate into heavenly abstraction, yet he grows more defined,
willful, stamped, the more he tries to become superhuman. The
more he labors to be sublime, the more earthly and pedestrian he
becomes, as if the cantankerous will for elevation itself excluded its
object. Because he is so manifestly a dung beetle that relishes his
corruption, a hunger artist haughty in his humility, we feel that we
know his character, indeed far better than he knows himself. Yet,
though he has precisely delineated features, this definedness exists
only in counterpoint to the sublimity to which he aspires; without
his ludicrous fantasy of Simeon in heaven, swathed in light and
wearing the martyr's crown, venerated by all men—"This dull
chrysalis / Cracks into shining wings" (ll. 153–54)—he would be

less incisive, more random, a creature of motiveless abjection. The visionary aspects of the poem act as a white background against which Simeon's silhouette grows visible, distinct. It is ironic that he acquires a sharp profile only by trying to slough off his face, to become traitless and beatified; but Tennyson likes to define personality by contrasting it with something that renders personality impossible. This is the key to the mystery of Tennyson's peculiar practice as a writer of dramatic monologues: shape and shapelessness; what a man is and what a man would like to mutate into; the verbal charm that brings him into being and the verbal charm that dispells him—these are forced together in the confines of the same rhetorical body, and the character acquires impetus, dramatic energy, from their tension.

Still, the coherence, the distinctiveness of Simeon Stylites is unusual in a character whose limbs and appendages are dropping from his body, someone who is less a man than the residue of a man, burnt to charcoal, the organic minimum. "St Simeon Stylites" is a humorous poem, and Tennyson liked to read it histrionically to amuse his friends; and yet, in the context of a poem that may have been begun when "St Simeon Stylites" was written, "The Two Voices" (1833), the martyr's absurd self-flagellation perhaps suggests Tennyson's anxiety about the nature of identity. "The Two Voices" does not posit delineated and striking characters, like Simeon, but instead offers half-personified figments of Tennyson's internal dialogue; as such it offers some clues to the process by which Tennyson created the characters of his dramatic monologues, the process by which almost unnamable psychic material is given a local habitation and a name, the process by which hidden, indistinct, awful matter is dragged into the light, given expression. "The Two Voices" is a psychomachia, but of an unusual kind, inconclusive, irresolute, with no assurance about the identity of the combatants; instead of the clearly defined warfare of appetite's siege against restraint (as in the classical psychomachia), we have a poet who attempts

(ll. 136–38)
>"As far as might be, to carve out
>Free space for every human doubt,
>That the whole mind might orb about."

Doubts revolve, the mind revolves, and no conclusions can be drawn in this planetary system of endlessly orbiting opinions. Most of the poem consists of a dialogue between the poet—by "the poet" I mean Tennyson's chief persona—and the first voice, the voice that urges suicide. What makes the poem confusing is that these antagonists employ similar imagery, similar trains of thought, are in fact difficult to tell apart. If there is any criterion for distinguishing them, it is that the poet generally tries to establish himself as a discrete person, small but unique, with a certain modest importance in the scheme of things, while his opponent, the bad voice, appeals to a vastness in which the individual is wholly swallowed up. In a poem like "St Simeon Stylites" a single character displays in himself the tension between shape and shapelessness, but in "The Two Voices" there is a division of role, a poet clinging to shape and a bad voice urging shapelessness:

(ll. 31–36)

> It spake, moreover, in my mind:
> "Though thou wert scattered to the wind,
> Yet is there plenty of the kind."
>
> Then did my response clearer fall:
> "No compound of this earthly ball
> Is like another, all in all."

Also, the poet insists on a measured hierarchy, while the voice insinuates its theory of gradualism; in the deleted section the poet asserts that

(Ricks, p. 537, ll. [7]–[9])

> "That individual unity
> Which each calls I, may never flee
> To many parts and cease to be"

while the bad voice denies that any being can pretend to integrity, definition:

(Ricks, p. 537, ll. [19]– [27])

> "And things" he said "which thou mayst cleave
> To many parts that each receive
> Another life, dost thou believe
>
> They feel thus one? So Nature spins
> A various web and knowledge wins
> No surety where this sense begins.

Nor whereabouts to fainter fades
Through tints and neutral tints and shades
Life and half-life, a million grades.

The bad voice's argument has some precedents in nineteenth-
century literature. Coleridge's Ordonio, the hero of *Remorse*, spec-
ulates that murder may be no sin because what we call death is not
death at all:

(2.2)

Say, I had lay'd a body in the sun!
Well! in a month there swarm forth from the corse
A thousand, nay, ten thousand sentient beings
In place of that one man. Say I had *kill'd* him!
Yet who shall tell me, that each one and all
Of these ten thousand lives is not as happy
As that one life, which being push'd aside,
Made room for these unnumber'd.

Hazlitt cites this passage in "On the Knowledge of Character"
(p. 114), and wonders whether it is not the source of his own
theory of human identity, of his own emphasis on its provisional
and mysterious qualities. A man wishes to think of himself as a
bounded, self-contained, authentic, independent entity; but mind,
as in Coleridge's "Dejection," may grow confused in the haze and
maze of abstract thought, and body is susceptible to this degeneration into competing protozoa. Tennyson's "The Two Voices" is a
dramatization of the competition between a man's urge to coherence, compact identity, and the contrary urge toward diffusion of body and soul. Hazlitt knew Coleridge pretty well, and
considered him a balked and cloudy genius, lost in unrealities:

(Hazlitt,
pp. 232–33)

*Mr. Coleridge has "a mind reflecting ages past"; his voice is like
the echo of the congregated roar of the "dark rearward and abyss" of
thought. He who has seen a mouldering tower by the side of a
chrystal lake, hid by the mist, but glittering in the wave below,
may conceive the dim, gleaming, uncertain intelligence of his eye:
he who has marked the evening clouds unrolled (a world of
vapours), has seen the picture of his mind, unearthly, unsubstan-
tial, with gorgeous tints and ever-varying forms—*

"That which was now a horse, even with a thought
The rack dislimns, and makes it indistinct
As water is in water."

The myth of Coleridge that Coleridge invented, and Hazlitt
helped to promulgate, was the myth of the dissolved man, the pure
intelligence blurred, uselessly sublime, in which imagination had
reached such heights of synthesis that no solid image obtained in its
ascent toward the One. Coleridge is the man who has lapsed,
yielded to what Tennyson called the bad voice. The passage that
Hazlitt quotes is from *Antony and Cleopatra;* the ruined Antony, his
armies defeated, his Cleopatra, as he thinks, a traitor, asks his friend
Eros whether he has ever looked at the melting images of bear or
lion or citadel or horse that one can behold in clouds; here is the
sequel:

	Eros.	It does, my lord.
(4.14.11–	*Ant.* My good knave Eros, now thy captain is	
14)	Even such a body. Here I am Antony;	
	Yet cannot hold this visible shape, my knave.	

Antony feels this dissolution of reputation kinesthetically, as if his
body were undoing itself along with his armies; it is a remarkable
passage, especially in a play so Nilotic, so infused with a sense of
slime made fecund by the sun. Little wonder that Hazlitt should
find this description of dispersing identity appropriate to a certain
strain of Romantic poetry. This sort of intuition, this feeling of
plasticity, of infinitely various shapes latent in one's being, can be a
source of exultation; but it is often the sinister exultation of the Soul
in "The Palace of Art," monstrously proud of her ability to become
Madonna, Ganymede, Cama, to mirror whatever she beholds. A
sane man will try to resist this feeling, to confine himself to a single
shape, as the poet does in "The Two Voices." For Tennyson the
sense that body and mind cannot retain a distinct shape can be
construed either as a revelation of higher truth—Loss of Self is the
motto by which Sir Galahad finds the Holy Grail, by which the
Ancient Sage attains transcendence—or as an invitation to suicide.
The idea of the body graduating into smaller bodies is a source of

terror. At the end of "The Vision of Sin" (1840–42) the orgy of skeletons slows, stops:

(ll. 209–12)

> Below were men and horses pierced with worms,
> And slowly quickening into lower forms;
> By shards and scurf of salt, and scum of dross,
> Old plash of rains, and refuse patched with moss.

And by 1868 Tennyson's Lucretius, another man weighing the advantages of suicide—I shall treat him in greater detail in a subsequent chapter—will remember that in death his atoms will disperse and reconstitute themselves "into man once more, / Or beast or bird or fish, or opulent flower" (ll. 247–48). In "The Palace of Art," in "The Vision of Sin," in parts of *In Memoriam,* in "Lucretius," the temptation to die is the temptation to identify oneself with nature, to become sublime; and it can be resisted only by the urging of the prosaic, the ordinary, just as the poet at the end of "The Two Voices" fortifies himself with a Sunday school tract illustration. Yet the temptation, the desire to mix oneself with the landscape, is hard to quell, and the equilibrium between the body and its ultimate relaxation, surrender of muscle tone, always precarious. The motto of the deranged sensibility, as we have seen before, is "I become what I behold"; and to disperse into atoms that mingle with grass and air is a demonic literalization of that motto. As always, whenever Tennyson goes too far in one direction, it reveals itself as an untenable goal, and there is a reversion to the mean: the too sublime always displays itself as a condition of terror, the too commonplace always displays itself as banal, with insufficient stress to permit vision or action.

The sympathy between Carlyle and Tennyson is clear if we compare the bad voice's description of the "various web" that nature weaves, in which the image of the body is the faintest of boundary lines among the "tints and neutral tints and shades," with the following passage from the "Organic Filaments" chapter of *Sartor Resartus:*

(p. 184)

> *"Wert thou, my little Brotherkin, suddenly covered-up within the largest imaginable Glass-bell,—what a thing it were, not for thyself only, but for the world! Post Letters, more or fewer, from all*

the four winds, impinge against thy Glass walls, but have to drop unread: neither from within comes there question or response into any Postbag; thy Thoughts fall into no friendly ear or heart, thy Manufacture into no purchasing hand: thou art no longer a circulating venous-arterial Heart, that, taking and giving, circulatest through all Space and all Time: there has a Hole fallen-out in the immeasurable, universal World-tissue, which must be darned-up again!"

"Such venous-arterial circulation, of Letters, verbal Messages, paper and other Packages, going out from him and coming in, are a blood-circulation, visible to the eye."

Carlyle argues too that we cannot descry the exact limits of a man, for we are each of us impinged upon by innumerable forces that alter us and are slightly altered by us. Carlyle defines these forces more exactly in the "Prospective" chapter: " 'Detached, separated! I say there is no such separation: nothing hitherto was ever stranded, cast aside; but all, were it only a withered leaf, works together with all; is borne forward on the bottomless, shoreless flood of Action, and lives through perpetual metamorphoses. The withered leaf is not dead and lost, there are Forces in it and around it, though working in inverse order; else how could it *rot?* Despise not the rag from which man makes Paper, or the litter from which the earth makes Corn' " (p. 53). It is as if, in "The Two Voices," the poet had to discover some way of clapping Carlyle's glass bell over himself, in order not to fuzz out into nonentity; but that, at the same time, Carlyle's seductive sense of sensuous reciprocity with the cosmos still compelled him—if only it could be made invigorating and not morbid.

The dialogue of "The Two Voices"—the competing voices that tug a man between self-definition and delirium, unboundedness—does not end with Tennyson and Carlyle, but continues, perhaps to this day; Walter Pater, about forty years later, gives Carlyle's argument new pungency in the Conclusion to *The Renaissance* (1873):

(Ed. Donald L. Hill, pp. 186–87)   *To regard all things and principles of things as inconstant modes or fashions has more and more become the tendency of modern thought. Let us begin with that which is without—our physical life. Fix upon it in one of its more exquisite intervals, the moment, for instance, of delicious recoil from the flood of water in summer heat. What is the whole physical life in that moment but a combination of natural elements to which science gives their names? But those elements, phosphorus and lime and delicate fibres, are present not in the human body alone: we detect them in places most remote from it. Our physical life is a perpetual motion of them—the passage of the blood, the waste and repairing of the lenses of the eye, the modification of the tissues of the brain under every ray of light and sound—processes which science reduces to simpler and more elementary forces. Like the elements of which we are composed, the action of these forces extends beyond us: it rusts iron and ripens corn. Far out on every side of us those elements are broadcast, driven in many currents; and birth and gesture and death and the springing of violets from the grave are but a few out of ten thousand resultant combinations. That clear, perpetual outline of face and limb is but an image of ours, under which we group them—a design in a web, the actual threads of which pass out beyond it. This at least of flamelike our life has, that it is but the concurrence, renewed from moment to moment, of forces parting sooner or later on their ways.*

It is a further shattering of the glass bell: the outline of the human body is a nearly arbitrary construct, even in its grossest, most supine state; as Yeats will express it (in his Introduction to *Fighting the Waves*), in what seems an unconscious commentary on this passage, the swimmer has himself become the wave. Mind and body alike are provisional, ever-shifting designs—Can You Find the Sailor Hidden in the Tree?—uncertain confluences of waves and particles.

Other voices are less enthusiastic about this dissolution, repeat Tennyson's qualms about the incipient polyps and amoebas into which our bodies will break down if we fail to maintain our self-control; the rhetoric of Coleridge's Ordonio, Tennyson's "Vision of Sin," attains something like its final form in T. S. Eliot's *Murder in the Cathedral:*

> I have eaten
> Smooth creatures still living, with the strong salt taste of

(*Complete
Poems and
Plays,*
p. 207)

living things under sea; I have tasted
The living lobster, the crab, the oyster, the whelk and the
        prawn; and they live and spawn in my bowels, and
        my bowels dissolve in the light of dawn.

This queasiness, this revulsion against tissue pullulating in one's own body, Jonah's fear of the whale growing in his intestines, suggests how intimate the terror of dissolution can become. To the body, the sublime is simply gangrene.

I have spoken as if the competition in "The Two Voices" were between a poet, who represents quotidian satisfaction, and a bad voice, who represents a perverted sublimity; but it is more complicated than that. The poet gets easily carried away by his rosy vision of life, with which he hopes to stop up the voice of despair. But whenever the poet makes extravagant claims—that man has dominion over all of nature (l. 21); that he will become the knight of truth and love, and "perish, wept for, honoured, known" (l. 149); that he will become a second Stephen, stoned for maintaining his religious vision in a hostile world but permitted to die blessed while "God's glory smote him on the face" (l. 225); that he will be vouchsafed an apprehension of a "Heavenly Friend" (l. 295) and "Vast images in glimmering dawn" (l. 305)—then the poet leaves himself open to attack. Whenever the poet pretends to be the mystic—the vast broken images (l. 305) seem derived from the early poem "The Mystic"—Tennyson makes the poet's claim to moral authority seem less tenable; the poet begins to sound presumptuous, and the overtones of the Soul in "The Palace of Art" start to be heard in his voice. When the poet compares himself to Stephen, he verges on the uncomfortable puffery of Simeon Stylites; and indeed if we think of a less playful version of "St Simeon Stylites" in which his loud self-abasement is predicated to one voice—the bad voice—and his cackling self-aggrandisement to another voice—the poet—we have the dialectic of "The Two Voices." Tennyson shows his irresolution, his inability to make a convincing final affirmation that the poet is correct and wise and that the bad voice is entirely bad, by making the poet and the bad voice difficult to tell apart. The bad voice infiltrates the poet's own rhetoric; and the cause of their collusion lies in the fact that their original separation was only a literary convention, that they are both equally Tennyson.

When the poet indulges in his flights of imaginary glory, the bad voice can either turn them inside out, display some greater abyss in which the glory vanishes, the fearful spheres of Pascal, or the voice can turn unsublime, empirical, point to the peaceful corpse:

> "Consider well," the voice replied,
> "His face, that two hours since hath died;
> Wilt thou find passion, pain or pride?
>
> "Will he obey when one commands?
> Or answer should one press his hands?
> He answers not, nor understands.
>
> "His palms are folded on his breast:
> There is no other thing expressed
> But long disquiet merged in rest."

(ll. 241–49)

In this manner poet and voice keep leapfrogging, adopting each other's tactics, sharing the same intuitions of incandescence—the bad voice speaks of the soul rending its chrysalis like a dragonfly, "A living flash of light" (l. 15), while the poet speaks of seeing the "distant gates of Eden gleam" (l. 212)—as if they differed only in interpretation.

I believe that the voice cannot be refuted by any argument of the poet's, for the poem adduces only the semblance of an argument, without genuine intellectual structure, an endless self-bickering; but the voice can be defeated, in a sense, by inclusion, by making it a necessary component in a larger, more complicated organizing of mental entities. I have alleged that the sum of Tennyson's speakers of dramatic monologues is Tennyson, and I hope to demonstrate this in the next chapters; here in "The Two Voices" we have a much-simplified version of this process, wherein several half-personified voices reveal themselves as partial aspects of a single large sensibility. Near the end of the poem the poet sees the happy family walking to church and hears a second voice saying,

"Be of better cheer" (l. 429), "Rejoice!" (l. 462). But this second voice, like the first, is mere ventriloquism, an ascription of a certain tonality to sentences, narrated visions, already in the head of the poet-persona. The poem shows us that it is hard to distinguish the life-enhancing from the life-denying; nothing is certain to be of one party or of the other. Yet by keeping open the possibility that what seems conducive to damnation, suicide, may in fact lead one to the opposite conclusion, the first voice is given a function in the poet's psychic economy. If "every cloud, that spreads above / And veileth love, itself is love" (ll. 446–47), then cloud making is also "labour working to an end" (l. 297); and the bad voice is a stimulation, a provocation to the discovery of the possibility of virtuous action. It is possible that the bad voice, which is the most confident, articulate, and subtle entity in the poem, may be identified with the high imagination, in its demonic phase; providing, for the most part, not distinct corporeal images, but vast and nebulous magnificences in which all definite forms are drowned.

The urge to speak, to utter oneself, always has a tendency to get out of control. The personages in Tennyson's poems usually begin by talking calmly of their circumstances, their histories, their emotional predicaments, but (as we shall see) as they get excited they start to make larger claims, preposterous overstatements of themselves, perplexing any hope of clear self-definition. This is the sense in which "The Two Voices" is a model for the dramatic monologues to come: every character has a bad voice inside him, urging him on to claim an infinite scope for his field of identity.

VI

Escape into Godhead

BEFORE "THE TWO VOICES" WAS COMPLETED, Tennyson learned that Arthur Hallam had died of a stroke in Vienna in September 1833 at the age of twenty-two. The black agitation of the two competing personages in this poem, one frantic to find a reason to die, the other frantic to find a reason to live, both grasping at irrationalities, suggests a mind in extremis. The stress of Hallam's death also provoked three dramatic monologues on characters of Greek my-thology, possibly four, if "Semele" was written at the end of 1833; all of them—"Ulysses," "Tithon," and "Tiresias"—depict the state of reeling. In "Œnone," as we have seen, the main theme was the creating and uncreating of images; the same is true of these mono-logues, though the intensity is greater. Œnone seemed, at the end, to go into trance, to shift from obsessive rehearsal of private woe into an oblivious incendiary rage; the 1833 monologuists are so eager to dismiss themselves, to dispel themselves, that they can scarcely bother to narrate the achievements, the distinctive features, of the selves they are abandoning. In this chapter we shall examine the change, the darkening, that Hallam's death wrought upon Tennyson's dramatic monologues; here the earthly muse has little to do, for the celestial muse is left to conceive these characters who are not so much people as pretexts for stating a vertigo of identity.

In "Ulysses" the great warrior knows that he has "become a name" (l. 11), that everyone already has heard Homer tell the *Iliad* and the *Odyssey;* merely to mention Troy or Achilles is enough to summon up the richly detailed story, the hero in high contour. His "hungry heart" (l. 12) has felt and suffered much, yet, he insists, it is not yet satiated. But this appetite for life is ambiguous:

(ll. 18–26)
> I am a part of all that I have met;
> Yet all experience is an arch wherethrough
> Gleams that untravelled world, whose margin fades

For ever and for ever when I move.
How dull it is to pause, to make an end,
To rust unburnished, not to shine in use!
As though to breathe were life. Life piled on life
Were all too little, and of one to me
Little remains.

He wants life, life, life—"More life, and fuller, that I want" ("The Two Voices," l. 399)—but, chasing the ever-receding vision of ocean past the Pillars of Hercules, he seems about to pass beyond those bournes from which no traveler returns. Tennyson wishes to extricate Ulysses from Homer's too settled verbal form, as if, smothered in words, Ulysses needed Dante, Shakespeare, Tennyson to summon up poetical energy, to free him for new adventure. Yet, for all of the unparalleled magniloquence, it sounds like an empty man's dream of repletion; the boat that awaits him and his already dead comrades may be, like the boat in the "Morte d'Arthur" (1833–34), the ship of death. To breathe *is* life. Telemachus, "decent not to fail / In offices" (ll. 40–41), seems to represent the principle that the business of life must go on, the principle of resolution, steadfastness; to Telemachus is surrendered Ithaca, the world of finite experience, while Ulysses investigates states of rapture and blessing, states pitched too high even for his epical self. It is the drama of "The Two Voices" once again, but now the commonplace, the bounded man, Telemachus, seems faintly contemptible, while the bad voice seems thrilling, irresistible. Ulysses speaks of gaining further renown, but he is broaching a region of whirlpools, the baths of stars, touching upon a condition of namelessness.

I am not sure that "Ulysses" is not the counsel of suicide, that Ulysses' invocations of sublimity are not those of the bad voice in "The Two Voices"; from this perspective, Telemachus represents the poet of "The Two Voices," finding satisfaction in the near and middle distance, in the slow but perceptible political progress of his island kingdom. The invitation at the end of the poem attempts to suggest that the stuff of new epics will arise from the voyage of Ulysses and his zombie mariners, but few poems are so *concluded* as "Ulysses":

(ll. 67–70)

that which we are, we are;
One equal temper of heroic hearts,
Made weak by time and fate, but strong in will
To strive, to seek, to find, and not to yield.

What words could follow these? "That which we are, we are" has nearly progressed into the divine "I am that I am"; and the last line, far from convincing us of the stern fortitude of a particular histor-ical character, suggests some larger-than-human ferocious implaca-bility. The anvil shocks exhaust Ulysses; his character lapses into these impersonal iambs. The strength of the language supersedes the strength of any putative speaker; as in certain passages in Shake-speare, we feel that the character on stage has stopped being human in order to be an occasion for a disengaged verbal creativity. In Homer's *Odyssey,* Odysseus plays a trick by telling the cyclops Polyphemus that his name is Outis, Nobody; and at the end of Tennyson's monologue Ulysses seems once again on the verge of becoming Nobody, a wraith in the Happy Isles receding even deeper into fantasy.

In "Ulysses" the emphasis is upon the speaker, upon the trans-shifting of the speaker into another mode of existence; in "Tithon" (1833; 1860) and "Tiresias" (1833; 1883), the emphasis is upon an image beheld by the speaker, an image that alters and shapes his life—these are poems like "Œnone," in which an imaginer seems to be inferred from an image. "Ulysses" seems to me, except for one line, "And see the great Achilles, whom we knew" (l. 64), an involved and morbid, deceptive poem, in which a desperate wish to escape, to flee, to perish is made to sound like noble life-fulfillment; "Tithon" and "Tiresias," which are oblique attempts to define Tennyson's relationship to the dead Hallam, seem to me, to the extent that they manifest preoccupation with the beloved rather than the mourner, healthier. It is as if Tennyson here were better able to make explicit his own emotion. The feeling of pervasive weakness is not disguised in great orotund willful bluster; Tithon luxuriates in his withering, claims to be nothing more than a phantom seeking dissolution:

(ll. 5–10)

Me only fatal immortality
Consumes: I wither slowly in thine arms,

Here at the quiet limit of the world,
A white-haired shadow roaming like a dream
The ever-silent spaces of the East,
Far-folded mists, and gleaming halls of morn.

One of the many feelings we feel when someone we love dies is
a certain resentment: why did he choose to inflict this punishment
on us, his death? why does he continue to enervate us with our
memories of him? "Tithon" investigates an imagination paralyzed
upon a single image, an image that returns every day but only as
cellophane unreality, never with the satisfying fullness of former
times, when the beloved was alive:

A soft air fans the cloud apart; there comes
A glimpse of that dark world where I was born.
Once more the old mysterious glimmer steals
From thy pure brows, and from thy shoulders pure,
And bosom throbbing with a fresher heart.
Thy cheek begins to bloom a fuller red,
Thy sweet eyes brighten slowly close to mine,
Ere yet they blind the stars, and thy wild team,
Spreading a rapid glow with loosened manes,
Fly, trampling twilight into flakes of fire.
'Tis ever thus: thou growest more beautiful,
Thou partest: when a little warmth returns
Thou partest, and thy tears are on my cheek.

(ll. 28–53)

Ay me! ay me! with what another heart,
By thy divine embraces circumfused,
Thy black curls burning into sunny rings,
With thy change changed, I felt this wondrous glow
That, gradually blooming, flushes all
Thy pale fair limbs: what time my moral frame
Molten in thine immortal, I lay wooed,
Lips, forehead, eyelids, growing dewy-warm
With kisses balmier than opening buds;
Anon the lips that dealt them moved themselves
In wild and airy whisperings more sweet
Than that strange song I heard Apollo sing,
While Ilion like a mist rose into towers.

The poem turns upon this contrast: once, the coming of Eos, Dawn, the immortal beloved, was a quickening of the whole body, a state of mutual vivacity, mutual shaping, as the sunrise resolved itself into a distinct face and the whisperings of Eos imparted a kind of sensuous body to Tithon, just as Apollo sang Troy into being; but now the dawn is a purely pictorial experience, for body is shriveled and eye alone senses the mysterious presence. Old age is a kind of lotos for Tithon, numbing every faculty save that of celestial vision, as if too great feeling had recoiled into anesthesia.

In the 1860 revision, "Tithonus," Tennyson altered the poem to heighten the discontinuity between Tithon-as-lover and Tithon-as-rememberer:

> Ay me! ay me! with what another heart
> In days far-off, and with what other eyes
> I used to watch—if I be he that watched—
> The lucid outline forming round thee; saw
> The dim curls kindle into sunny rings.

(ll. 50–54)

Tithonus is not quite sure that he is the man who was once Eos' lover; he has grown so spectral, so personally dim, that he cannot know that the image in his head once had reality. The image of Dawn has lost pertinence, is growing cold:

> Coldly thy rosy shadows bathe me, cold
> Are all thy lights, and cold my wrinkled feet
> Upon these glimmering thresholds, when the steam
> Floats up from those still fields that dream below.
> Release me! so restore me to the ground;
> Thou seest all things, thou wilt see my grave:
> Thou wilt renew thy beauty with the morn;
> I earth in earth forget these empty courts,
> And thee returning on thy silver wheels.

("Tithon," ll. 56–64)

Tithon is, like Œnone, an imaginer whom Tennyson has summoned to account for a particular image; but he is scarcely a recognizable character, without even Œnone's or Ulysses' rhetorical simulacrum of character, only a kind of aspic that melts and runs while the thing embedded in the aspic remains indestructible, bril-

liant. Tithon is in love with a state of incipience, with a half-image
that keeps trying to kindle itself into full resolution, complete
acuity; but Dawn, like youth, cannot be retained, must change itself
every day into the full sun at which no man can gaze.

I believe that this process of focusing and unfocusing in Tithon's
imagination is related to the alternation of obsessiveness and eva-
siveness with which the image of the dead exasperates us; when we
would forget, it will not let us go; when we would remember, it
slips away from us, as Tennyson dramatizes in *In Memoriam* 70:

> I cannot see the features right,
> > When on the gloom I strive to paint
> > The face I know; the hues are faint
> And mix with hollow masks of night;
>
> Cloud-towers by ghostly masons wrought,
> > A gulf that ever shuts and gapes,
> > A hand that points, and pallèd shapes
> In shadowy thoroughfares of thought;
>
> And crowds that stream from yawning doors,
> > And shoals of puckered faces drive;
> > Dark bulks that tumble half alive,
> And lazy lengths on boundless shores;
>
> Till all at once beyond the will
> > I hear a wizard music roll,
> > And through a lattice on the soul
> Looks thy fair face and makes it still.

(ll. 1–16)

The cloud-towers may remind us of the towers of Troy, congealed
from a cloud by music, to which Tithon compares himself; the
poem is a remarkable depiction of the dejected imagination, hunt-
ing through a repertory of possible vaguenesses that refuse to focus
themselves properly, until the desired face simply, effortlessly, in-
voluntarily, appears. In "Tithon" the face half-appears, tantalizes,
will not leave him in peace and will not embody itself satisfactorily.
The poem is a remarkable record of a sensibility that has lost every
faculty but the imagination, and in which even the imagination is
competent to find only one ever-fleeing image.

Christopher Ricks has noted that, in Jacob Bryant's *New System of Ancient Mythology* (1807), a book in Tennyson's library, Bryant says that "Tithonus, whose longevity is so much celebrated, was nothing more than one of these structures, a Pharos, sacred to the sun" (Ricks, p. 1117). This does much to explain why Eos' whispers remind Tithon of Apollo's incantation of Troy's towers; and the idea of Tithon as a lighthouse may recall the lighthouse to which the Soul was compared in "The Palace of Art" as well as the complicated optical apparatus in the Lady of Shalott's high dwelling, for Tithon has in a sense withered into a camera obscura. His mind has nothing in it but dim self-loathing and grief, except insofar as it provides a film on which to register the sunrise each morning. Disembodied, he painfully remembers the body's former pleasures. The image has detached itself, retains all ardor, all glory, while the imaginer gutters out, a spent candle. In poems like this Tennyson seems to be trying to lose himself—his personae evolve by a steady weakening—while he seizes the sacred dead image as firmly as possible. The death of J. M. Synge affected Yeats, though Yeats never wrote a full *In Memoriam:* "3. We pity the living and not such dead as he. He has gone upward out of his ailing body into the heroical fountains. We are parched by time. 4. He had the knowledge of his coming death and was cheerful to the end, even joking a little when that end had all but come. He had no need of our sympathies. It was as though we and the things about us died away from him and not he from us" (*Autobiography, The Death of Synge,* no. 17). This is close to the mood of "Tithon." Hallam is dead, but, like Eos, a fiery, heroical, indissoluble thing; and Tennyson is alive, but, like Tithon, parched, poor, feeble, deprived, trying to subsist on a diet of bright shadows. I have said that Tennyson found it difficult to speak in a voice of just the proper size; and in "Tithon," far from achieving an agreeable conversational tone, Tennyson fines his voice down to a cricket's whisper, almost no voice at all.

In the mythological poems written just after Hallam's death, Tennyson both conceals and expresses the nature of the sorrow; the impersonations are curiously eccentric, wobbly, the masks slightly askew. The poems all have at their center something raw, incomplete, unresolved, as if to confess that their author was attempt-

ing to treat a matter not quite digested. Unfocused speakers keep
trying to clarify unfocused images, a continual grappling with
dazzling confusion. To read the poems in sequence is to watch a
poet ransacking a library in the search for a proper equivalent to his
turbulent emotional state but finding that none of the analogies is
exactly right, not Ulysses, Tithon, Tiresias, Madonna, Ganymede,
Asiatic dame. Because the poet does not seem to know precisely
what he wishes to express, any character suggesting exalted pathos
will do, as long as the character is seized by some blighting or
ennobling fit of vision, the Spirit of Prophecy familiar to us from
"Armageddon" on. Sublime emotion never has any exact tenor, is
but a limit of convergence where the extremes of joy, terror, grief,
pity all meet; and so it encourages a certain arbitrariness of feeling in
poems that approximate it. Each of the monologues suggests someone blasted by an image at once inaccessible and immediate, all-
compelling.

If "Semele" belongs to this sequence, it shows the most extreme engorgement of the eyeball, for Semele was struck dead by
the sight of Zeus:

> I wished to see Him. Who may feel
> His light and live? He comes.
> The blast of Godhead bursts the doors,
> His mighty hands are twined
> About the triple forks, and when He speaks
> The crown of sunlight shudders round
> Ambrosial temples, and aloft,
> Fluttering through Elysian air,
> His green and azure mantles float in wavy
> Foldings, and melodious thunder
> Wheels in circles.
> But thou, my son, who shalt be born
> When I am ashes, to delight the world—
> Now with measured cymbal-clash
> Moving on to victory;
> Now on music-rolling orbs,
> A sliding throne, voluptuously

Panther-drawn,
To throbbings of the thunderous gong,
And melody o' the merrily-blowing flute;
Now with troops of clamorous revellers,
Merrily, merrily,
Rapidly, giddily,
Rioting, triumphing
Bacchanalians,
Rushing in cadence,
All in order,
Plunging down the viney valleys—

The lightning bolt, the thunder, the burning majesty shatter not only Semele but the poetic meter as well. Yet after the immanence of the god; after the intolerable light, the sun's corona, the thunder's magnification of its lord; after the disturbance of the cochlea's equilibrium, there comes a sense of direction, of clarity. The visual and metrical chaos resolves into a detailed image, a dactylic rhythm; Semele dies, but in death gives birth to Dionysus and his outspilling energies. I take this as a simple allegory of something difficult to say directly, the fact that the death of Hallam made Tennyson feel first that something in him had died—the bolt strikes Semele dead—and then that he felt great creative energies loosed by Hallam's death—Dionysus rushes forth in his giddy chariot, but rushes "in cadence." "Semele" is in this sense the antidote to "Tithon": instead of lingering in Struldbruggian immortality she perishes instantly, but her perishing is a kind of metamorphosis, a deliquescing into a new god, in fact into a whole parade; as if beneath the black mourning clothes, the loud and protracted lamentation over Hallam's death, there was in Tennyson a suppressed hilarity, a hidden exultation in the exercise of his potential faculties. It would not have been easy for Tennyson, a man who seems to have been pious in the religion of emotion, to admit to himself how useful Hallam's death was; and indeed "Semele" was but an unpublished fragment, as if its movement into indecorous delirium made its author somewhat uncomfortable.

Of these monologues of 1833, "Tiresias" is perhaps the fullest and richest, the most satisfactory embodiment of Tennyson's emotional state, his feeling of maimed exaltation. Tiresias beholds the divine vision, but, unlike Tithon, he is not stupefied; unlike Semele, he is not killed; unlike Ulysses, he is not moved to megalomania:

> There in a secret olive-glade I saw
> Pallas Athene climbing from the bath
> In anger; yet one glittering foot disturbed
> The lucid well; one snowy knee was prest
> Against the margin flowers; a dreadful light
> Came from her golden hair, her golden helm
> And all her golden armour on the grass,
> And from her virgin breast, and virgin eyes
> Remaining fixt on mine, till mine grew dark
> For ever, and I heard a voice that said
> "Henceforth be blind, for thou hast seen too much,
> And speak the truth that no man may believe."
> Son, in the hidden world of sight, that lives
> Behind this darkness, I behold her still,
> Beyond all work of those who carve the stone,
> Beyond all dreams of Godlike womanhood,
> Ineffable beauty, out of whom, at a glance,
> And as it were, perforce, upon me flashed
> The power of prophesying—but to me
> No power—so chained and coupled with the curse
> Of blindness and their unbelief, who heard
> And heard not, when I spake of famine, plague,
> Shrine-shattering earthquake, fire, flood, thunderbolt.

(ll. 38–60)

The eyes of the goddess burn out Tiresias' eyes; but he is left with an ineradicable afterimage, the lineaments of Athena, to haunt him forever—"Behind this darkness, I behold her still." As in "Tithon" the Real Presence decays into an image, and displays, if not hostility, at least an ambiguous affection; but in "Tiresias" the image is an abiding source of power, for his gift of prophecy seems to be imparted directly by the picture, gold inhering in blackness. The eyes of imagination open as the physical eyes shut—the low muse is disabled, one might say, in order to enable the high muse. Something has been confronted—it is of course Hallam's death dressed up in another *son et lumière* show—which effaces and renders unimportant everything else; but, whereas Tithon huddled in a catatonia intermitted by a single image, Tiresias' imagination contains not only the one great steady image but much else as well, a world of prophecy. In this way the poem resembles "Semele," for from the catastrophe, the blinding insight, there comes a blessing, a doubtful blessing.

We remember that in "Œnone," a poem written well before Hallam's death, the nymph urged Paris to choose Athena in the Judgment. There Athena promised Paris not only "Self-reverence, self-knowledge, self-control" (l. 142), but other benefits as well:

> "If gazing on divinity disrobed
> Thy mortal eyes are frail to judge of fair,
> Unbiased by self-profit, oh! rest thee sure
(ll. 154–59)
> That I shall love thee well and cleave to thee,
> So that my vigour, wedded to thy blood,
> Shall strike within thy pulses, like a God's."

Athena is no mere schoolmistress urging self-restraint and other dismal virtues, but a woman holding out a promise of ecstatic union with a goddess; her love is not sexual but a provocation to a kind of apotheosis. Phrased only slightly differently, this coaxing would sound much like Satan's temptation of Adam and Eve. But I have quoted a revised version; the original passage was as follows:

> "So shalt thou find me fairest, so endurance,
> Like to an athlete's arm, shall still become
(Ricks,
> Sinewed with motion, till thine active will
p. 393, ll.
> (As the dark body of the Sun robed round
[10]–[16])
> With his own ever-emanating lights)
> Be flooded o'er with her own effluences,
> And thereby grow to freedom."

Something of Tiresias' description of Athena downstopped, fading to black, may have come from this simile from "Œnone," the dark sun hidden in its own out-streaming light. Tiresias is like a Paris who has chosen the right goddess but who has not altogether enjoyed that goddess's favor. Self-knowledge and self-control are indeed his, and prophetical fervor strikes in his pulses; he has half become a god, but at great cost, for his human component has become battered, crippled. As Tennyson matures, sublimity becomes increasingly expensive.

As a rhetorical personage, Tiresias has greater definition than any of Tennyson's earlier characters, except for the comedian St. Simeon Stylites. He alone has a clear social function; Ulysses abdicates from Ithaca, Tithon revolves on a private planet too far from the sun, but Tiresias prevents the destruction of Thebes with his persuasive advice to Menoeceus. Tiresias is consistently sage, knowledgeable, severe but temperate, painstaking, politically astute—"the tyranny of one / Was prelude to the tyranny of all" (ll. 72–73), disappointed that his wisdom is unheeded, but not bitter; he has considerable profile, distinction. And yet he is above all the vessel of imagination, and imagination leads always to a realm without firm contour, where images slip, slide, and will not stay still. If Athena's shape remains constantly before him, it is nevertheless only a residuum, a zero image in a blind eye; and his prophecies are rehearsals of dissolving things:

> Menoeceus, thou hast eyes, and I can hear
> Too plainly what full tides of onset sap
> Our seven high gates, and what a weight of war
> Rides on those ringing axles! jingle of bits,
> Shouts, arrows, tramp of the hornfooted horse
> That grind the glebe to powder! Stony showers
> Of that ear-stunning hail of Arês crash
> Along the sounding walls. Above, below,
> Shock after shock, the song-built towers and gates
> Reel, bruised and butted with the shuddering
> War-thunder of iron rams.

(ll. 88–98)

Again we see Tennyson's fascination with the idea of a city erected by a song, Amphion's song; and his complementary fascination with the rhetoric that unbuilds cities, the song that can undo what a song once did. Tiresias manages to forestall his own

imagination by persuading Menoeceus to sacrifice himself in order
to appease Ares' wrath; but, though the city is spared, Menoeceus
must die. It is as if Ulysses ordered Telemachus to commit suicide in
order to save Ithaca; now the prosaic, workaday world has itself
been infected with morbidity, as the aftershocks of Hallam's death
keep spreading through Tennyson's versions of the cosmos. At last
Tiresias, for all his success in establishing a sound, secure public
identity, wishes to die, to be assimilated whole into the Elysium of
his intuition, where he will join the kings of old:

>   —and these eyes will find
> The men I knew, and watch the chariot whirl
> About the goal again, and hunters race
> The shadowy lion, and the warrior-kings,
> In height and prowess more than human, strive
> Again for glory, while the golden lyre
> Is ever sounding in heroic ears
> Heroic hymns, and every way the vales
> Wind, clouded with the grateful incense-fume
> Of those who mix all odour to the Gods
> On one far height in one far-shining fire.

(ll. 167–77)

The fire of the gods, which receded into darkness when he saw
Athena bathe, will shine forth again before his restored eyes. He is
still a spectator and not a participant, a voyeur of sorts, but he has
attained the denatured, characterless integrity of a god. The imaginer, freed from terrestrial vagueness, has been translated into the
kingdom of his images, a refuge acceptable in death. This happy
ending was not, of course, available to the historical Tennyson,
who could not readily join the bright image of Hallam dead; but as a
believer in the immortality of the soul Tennyson could well permit
himself such a dream of the heaven of art.

 Why does Tennyson continually imagine Hallam's death as
the teasing and painful apparition of a god? Because he wishes to
show something shocking, sudden, unforgettable; because Hallam's image had taken its final form, sharp, immutable, lavishly
dwelt upon; because the death of someone so gifted, so young,
seemed uncanny, the result of divine intervention—"God's finger

touched him, and he slept" (*In Memoriam* 85.20); because the contemplation of the persistence of identity after death abstracted Tennyson from the themes of the world of experience, put him in touch with the billowing sublimities he had dealt with in his early visionary poems; because he loved him. Hence Hallam, in death, becomes a celestial muse, the Spirit of Prophecy, an ambiguous inspiration, for when higher things are revealed, the lower life is blighted; every epiphany demands a sacrifice. The wizard in "Merlin and Vivien," who first learned the spell of the prison-without-walls, pored over the mysteries written in his book until he gained all spiritual wisdom, but he paid a price: he

> Read but one book, and ever reading grew
> So grated down and filed away with thought,
> So lean his eyes were monstrous; while the skin
> Clung but to crate and basket, ribs and spine.
> And since he kept his mind on one sole aim,
> Nor ever touched fierce wine, nor tasted flesh,
> Nor owned a sensual wish, to him the wall
> That sunders ghosts and shadow-casting men
> Became a crystal, and he saw them through it,
> And heard their voices talk behind the wall,
> And learnt their elemental secrets, powers
> And forces; often o'er the sun's bright eye
> Drew the vast eyelid of an inky cloud,
> And lashed it at the base with slanting storm.

(ll. 620–33)

This lemur has starved away his body, become all eye; his vision can penetrate into and inform the realm of elemental forces, can outstare the sun and control all transparencies and opacities. Tiresias is less withered but less masterful, a groping prophet and a limited magician, but he dreams of attaining this sort of expertise, this passing-away into mystery. When Tennyson published "Tiresias" in 1885, about fifty-two years after he wrote it, he framed it with a fine verse epistle "To E. FitzGerald," knowing well that his friend, the translator of the *Rubáiyát*, had much preferred such earlier poems to his recent works; in the preface Tennyson remembers how he once tried to adopt FitzGerald's vegetarian diet:

And once for ten long weeks I tried
Your table of Pythagoras,
And seemed at first "a thing enskied"
(ll. 14–20)   (As Shakespeare has it) airy-light
To float above the ways of men,
Then fell from that half-spiritual height
Chilled, till I tasted flesh again.

It is interesting that Tennyson seemed to feel that the publication of
"Tiresias," in which a prophet tries to hoist himself into a land of
perpetual vision, required this prefatory apology, in which the poet
humorously explains his inability to live, like Sir Galahad or the
wizard of "Merlin and Vivien," in the lofty and rarefied country of
meatless insight. The prophetic mode is somewhat frigid and exclusive, sustainable only in extreme grief or rapture; Will Waterproof's inspiration, derived from beer and hearty food, is more to
Tennyson's taste than the inspiration of incorporeality, blindness.

Tiresias, Tithon, and Semele each behold a different god, and
each is changed differently by the beholding. Yet it is possible to
infer a personage common to all three poems—I call him Tennyson, though I know that the historical Alfred Tennyson eludes any
effort to define him from his verbal inventions—a personage who
expresses different aspects of his injury through these varying
masks. We have seen in the *Idylls of the King* that Arthur is a
hypothetical limit to the whole body of his knights, a bland featureless entity whom each knight, when not deviant from uprightness,
approaches. "Tennyson," similarly, is a hypothetical limit, the
point of convergence of his monologuists, derived by extrapolation. Tennyson never seems to have been certain to what extent
human beings are ultimately differentiable: the Idealist (1829), who
is earth and stars and sea, admits one restriction in his bloated self—
"I am all things save souls of fellow men and very God!" ("The
Idealist," l. 18), and this doctrine is evidently part of "The Higher
Pantheism" (1867) as well—"For is He not all but that which has
power to feel 'I am I'?" (l. 8); but, although Tennyson seems to
wish to retain some degree of individuation, he also dreams of our
race as a single organism, a jellyfish or polyp colony, in which all

men are ingredient (as we can see from a couplet deleted from "Locksley Hall Sixty Years After"): "When the great elastick name will flash through all from end to end, / Make, as in the simple body, every member friend with friend" (Ricks, p. 1366). It is not surprising, then, that we should feel a subsistent indwelling unity among the characters who appear in Tennyson's poems. Like the voices in "The Two Voices," Tithon, Tiresias, Ulysses, and Semele are only aggregated tonalities sharing a common vision, a common intelligence.

I have described Tennyson's method of establishing character as a counterpoint between the ordinary paraphernalia of human distinctness—quirky traits, idiosyncratic gestures, palsied limb, or aquiline nose—and some lapsing into luminiferous ether in which no innate feature whatsoever can exist. "The Holy Grail" (1868) suggests a refinement of this thesis. Each knight granted a vision sees a different Grail; it is as if individuality arose from the defeats in our apprehension of the sublime, as if each knight's aperture of personality were too narrow to take in the whole—but from the sum of partial responses one might devise a composite and integral Grail. As in Keats's parable of the Vale of Soul-making, individuation is deformity. Percivale's sister, an ascetic nun, sees the Grail in a shaft of cold moonlight, rose-red, beating like a living heart (l. 118); the assembled knights of the Round Table cannot see the Grail at all, but can see the luminous cloud that hides it (l. 189); Galahad sees the Grail during the Eucharist, in the shape of a "fiery face, as of a child / That smote itself into a bread, and went" (ll. 466–67)—and the apparition follows him wherever he goes, like the indelible image of Athena in back of Tiresias' eyes; Percivale sees the Grail from a great distance, a meteor adding a red shimmer to the Spiritual City into which Galahad has been translated, a second Elijah (l. 530); Bors, through one miraculous chink in his prison of great stones, also sees the Grail as a kind of meteor, "In colour like the fingers of a hand / Before a burning taper" (ll. 690–91). Each witness betrays his inmost self in his account of what he beholds.

The most virtuous are granted the most sustained and vibrant, lucid visions: Percivale's sister sees a heart, Galahad a child's face, and we suspect that an unobstructed eye would discover that the

Grail was fully human in its lineaments, an *imago dei,* abiding night and day. To the less sanctified the Grail is only a brief glimmer, a Gleam pursued and glimpsed afar, only a little more than the will-o'-the-wisp the quest for which is denounced by Arthur (l. 319). But even to Bors, a rough, practical, unassuming knight, the Grail is somewhat corporeal, colored like the translucent webs between our fingers—Tennyson may have remembered that Guenevere in William Morris's "The Defence of Guenevere" (1858), mad with her own beauty and the beauty of a spring day, holds her hand up to the sun and wonders that her hand is not wholly transparent (l. 123), for images of sublimity are often accompanied with hints of narcissism, self-dissolution. Heart, face, and hand, a living body assembles itself member by member into the Grail. The Grail burns Lancelot because his sin is inextricably rooted in his heart (l. 774); because he cannot overcome his viciousness the Grail scalds him as a devil is scalded by holy water. Thus the determinant of identity lies in one's imaginations of the supernatural—the Grail is a kind of Rorschach test in that its configurations reflect a man's deepest image of himself.

Psychology, then, is a matter of relationship to God. In the 1833 monologues the god appears as Zeus, Eos, Athena, perhaps Achilles as well, for potency, light, wisdom, and fortitude must be summoned to aid in the crisis; but the epitome of each of those virtues, Arthur Hallam, has passed away, and therefore the poet invokes a small troop of partial intelligences, Semele, Tithon, Tiresias, Ulysses, each of whom is qualified to enact some vision of absence, some vestige of presence. In these poems various divine images fade and disperse, and the sum of these outlines is the deteriorating face of Hallam, not quite preservable in memory; and the sum of these imaginers is Tennyson, who displays the full range of yearning exaltation, self-abnegation, eulogy, even envy. Yet though one may accuse the author of exaggerated grief, self-pity, bombast, there is also a kind of triumph, for at the center of each of the monologues is an almost contentless creativity, as if Tennyson's final consolation were to become a spectator of the operations of his own genius. This is a reason why the dramatic monologues on

Hallam's death constitute such a magnificent achievement: the faculty of invention is seldom so successfully dramatized, so rawly displayed. The man is stunned, enfeebled, flebile, while the imagination becomes hyperactive, so feverish that images wildly appear and disappear, mutate into other images.

VII

Anonymity Speaks

IN THE DRAMATIC MONOLOGUES written in the years after 1833, Tennyson, far from settling down into more stable and amenable personae, posits still more bewildered, wretched, disoriented speakers; the earthly muse seems unable to tame, to quiet down and shore up, these heaven-storming ranters. Indeed these later monologues, to be examined in this chapter, constitute for the most part a less impressive achievement than those associated with Hallam's death; the shapelessness of the personae is employed to less telling effect. "Locksley Hall" (1837–38), like "Ulysses," demonstrates how the exercise of supreme rhetorical power undermines any cohesiveness or unity attributable to the speaker; the poem is a heap of random tirades, and its speaker is a monstrous drifting thing, an abstract vehemence raging against the world or congratulating himself, congratulating the world or raging against himself. In "The Two Voices" Tennyson maintained at least the illusion of structure by dividing the speeches among three entities: a puzzled poet, a bad voice urging suicide, and a good voice urging happiness; but in "Locksley Hall" these three tonalities are hopelessly snarled, and the speaker passes rapidly back and forth from mania to depression without any ballast of identity. Character is a sort of inertia, a mass of predication; but the speaker of "Locksley Hall" is weightless, windy, all energy and no mass, a bundle of keen, fitful gusts. He is exceedingly self-preoccupied, but does not seem to know just which of his many selves to be preoccupied with: "Love took up the harp of Life, and smote on all the chords with might; / Smote the chord of Self, that, trembling, passed in music out of sight" (ll. 33–34). Self is constituted only so long as it is agitated by some overwhelming emotion; then it vanishes, and the speaker flounders in nonentity until a new emotion sings him into selfhood once again. Behind this couplet, I believe, were the harps of Amphion,

Apollo, Orpheus, all those kinetic and creative songs; and also, perhaps, the Aeolian harp beloved by Coleridge and Shelley, the symbol of the imaginative man who is himself sleeping, silent, the mere resonating cavity of superhuman forces. But in Romantic poetry the poet is often confident that he can vibrate with the forces that inspire him; in Tennyson the sensitive man remains curiously passive, for all his expostulatory vigor. It is as if the speaker's emotion existed outside him, and he must wait for it to strike, like the Greek hero who is frail and witless until a god animates him. Near the end of "The Holy Grail" Arthur explains the discrepancies in the knights' reports of the Grail:

> " 'Blessèd are Bors, Lancelot and Percivale,
> For these have seen according to their sight.
> For every fiery prophet in old times,
> And all the sacred madness of the bard,
> When God made music through them, could but speak
> His music by the framework and the chord;
> And as ye saw it ye have spoken truth.' "

(ll. 870–76)

The Grail, like all divine things, cannot be known directly, only grasped in some sensuous apparition; each vessel comprehends in its own fashion, lute, theorbo, and viol, each gives out its characteristic sound though the same plectron is used, a broken consort. We see once again that personality manifests itself as a response to some transpersonal intuition; only against a bright celestial background can the silhouette of a particular figure make itself visible; it is sublimity that plucks the chord of self. What is disturbing about "Locksley Hall" is that the chord of self seems to be not one chord but the whole chromatic scale; well might one instead speak of the discords of self. The whole harp seems too highstrung and not in proper tune. In "Aylmer's Field" (1862–63), Leolin's stress over his inability to marry Edith reaches such a pitch that a friend warns him, "Screw not the chord too sharply lest it snap" (l. 469), and the companions of the speaker of "Locksley Hall" must have similar anxieties.

Just as the speaker has no steady sense of self, he has no steady sense of fact; he is prey to competing enthusiasms and revulsions, provoked not by stimuli in the external world but by arbitrary surges and ebbings of passion—"So I triumphed ere my passion sweeping through me left me dry" (l. 131), he says at one point of transition between a frenzied vision of technological utopia and a frenzied indictment of his paltry, jaundiced self beholding a society starving and diseased. In "Locksley Hall" it is as if the libido had been given a speaking voice. The rhythm of the poem is controlled by sexual tension: when the speaker first visits Locksley Hall he recapitulates adolescent fantasies of the erotic sublime, a world in which Pleiades, robin, lapwing, and young man have all grown overvivid, mingled, acute, aberrant; but this fantasy deflates disastrously as he remembers how his human passion was balked by Amy's inability to marry him, and so it is replaced by an equally fantastical vituperation of Amy, a recounting of her imagined misery in marriage. As a human being the speaker has come to nothing, is merely a wind, or a reed buffeted in the wind; but, like Tiresias, his prophetic and visionary faculties have become engorged as his ordinary life has shriveled. The speaker may wear modern clothes, but he is prehistoric, mythological, too sublime to be a man. Cupid, not permitted to sleep with Psyche, tries to shake the frame of the world, to seize up everything in his overspilling moods of love and hate. Later in the poem the speaker tries to shake off his desolation, tries to cheer himself with a fantasy of a savage woman, the anti-Amy, all sex and no brain, with whom he will sport in an Eden full of goats and parrots and rainbows, a perpetual summer; but he revolts in horror from these thoughts, for he is a civilized man, "the heir of all the ages" (l. 178)—he cannot accept any specifying of an object for his sexual feelings, for he is finally infatuated with a generalized, visionary, sublimated libidinousness that will find no relief or realization in any human society and yet must remain wretched precisely because it is denied any discharge. It is therefore a poem that cannot really end, for there is no solution, no way of stopping this wild oscillation. The speaker is, for all his violence, a phantom of halting emphases, undifferentiated energies, polymorphous, amorphous, a black megaphone that will amplify any message whatsoever.

Forty-nine years later Tennyson picked up once again this

megaphone, this figment of trochaic octameter, in order to declaim "Locksley Hall Sixty Years After" (1886). By the end of the nineteenth century the genre of the dramatic monologue was much more sophisticated, and the later poem employs several formal advancements. The monologues of the 1830s sometimes posited interlocutors—a vague throng of companions or onlookers—but they were, except for Menoeceus in "Tiresias," shadowy figures, mere excuses for shapely narratives; even Tiresias described himself and his situation in aria, so to speak, not recitative. "Locksley Hall Sixty Years After" attempts in places a chatty tone, smuggles in some of the exposition and stage setting in conversational asides, even tells us how to infer the grandson's responses and remarks from the old man's speech. Yet I share the feeling of many of Tennyson's readers that something is amiss in the poem. Sixty years later the speaker of "Locksley Hall" has found what he lacked, a core, a stable sense of self and world; he has entered history, has married and had a son, mended "the broken chain that bound me to my kind" (l. 52); his vain fantasies of Amy's marital squalor have been replaced by mature regret about Amy's early death and the brevity of her marital happiness, by mature respect for the good deeds and benign temper of her husband. In short, the speaker has descended into humanity, become a person. However, this character, once established, discredits itself immediately, for we do not know how to reconcile the expostulating, ranting, rapturous, fulminating speaker we knew from the earlier poem and whom we still find sixty years later with the generous old codger that the later poem posits. The speaker of "Locksley Hall" was, above all, enamored of his feeling of amplitude; he railed against Amy for stooping to marry someone with "a range of lower feelings and a narrower heart than mine!" (l. 44), and found intolerable the "narrow foreheads" (l. 175) of his imaginary barbarian wife and children. The speaker of "Locksley Hall Sixty Years After" has become narrow, as all men must, for no one can retain into old age a state of indefinite potentiality; and yet he still pretends to the old rhetorical width of being. He is a chimera, half a plausible old fellow instructing his grandson in a dramatic monologue, half a mere mouthpiece of vehemence, a "dying actor" (l. 152) contorting himself, elocuting to no one in particular. As an actor, he is not convincing, for he keeps forgetting his major role to digress lumpily among spoiled dreams. The mighty organ-voice of Milton sounds strange in the speaker's quavery old throat; but indeed it would sound strange attributed to any contemporary Englishman, for the poem's rhetorical outbursts do not really tend to define anyone at all, except perhaps some disfigured Dostoevskian hysteric. The celestial muse and the earthly muse cannot agree on a single definition of the speaker, and so he suffers from their competing foci.

In "Locksley Hall" the speaker had a good deal of faith in those twin instruments of sublimity, visionary art and visionary science, though his visions were continually infected by sexual frustration; in "Locksley Hall Sixty Years After" agencies that blight visionary hope have greatly proliferated, and the speaker wavers wildly— "Chaos, Cosmos! Cosmos, Chaos!" (ll. 103, 127); "Forward, backward, backward, forward" (l. 193)—but he has, to a large extent, become equally disillusioned with art and science. It is hard for him to work up a bout of enthusiasm, because he is so conscious of the defectiveness of his vehicles of hope. The spirit of Wordsworth, so beneficent in "Locksley Hall," has been replaced by the spirit of Zola:

> Set the maiden fancies wallowing in the troughs of
>   Zolaism,—
> Forward, forward, ay and backward, downward too into
>   the abysm.

(ll. 145–48)

> Do your best to charm the worst, to lower the rising race
>   of men;
> Have we risen from out the beast, then back into the
>   beast again?

Zola is, like Tristram in "The Last Tournament" (1870–71), a backwards Orpheus:

> "And thank the Lord I am King Arthur's fool.
> Swine, say ye? swine, goats, asses, rams and geese

(ll. 320–31)

> Trooped round a Paynim harper once, who thrummed
> On such a wire as musically as thou
> Some such fine song—but never a king's fool."

And Tristram, "Then were swine, goats, asses, geese
The wiser fools, seeing thy Paynim bard
Had such a mastery of his mystery
That he could harp his wife up out of hell."

Then Dagonet, turning on the ball of his foot,
"And whither harp'st thou thine? down! and thyself
Down!"

This sort of regressive art, by which Eurydice is lured back to hell, by which Circe turns Ulysses' men into swine, calls into question all the healing, elevating powers that art claims to possess; the only magic that the speaker of "Locksley Hall Sixty Years After" credits is black magic.

Science has similarly grown disreputable. In "Locksley Hall" the speaker announced grandly, "Let the great world spin for ever down the ringing grooves of change" (l. 182)—Tennyson had the odd myopic notion that trains ran in grooves rather than on tracks—but Sixty Years After the speaker's grandson is delayed by technological breakdown: "Wrecked—your train—or all but wrecked? a shattered wheel?" (l. 215). As for the airy tales of science, the cosmological discoveries that expanded the spirit of the speaker of "Locksley Hall," they too have soured Sixty Years After; he clenches himself and tries to recall sublime poetry, Sappho's vision of the evening star, but feels checked by the deathliness that science attributes to the heavens: "Dead the new astronomy calls" the moon (l. 175); "the sun himself will pass" (l. 182). The recollection of Sappho helps the speaker to affirm his faith in the Higher Pantheism, but clearly there are trends in both art and science that tend to defeat his philosophy. As polemical antidemocrat, as Higher Pantheist, as good old grandfather, the speaker resists assembly into a human being; but the passages of greatest imaginative intensity are perhaps those in which the speaker most resembles Tiresias prophesying the burning of Thebes, the passages in which the speaker depicts his society disarticulating itself, sinking to darkness, as if civilization itself were cyclothymic, manic-depressive, degenerating like the speaker into incoherence, preposterousness. "Set the feet above the brain and swear the brain is in the feet"

(l. 136); this is the speaker's image of a topsy-turvy society, but it could serve, as well, as a picture of his own jumbled nature, the severed members of various personae sewn together and called a speaker.

One component of the identity of the speaker of "Locksley Hall Sixty Years After" is derived from "The Ancient Sage" (1885), written in the previous year. "The Ancient Sage" would be, except for the scene setting in the first eight lines, a strict dramatic monologue, and a more integrated poem than "Locksley Hall Sixty Years After." The interlocutor is not the callow and opinionless grandson of "Locksley Hall Sixty Years After," but a genuine antagonist, a young Epicurean from whose light-minded poem the Ancient Sage reads passages, that he may refute them. The Ancient Sage seems at times almost a caricature of the transcendentalist—he is loosely modeled on Lao-tze—but his character partakes of some of the crispness, the sharp outline of caricature. It is as if the effort of confuting the seize-the-day frivolity of his follower imparted a certain distinctiveness to his cloudy meditations; he takes the concrete imagery of his follower's poem and twists it to illustrate his own themes:

> "And idle gleams will come and go,
> But still the clouds remain;"

(ll. 240–46)   The clouds themselves are children of the Sun.

> "And Night and Shadow rule below
> When only Day should reign."

And Day and Night are children of the Sun,
And idle gleams to thee are light to me.

The third of these lines is the moral of "The Two Voices," and we again see how arbitrary is Tennyson's choice to assign certain tonalities to different speakers; it is all one stream of thought, though it may be broken into two or three or more voices. This method, whereby all furious debates collapse into the single intelligence of the poet in whose mind they take place, gives Tennyson's poetry a certain cohesiveness and strength, a unity of development; but it can be confusing to the reader who expects the characters in a poem to have a greater degree of autonomy than Tennyson gives them. The Ancient Sage has profile because he is consistently engaged in a single task, the subverting of all sensuous evidence of the world's transitoriness to reveal the manifestations of eternal power—"Force is from the heights" (l. 14) and trickles down everywhere around us. The Ancient Sage also has certain attractive character traits, including a gruff, strong patience with his follower's witty obtuseness. The follower is no atheist, but believes that there is no connection between God and nature: "'The nameless Power, or Powers, that rule / Were never heard or seen'" (ll. 29–30), while the Ancient Sage believes in a continuous transition of force between the domain of the spirit and the created world that expresses it, that is upheld by it.

The Ancient Sage also has a concomitant theory of personality:

> for more than once when I
> Sat all alone, revolving in myself
> The word that is the symbol of myself,
> The mortal limit of the Self was loosed,
> And past into the Nameless, as a cloud
(ll. 229–39)   Melts into Heaven. I touched my limbs, the limbs
> Were strange not mine—and yet no shade of doubt,
> But utter clearness, and through loss of Self
> The gain of such large life as matched with ours
> Were Sun to spark—unshadowable in words,
> Themselves but shadows of a shadow-world.

This is almost a versification of a prose passage Tennyson had written about ten years earlier, already cited at the beginning of this study, in which he described

> *a kind of "waking trance" (this for lack of a better word) I have*
> *frequently had quite up from boyhood when I have been all alone.*
> *This has often come upon me through repeating my own name to*
(Martin,   *myself silently, till all at once as it were out of the intensity of the*
pp. 28–29)   *consciousness of individuality the individuality itself seemed to*
> *dissolve & fade away into boundless being—& this not a confused*
> *state but the clearest of the clearest, the surest of the surest, utterly*
> *beyond words—where Death was an almost laughable impos-*

sibility—the loss of personality (if so it were) seeming no extinc-
tion but the only true life.

This paroxysm, this sudden access, this feeling of individuality
growing most distinct at the moment of its supersession, is the
innermost subject of most of Tennyson's dramatic monologues. I
have said that, even in a humorous monologue like "St Simeon
Stylites," Tennyson could succeed in defining a character, in im-
parting a recognizable timbre to his voice, only by counterpointing
him against some vision or audition of that same character translated into a state of high indistinctness, anonymity. Tennyson in the
1830s kept inventing waning images of gods to balance his waxing,
increasingly definite spectators, but it is clear that Tennyson found
in himself both the god and the spectator, both the sense of self and
the sense of some larger field into which the self melted. Well may
Tennyson have declared of *In Memoriam:* "It is rather the cry of the
whole human race than mine. . . . It is a very impersonal poem as
well as personal" (Ricks, p. 859); the whole race's voice is always
threatening to surge up from the back of his throat.

I believe that the constraints of this doctrine or intuition were
responsible for much of the oddity, the impalpability, the sense of
strain in many of the dramatic monologues; it is hard to depict
characters who realize themselves most distinctly just as their
boundaries are blurring away. The fear of gradualism in "The Two
Voices," the fear of collapsing into a pile of one-celled creatures, is
simply the malignant inversion of this feeling, its materialistic
parody.

I have alleged that the Ancient Sage does have a genuine
character, at least when compared with the speaker of "Locksley
Hall Sixty Years After," in whom the trick of revealing character
at the moment of dissolution fails; but the Ancient Sage will
always seem a pallid logician next to Tithon or Tiresias or Ulysses, less a personality than a theory of personality given a voice.
Yet this is one of Tennyson's most directly autobiographical
poems, in which he reveals not only his old "waking trances" but
his equally persistent feeling, from earliest youth, called "The
Passion of the Past" (l. 219), the remote nostalgia for some antenatal unity of beginnings and endings, the intuition of eternity.

Precisely because the poem is set in a distant mythological time and place, because the Ancient Sage is half resolved into the divine, Tennyson can attribute intimate matter to him without fear of falsifying; indeed the Ancient Sage is a character in a tense equilibrium between his follower's worldliness, his sharp-eyed specificity of observation, and a state of anonymity. If one repeats a word over and over— *Tennyson Tennyson Tennyson Tennyson*—it lapses into a pure pattern of sound, patter of sound, smooth dactyls that denote nothing and no one but are still saturated with feelings of propriety, of belonging. Many of Tennyson's characters are happily anonymous, like the male protagonists of "Locksley Hall," *Maud*, and *The Princess;* and many of Tennyson's characters dwell lovingly on their own names: Simeon Stylites keeps saying "I, Simeon" as if mere repetition could elevate it into sainthood; the speaker of *Maud* hallucinates that someone is crying his name (1.6.8.261); in "I Loving Freedom for Herself" Tennyson mentions the cuckoo "that loves / To babble its own name" (ll. 7–8); and several of Tennyson's lovers swoon when they hear their name on their beloved's lips—"From thy rose-red lips MY name / Floweth" ("Eleänore," ll. 133–34); and in "The Lover's Tale" Julian exclaims,

> my name has been
> A hallowed memory like the names of old,
> A centred, glory-circled memory,
> (1.434–40) And a peculiar treasure, brooking not
> Exchange or currency: and in that hour
> A hope flowed round me, like a golden mist
> Charmed amid eddies of melodious airs.

Knowledge of one's own name is conducive to golden mist, vertigo, namelessness.

As the feeling of one's identity grows more intense, it kindles into abdication and surrender of identity. The Ancient Sage's subtlest image of this transduction is in a reply he makes to his follower's attempt to diminish the significance of life:

> "For all that laugh, and all that weep,
> (ll. 187–94) And all that breathe are one

    Slight ripple on the boundless deep
    That moves, and all is gone."

But that one ripple on the boundless deep
Feels that the deep is boundless, and itself
For ever changing form, but evermore
One with the boundless motion of the deep.

If D. H. Lawrence had written this, we would not have been surprised, for Lawrence often spoke of vividly living things as waves, claimed that all true form was dynamic, a shimmer of plasm, and the outer shape a dead husk; but in Tennyson such a passage seems adventurous. A wave has no static identity, can be said to exist only insofar as it moves; it is a fragile complex, but it propagates itself infinitely, maintains itself across a whole Atlantic of time. It seems that a man has a name, a history, only to the extent that he feels himself a tenuous, tenacious agitation of something within him nameless and timeless. Elsewhere Tennyson seems to have thought of identity, boundedness, as a kind of retraction, just as the God of *Paradise Lost* withdraws himself to allow room for men, planets, stars. Near the end of his life Tennyson attended séances to discover news of his dead son Lionel, and he described the world of spirit as "a great ocean pressing round us on every side, and only leaking in by a few chinks" (Martin, p. 557). The Ancient Sage, like Tiresias and Semele, feels the flood about to pour in, and knows his outline most acutely at the moment of implosion.

    These doctrines of selfhood, according to which the self can define itself only in relation to the huge hydraulic pressure that squeezes it on all sides, may help to explain the most puzzling feature of Tennyson's long career as a writer of dramatic mono-logues, the fact that his most impressive acts of characterization tend to occur in the most mythy and abstract characters, those farthest removed from pedestrian nineteenth-century England. The earthly muse had many gifts for Tennyson, but could not offer him—as we saw earlier in comparing "The Gardener's Daughter" to "The Palace of Art"—many convincing speakers of dramatic monologues. Sometimes in middle and old age Tennyson would revive a character from a poem of his youth and outfit him in plausible, relatively modern dress, convert him from a demigod into a credible pathetic fellow. For instance, "Ulysses" (1833) could be resurrected, with a little plastic surgery, as "Columbus" (1879–80), degraded from an idle king into an arrogant explorer cast into a dungeon, yet for all his fretful squalor still dreaming of using the wealth he plundered from the New World to launch a crusade to free the Holy Land, still "ready to sail forth on one last voyage" (l. 233). Faint traces of the old superhuman resonance may linger, but the poem sinks, a sodden treasure ship, under the weight of accreted homely details of Columbus's history and personality, borrowed from Washington Irving's biography; the characteristic touches that should enliven the monologue, make it pungent, instead give an impression of slackness or luridness or even unintended humor, as when Columbus, complaining of "spasms that grind / Bone against bone" (ll. 216–17) recalls the theatrical morbidity of Simeon Stylites. The nimbus of the sublime is too dim, and Tennyson had little gift for depicting life at its lower pitches, in its more ordinary and affable states.

Somewhat more successful than "Columbus" is "Romney's Remorse" (1889); Romney's remorse is identical to the remorse of the Soul in "The Palace of Art" (1832), except that it is now attributed not to an allegorical figment but to an actual, somewhat talented painter, who, when young, abandoned his wife and child to perfect his skill, a somewhat overzealous reaction to Joshua Reynolds's idea that marriage spoils an artist; he returned to his wife after many years and she nursed him in his final illness—FitzGerald suggested this story as a theme for a poem. Tennyson imagines Romney, mad and desolate, pleading for her forgiveness as he dies. He repents that he lived in a world of images, a false "Heaven of Art" (l. 38); now "The coloured bubble bursts above the abyss" (l. 51). The soul in "The Palace of Art" showed genius naked, full of terribilita, while Romney has nothing immoderate in him, seems mediocre; we do not feel that, if he had in his youth renounced art in favor of human tenderness, he would have deprived the world of many great paintings. By making him too human, Tennyson has lost the sense of spaciousness, of grandeur, which would have given point to his moral choice.

But in one point "Romney's Remorse" is superior to "The Palace of Art": the hasty ending of the earlier poem did not clarify the relation between the life of good deeds and aesthetic life—why should exclusive devotion to art make one morally unfit? Why should moral action make one aesthetically fit?—whereas "Romney's Remorse" cleverly illustrates the formal similarities between ethical and aesthetic behavior. Romney tells his wife of a recent dream, a new subject to paint:

> I dreamed last night of that clear summer noon,
> When seated on a rock, and foot to foot
> With your own shadow in the placid lake,
> You claspt our infant daughter, heart to heart.
> I had been among the hills, and brought you down
> A length of staghorn-moss, and this you twined
> About her cap. I see the picture yet,
(ll. 69–83) Mother and child. A sound from far away,
> No louder than a bee among the flowers,
> A fall of water lulled the noon asleep.
> You stilled it for the moment with a song
> Which often echoed in me, while I stood
> Before the great Madonna-masterpieces
> Of ancient Art in Paris, or in Rome.
>   Mary, my crayons! if I can, I will.

An image remembered from life, Madonna and child, produces aesthetic emotion; this suggests that it is hard to draw the boundary between the feelings evoked by great art and the warm plebeian feelings anyone might feel in the presence of his family. Art at its best is not exclusive of life but a representation of its richest, creamiest aspects. The water-reflection of wife and child seems a further stimulus to Romney's painterly imagination; but soon he remembers how their child died during his long dereliction, and he scatters his crayons on the ground:

>   Down, you idle tools,
(ll. 107–13) Stampt into dust—tremulous, all awry,
> Blurred like a landskip in a ruffled pool,—

Not one stroke firm. This Art, that harlot-like
Seduced me from you, leaves me harlot-like,
Who love her still, and whimper, impotent
To win her back before I die.

Again, there may be some vague reminiscence of Prospero's cast-
ing-away of the implements of his magic. Romney, having be-
trayed life for art, knows that his art can only falsify life, knows that
any representation he could make from his memory of fatherly bliss
would be a distortion, an ugliness. Treachery to one's deepest
feelings renders art idle and vain; he is damned in his painting as
well as in his soul, and he imagines a Judgment Day in which
adulterers and wife-murderers find his aestheticism a sin more
contemptible than any of theirs. Possibly we are to hear in this
passage a hint of perverse pride, for the artist thinks himself, like St.
Paul or St. Simeon Stylites, the chief of sinners. At the end of the
poem Romney touches on his thread of hope:

I love you more than when we married. Hope!
O yes, I hope, or fancy that, perhaps,
(ll. 150–54)   Human forgiveness touches heaven, and thence—
For you forgive me, you are sure of that—
Reflected, sends a light on the forgiven.

What interested FitzGerald in Romney's story was the idea that
"this quiet act of hers [nursing the man who deserted her] is worth
all Romney's pictures! even as a matter of Art, I am sure" (Ricks,
p. 1418). These last lines delicately suggest that good deeds, like
good works of art, are *reflections* of light, representations of loftiness, and therefore conducive to heaven. The Christ child in Rapha-
el's Madonnas and the conduct of Romney's wife are each an *imago
Christi;* the fissure between art and life is by this strategy of reflections bridged. To a certain extent life itself can possess the grace, the
economy, the firmness of gesture to which art aspires; the earthly
muse, toiling unobtrusively in low precincts, can rival the stormy
charms of her celestial counterpart.

The story of Romney's death has some historical basis, but it is
largely Tennyson's invention. If Tennyson had been the Victorian

sentimentalist he has at times been taken for, he would have developed the story along the following lines: the decayed painter, at
last understanding the magnitude of his wife's sacrifice and of his
own depravity, picks up his crayons—Tennyson knew from biographical sources that Romney's skill at drawing was unimpaired in
his later years—and sketches the old scene, wife and baby seated on
rock and reflected in lake, with sudden luminous power, a masterpiece, after which wife and husband embrace, all forgiven as virtuous action resolves into fine art. But this is not the line that
Tennyson chose: instead the artist must destroy his tools, must
renounce art in order to obtain salvation. The closing of the breach
between art and life is only a kind of undertheme in the poem, a
premonition accomplished by manipulating imagery, for in the
actual plot Romney must decide between the hell of art and the
heaven of atonement. Good art, the art of goodness, exists, but it is
not available to Romney; he must abandon his vocation, unmake
himself to accomplish his death.

Tennyson has known ever since "The Palace of Art" that the
artist will wither away if he keeps himself apart from the richness,
the panoply, of human action; but he cannot quite see how the artist
can launch himself into the roil, the ethical complexity of life, and
still be an artist. As in Arnold's *Empedocles on Etna,* the artist either
asphyxiates on his mountaintop or goes mad from the babbling of
the crowd. Reverie and deed, the sublime and the commonplace,
still seem incompatible in the limits of a single human brain.

VIII

Escape from Lucretius' Heaven

IF IN HIS LATER YEARS Tennyson experimented with dramatic monologues built around comparatively unexceptional speakers, recognizably "modern" characters who nevertheless manage to impinge upon the abyss, he also tried to imagine this experience, this verging on the ultimate, from the opposite direction, from the perspective of a god. "Demeter and Persephone" (1887) is one of Tennyson's best poems, and some of its shivery power is drawn from the fact that the goddess herself speaks; it is as if one of the divine images beheld in the monologues of the 1830s—Eos, Athena, Zeus—at last gave us a version of how it feels from the other side. Instead of a man trembling on the edge of dissolution or apotheosis, we have a goddess puzzling over epiphany.

Tennyson in many poems in his youth—"Armageddon," "Tithon," and "Tiresias," to mention a few—investigated with care the spidery sensations of a man's accession to deity; but how did he imagine that the god feels about the approach of men? Keats found this matter so troubling that he broke off *Hyperion* at the moment the shuddering Apollo attains his godhead, as if empathy with an attained divinity were beyond his gifts. In his earlier poems Tennyson relied closely upon classical models when treating the emotions of gods, as if he too were not altogether confident in his imagination; for instance, Tiresias' vision of himself lolling among the superhuman does not stray far from Pindar's "Dirge on Elysium." There it seems that the gods dwell in a state of playful and insipid strength. Tennyson's Lotos-Eaters, who are in a sense damned without knowing it—damned, just like Adam and Eve, for wishing to be as gods—have a precise sense of which divine stance they wish to imitate:

(ll. 153–64)

Let us swear an oath, and keep it with an equal mind,
In the hollow Lotos-land to live and lie reclined

On the hills like Gods together, careless of mankind.
For they lie beside their nectar, and the bolts are hurled
Far below them in the valleys, and the clouds are lightly
    curled
Round their golden houses, girdled with the gleaming
    world:
Where they smile in secret, looking over wasted lands,
Blight and famine, plague and earthquake, roaring deeps
    and fiery sands,
Clanging fights, and flaming towns, and sinking ships,
    and praying hands.
But they smile, they find a music centred in a doleful
    song
Steaming up, a lamentation and an ancient tale of wrong,
Like a tale of little meaning though the words are strong.

This too is based on a classical source, Lucretius' account of the gods who reside far above clouds and winds and snow, peaceful, immaculate, cushioned and laughing; but Lucretius' gods are simply deaf, while the gods of the Lotos-Eaters take aesthetic delight in human suffering, hear the lamentation of our race at such a distance that it modulates into music, an exquisite song in a foreign language, expressive but expressive of nothing in particular. It is the aesthetic heresy; "The Lotos-Eaters" (1830–32, though the passage just cited was added in 1842) was written at the same time as "The Palace of Art," and in a sense the Lotos-Eaters have been more successful than the Soul of "The Palace of Art" at assimilating themselves into the proper involution, unnaturalness, languor, and delirium of the gods; the Soul, by contrast, was too flighty, self-congratulatory, consciously superb. The gods feel nothing, then, but a disengaged and involved mildness, a mansuetude that does little to mitigate their general anesthesia.

The Lotos-Eaters' eerie sympathy with a transcendence that smiles at men's pain was one of the first signs that Lucretius would be one of the patron saints of nineteenth-century English poetry; the temperature of great art, already low when Keats's Grecian urn displayed its cold pastoral, was sinking rapidly below freezing. In one of Matthew Arnold's earliest poems, "The Strayed Reveller" (about 1847–48), the happy gods turn their shining eyes to earth and see picturesque centaurs prancing and snuffling, picturesque Indians reaping melons grown on great rafts in a mountain lake. But the human bard sees instead furious centaurs struggling in vain against the Lapiths, against Hercules, or Indians tossed in their boats by storms, their melons spoiled by worms. The Youth, Arnold's protagonist, envies the divine disengagement and tries to induce it in himself by wine and frenzied dancing. As in "The Lotos-Eaters," narcosis and ecstasy are supposed to terminate in a state of continuous delectable unfeeling. Later in the century Swinburne and Wilde will apply Lucretian rhetoric to their houses of art—abodes that no wind will ever shake nor clouds sprinkle with rain nor snow mar with bitterness—usually with a certain unstated anxiety that the invariant tingling, buzzing, jingling of the nerves by Giorgione, or attar, or velvet, or the diminished seventh, may lead to monotony or exhaustion.

Lucretius' vision of the gods comes from a poem counseling against the fear of death; and sometimes in nineteenth-century poetry it seems that death is a state of aesthetic delight. When Tennyson, in "The Two Voices," records that a voice advised him to inspect the face of a corpse and to note the extreme calm suggested by the expression, he is employing the sort of sinister consolation often found in Lucretius' *De rerum natura;* and it is an underlying theme of "The Palace of Art" that the glorification of art leads to the glorification of death. Swinburne's Proserpine is simply death given a fancy name:

> Pale, beyond porch and portal,
>   Crowned with calm leaves, she stands
> Who gathers all things mortal
>   With cold immortal hands;
> Her languid lips are sweeter
> Than love's who fears to greet her
> To men that mix and meet her
>   From many times and lands.
>
> She waits for each and other,
>   She waits for all men born;

(ll. 49–72)

Forgets the earth her mother,
   The life of fruits and corn;
And spring and seed and swallow
Take wing for her and follow
Where summer song rings hollow
   And flowers are put to scorn.

There go the loves that wither,
   The old loves with wearier wings;
In all dead years draw thither,
   And all disastrous things;
Dead dreams of days forsaken,
Blind buds that snows have shaken,
Wild leaves that winds have taken,
   Red strays of ruined springs.

In this poem, Swinburne's "The Garden of Proserpine" (1866), oblivion is made erotic, given a personality, a dim vast body pleased by the sensations of a growing chilling, an equilibrating, scattering, disordering; on her papillae she tastes the corruption of the whole world's harvests and she watches all things intestine diminish and disperse before her obtunding gaze. She dwells in the underworld, not the upper air, but she resembles Lucretius' gods in that she has surpassed the weather, as Swinburne shows:

Then star nor sun shall waken,
   Nor any change of light;
Nor sound of waters shaken,
   Nor any sound or sight;
Nor wintry leaves nor vernal,
Nor days nor things diurnal;
Only the sleep eternal
   In an eternal night.

(ll. 89–96)

It seems that any man can choose to be a god, dissolute and dispassionate, interesting, if only he will die. We have already noted, in connection with "The Two Voices," Tennyson's fascinated fear of the breakdown of the body after death, as if a corpse's nervous system could *feel* the muscular tension of rigor mortis, the teasing retraction of flesh around the indiscreet bone, as if death offered a superior sensory acuity. But Tennyson, Arnold, Swinburne, Wilde, all dream of a species of death that would combine the most attractive features of life and death, an immersion into the greater intensities of feeling attributed to the inorganic world—sun, volcano, the tides of ocean—but also an attained refuge, an apathy without end. It seems that the most sublime muse is Proserpine, the Muse of Death. This not wholly consistent fantasy is expressed in Arnold's *Empedocles on Etna* (1852), in Swinburne's *Atalanta in Calydon* (1865)—there Meleager desires to become "What the flower of the foam is / In fields of the sea" (ll. 2134–35), an image somewhat similar to the Ancient Sage's picture of himself as a ripple—and in Tennyson's "Lucretius" (1865–68).

Tennyson goes further in "Lucretius" than in any of his previous monologues in imagining what it means to be a god. Lucretius is not sure that his imagination is correct—he entertains the possibility that the gods may be, not, as he thinks, the impersonal forces of nature to which we ascribe a human personality, but instead the jealous and peculiar deities of conventional religion, as he wonders whether a personal Venus has not infected his mind with sexual corruption (l. 67)—but nevertheless his imagination is abundant and specific, as we see when he explains to the gods his use of the term *Venus:*

> "I take
> That popular name of thine to shadow forth
> The all-generating powers and genial heat
> Of Nature, when she strikes through the thick blood
> Of cattle, and light is large, and lambs are glad
> Nosing the mother's udder, and the bird

(ll. 95–113)   Makes his heart voice amid the blaze of flowers:
> Which things appear the work of mighty Gods.

> "The Gods! and if I go *my* work is left
> Unfinished—*if* I go. The Gods, who haunt
> The lucid interspace of world and world,
> Where never creeps a cloud, or moves a wind,
> Nor ever falls the least white star of snow,

Nor ever lowest roll of thunder moans,
Nor sound of human sorrow mounts to mar
Their sacred everlasting calm! and such,
Not all so fine, nor so divine a calm,
Not such, nor all unlike it, man may gain
Letting his own life go. The Gods, the Gods!"

The lines about cloud, wind, and snow are a close translation of that passage in Lucretius which Tennyson has previously used to good effect in "The Lotos-Eaters," and in "Morte d'Arthur," in a description of Avilion. What would it feel like to be a god? A dead man would not actually be a god, but he would experience to a lesser degree the same feelings—on one hand, the sense of floating, or imperturbability, of suspension in outer space, and, on the other hand, the sense of disintegrating into atoms pulled and pushed and mingled and recombined into new forms, the intimate sense of the operation of blind force. These sensations are divine but easily attributable to actual corpses, if corpses could feel. As a philosopher Lucretius tries to sustain his intellectual belief in his materialistic, denatured deities, mere scientific principles, the gusts of spring or the winds of war, remote from men's passion because they do not exist as men; but as the love potion crazes the smooth glass of Lucretius' mind—his wife slipped it to him, as we learn in the preamble, in order to compel him to pay more attention to her—he feels the world around him breaking into human and subhuman forms; he changes from a debunker of myth into a mythmaker, full of archaic imaginative power:

For look! what is it? there? yon arbutus
Totters; a noiseless riot underneath
Strikes through the wood, sets all the tops quivering—
The mountain quickens into Nymph and Faun;
(ll. 184–99)   And here an Oread—how the sun delights
To glance and shift about her slippery sides,
And rosy knees and supple roundedness,
And budded bosom-peaks—who this way runs
Before the rest—A satyr, a satyr, see
Follows; but him I proved impossible;

> Twy-natured is no nature: yet he draws
> Nearer and nearer, and I scan him now
> Beastlier than any phantom of his kind
> That ever butted his rough brother-brute
> For lust or lusty blood or provender:
> I hate, abhor, spit, sicken at him.

The gods try their best to remain noble, detached, impersonal, to stand upright in Elysium as half-carved statues, monoliths captioned with the names of forces, but they cannot maintain this stiff abstract posture, must find themselves quickening into the genii of these rutting landscapes. Lucretius, who proved that the afterlife was a fable, who

>   told a truth
> (ll. 259–61)   That stays the rolling Ixionian wheel,
>   And numbs the Fury's ringlet-snake

tries to maintain his high disillusionment, tries to muster arguments to convince himself of the impossibility of satyrs; but his brain, which the philter has made fecund with sexual images, cannot dismiss the shivers and shimmers from the scene around him. Lucretius would like to cultivate detachment, that species of the sublime which renders a man invulnerable to the lower world; but instead he finds derangement, another sort of sublimity altogether, whereby the contemplated world grows scarily expressive of heaving inner impulses. He considers himself, at this moment in the poem, perfectly estranged from the gods, sunk to the level of a beast; and at the end of the poem he stabs himself to death in order to attain his "Passionless bride, divine Tranquillity" (l. 265), that is, unbeing.

However, his conception of divinity is dubious. W. H. Auden, in "In Praise of Limestone" (1948), speaks of the modern poet whose "antimythological myth" is questioned by presentiments of mythological beings everywhere in a certain Italian landscape, a landscape in which stone seems effortlessly to shape itself into temple. It seems to me likely that Lucretius is the sort of poet whom every age will find "modern," skeptical, reasonable, lucid; but his antimythology is also a myth, his disenchantment another kind of magical act. He imagines gods that appeal to the cerebral cortex's desire to disengage itself from the rest of the man, to hover in the air as a naked thinking film; but, pricked by desire, he might well have noticed how easily other sorts of gods come forth to answer to other human desires, how arbitrary all god-construction is. The possibility is open that he knows more about Venus in his state of venereal excitement than he does when recumbent in philosophy; that his vision of satyrs howling, nymphs moaning, has more godhead in it than his vision of deities careless, cloudless, eyeless, earless. What a man cannot confront about himself always detaches into a bad voice, or a pseudoperson, or a god, and then persecutes and ravages him.

Lucretius is like Tennyson's earlier characters, Ulysses, Tithon, Tiresias, in that he wishes to be relieved of the burden of identity, to be translated into another, finer tone—though his idea of refuge, a refuge discussed into atoms, is bleaker and less attractive than theirs; "Lucretius" differs from the poems of the 1830s, however, in that it seems to show a cultural era striving toward a suitable conception of the realm of the gods. T. S. Eliot would not have needed to look further than "Lucretius" or "The Two Voices" to illustrate his notion of the dissociation of sensibility—it is possible that he did look no further—for in "Lucretius" mind and body have competing, mutually exclusive fantasies of divinity, and each maddens the other. I believe that Tennyson intended the poem as an indictment of an age that found no true sacredness in things, an age that saw the gods only as figments of philosophers or pornographers, Kant or Zola. Lucretius represented to Tennyson the specious sublime, a vision exalted but strangely warped, vacillating between drunkenness and catatonia, just as Arnold's Empedocles found himself perishing either from the rarefied air on Etna's summit or from the vain babble of life in the valley. "Lucretius," like "Balin and Balan," investigates the decay of mythology: as myths lose their efficacy they become fairy tales to amuse children, or, Vico-fashion, the halting attempts of primitive man, incapable of abstraction, to explain natural phenomena with his impoverished vocabulary.

And yet, though Tennyson seems to deprecate those nymphs and satyrs, the consequences of setting Lucretius' maiden fancies wallowing in the troughs, it is possible that they manifest a more religious view of nature than does Lucretius' atomic theory. For Tennyson, as for any good post-Romantic, the subconscious contains more impressive truths than the upper mind. In "Tithon," "Tiresias," and "Semele," the god labored to appear, in some sense, to his worshiper; "Tithon," especially, showed the pain of immanence, Eos' slow shaping of herself from the bright sphere of the dawning sun into a whole and exact woman, a goddess. In "Lucretius" the gods seem to abet Lucretius' wife, to wish to recapture some of their pagan vitality, to become willful and urgent, personal, deranged and deranging. They can achieve this only in distorted form, in a grotesque exaggeration of their carnality, their barbarism, but in the eyes of Lucretius any image of the gods that is not a vacant transcendence would be likely to appear so; to be human is to be bestial, so enthralled is Lucretius by the huge inane. Lucretius is heretical in the same manner as the flippant follower of the Ancient Sage in that he believes that power is so far detached from human life that it is for all purposes negligible; the potion may destroy him, but it also breaks him out of his aloof contemplation, puts him into the current of living things—the forces of generation, Eros and Thanatos, begin to move through his petrified heart. It is a kind of sagacity. Like the Soul in "The Palace of Art," much of Lucretius has atrophied from his intellectual prepossession, and his body exacts its revenge.

No god known to Lucretius, neither his enskied parallelepipeds nor his satyrs, equally fantastic and partial, can be the agent of his salvation; but a god who answers prayer, a potent and personal god, is not entirely excluded from his philosophy, as we can see from his apology to Venus:

> "Nay, if thou canst, O Goddess, like ourselves
> Touch, and be touched, then would I cry to thee
> To kiss thy Mavors, roll thy tender arms
> Round him, and keep him from the lust of blood
> That makes a steaming slaughter-house of Rome."

(ll. 80–84)

Homer's deities do not offer the consolations of Christ, but they are perhaps the best of the options open to Lucretius. Even as he addresses Venus, he tells her that mythology has told nothing but lies about her, that the story of Adonis must be a fabrication because it says she " 'wept / Her Deity false in human-amorous tears' " (ll. 89–90); but "Lucretius" is nevertheless a vehicle by which the gods seem to shake themselves free from a false abstraction, a false frigidity, work toward a more puissant, vital myth, even though they refuse to be confined by any specific body of myths.

By the time of "Demeter and Persephone" (1887), about twenty years after "Lucretius," the Greek gods had at last arrived at a satisfactory mythical form:

> Faint as a climate-changing bird that flies
> All night across the darkness, and at dawn
> Falls on the threshold of her native land,
> And can no more, thou camest, O my child,
> Led upward by the God of ghosts and dreams,
> Who laid thee at Eleusis, dazed and dumb
> With passing through at once from state to state,
> Until I brought thee hither, that the day,
> When here thy hands let fall the gathered flower,
> Might break through clouded memories once again
> On thy lost self.

(ll. 1–11)

Demeter, a goddess, strives to render her goddess-daughter Persephone un-Lucretian, strives to inculcate in her as much of the human as she can. A manuscript of these lines shows, instead of lines 10–11, the following: "might have power to disentrance / Thy senses" (Ricks, p. 1374); there it is clearer that Persephone, as Queen of the Dead, lives in a condition rather like that of the Lotos-Eaters; involved and dim, apathetic. As Persephone recovers her lost self, her lost affect, her face no longer resembles Pluto's; instead of being shadowy and iconic she becomes brilliant, fruitful:

> A sudden nightingale
> Saw thee, and flashed into a frolic of song
> And welcome; and a gleam as of the moon,

(ll. 11–28)

When first she peers along the tremulous deep,
Fled wavering o'er thy face, and chased away
That shadow of a likeness to the king
Of shadows, thy dark mate. Persephone!
Queen of the dead no more—my child! Thine eyes
Again were human-godlike, and the Sun
Burst from a swimming fleece of winter gray,
And robed thee in his day from head to feet—
"Mother!" and I was folded in thine arms.
      Child, those imperial disimpassioned eyes
Awed even me at first, thy mother—eyes
That oft had seen the serpent-wanded power
Draw downward into Hades with his drift
Of flickering spectres, lighted from below
By the red race of fiery Phlegethon.

Arthur's knights looked just like Arthur, when inspired by virtue; but now Tennyson prizes, not a divine identicality of feature, but a human diversity; and Persephone and Demeter embrace like daughter and mother in any human recognition scene.

Instead of Lucretius' two versions of the gods—those of archaic mythology and those of modern science, the former flagitious or vengeful, too human, the latter the disembodied laws of motion—"Demeter and Persephone" posits two great phyla of deities, those of earth and those of the underworld: the terrestrial gods are personal, vivid, energetic, the locus of many colorful tales, while the chthonian gods are spectral and oblivious, beyond cloud or wind or snow. When Persephone first comes to the light she awes her mother with her "imperial disimpassioned eyes," eyes like those of Lucretius' careless sublime gods, or like those of the colossus of the Mystic's dream, "One mighty countenance of perfect calm, / Awful with most invariable eyes" ("The Mystic," ll. 23–24). Hell is ether and drifting, earth is oxygen and emotion. The sublimity of detachment must be replaced by the sublimity of magnified passion; in Tennyson's early poem " 'Pierced through with knotted thorns of barren pain' " (1832), the poet imagines himself walking on a volcanic plain, hearing through yawning rifts the scummy sulfur seething far below, while in "Demeter and Persephone" Demeter fears that the ground will give way and "The shrilly whinnyings of the team of Hell . . . Jet upward through the midday blossom" (ll. 44, 47). When a goddess moves, the earth lauds her, does her homage; crocuses break out under Persephone's feet (l. 50), exactly as they did for Hera, Athena, and Aphrodite in "Œnone" (1830–32).

Yet for all this metamorphic fury it is still recognizably human emotion, on a larger scale; the whole pathetic earth may express the goddess's shuddering or magnanimity or grief, but it is human shuddering, human magnanimity, human grief, granted greater resources of expression. Demeter, sick with Persephone's long absence, finds herself envying "human wives, and nesting birds" (l. 52), and indeed the whole thrust of the poem is to humanize the gods. Demeter is Earth Goddess but nevertheless the most genial of companions to man. This is the end point of all the contractions into human shape, the difficult focusings of Eos, Athena, Zeus: Demeter is any sorrowing mother overjoyed at the return of the prodigal daughter, yet supported by the full apparatus of halos, quiverings, mythy resonance. We feared that the gods lived stunned and anesthetized, as Lucretius thought, but no, they have the full range of feeling, greater than human. The countermovement is complete: as men have striven to be gods, so the gods have striven to be men; form yearns for formlessness, formlessness for form. The earthly muse yearns to dress herself in a seraph's alb and aura, the heavenly muse to wear a cotton blouse and knit stockings.

The poem, like most of the monologues of the 1830s, ends with a prophecy: Demeter predicts that she and her kind will be replaced by "younger kindlier Gods," as Tennyson pursues a line of thought derived from Aeschylus, and Keats's *Hyperion* (as Christopher Ricks and Douglas Bush point out); her prophecy differs from Keats's, however, in that Keats's Oceanus predicted an evolution into beauty, while Tennyson wishes to attribute to Demeter a vague intuition of Christ:

(ll. 130–51)

                    Gods,
   To quench, not hurl the thunderbolt, to stay,

Not spread the plague, the famine; Gods indeed,
To send the noon into the night and break
The sunless halls of Hades into Heaven?
Till thy dark lord accept and love the Sun,
And all the Shadow die into the Light,
When thou shalt dwell the whole bright year with me,
And souls of men, who grew beyond their race,
And made themselves as Gods against the fear
Of Death and Hell; and thou that hast from men,
As Queen of Death, that worship which is Fear,
Henceforth, as having risen from out the dead,
Shalt ever send thy life along with mine
From buried grain through springing blade, and bless
Their garnered Autumn also, reap with me,
Earth-mother, in the harvest hymns of Earth
The worship which is Love, and see no more
The Stone, the Wheel, the dimly-glimmering lawns
Of that Elysium, all the hateful fires
Of torment, and the shadowy warrior glide
Along the silent field of Asphodel.

What is Demeter saying? It is not simply that she foresees an earthly paradise of perpetual spring, for there will be autumn then too. It is as if she were trying to understand that Persephone should descend into hell, not in order to preside over it but to harrow it; that Persephone's resurrection should be not cyclic, seasonal, but once and for all; and that she should take with her the souls of resurrected men—so that there might be some state which was at once spring and autumn, a sprouting and a reaping, an exuberance and a satisfaction. Demeter is the goddess of the earth and, bound inevitably to the cycle of the seasons, has difficulty in conceiving an eternity that is a state of salvation, is not the listless insubstantial afterlife of Greek thought, in which the dead Achilles tells Odysseus that it is better to be a yeoman farmer on earth than the lord regent of the kingdom of the dead. Tennyson at the end of "Demeter and Persephone" unwrites the ending of "Tiresias," the old poem published two years before, which presents the classical

Elysium as attractively as possible; Demeter does not know exactly what she wants, but she knows she wants something else. She is groping after a new chastened identity, that of the Virgin Mary, just as she is struggling to convert Persephone into Christ; Enna, the whole tissue of Greek mythology, is growing thin, translucent, and another order of myth is felt underneath it. Although she is moving away from Lucretius' conception of the gods as faceless translunar loafers—a conception here relegated to the Plutonian netherworld—toward an idea of godhead suffering and exulting along with man, concretely present, she is still Lucretian to the extent that she wishes to debunk certain mythologies. Lucretius congratulated himself for bringing Ixion's wheel to a halt and plucking the snakes from the heads of the Furies; similarly, Demeter predicts that the Stone and the Wheel—Sisyphus and Ixion—will vanish, with all the gibbering souls of the classical cobwebby hell, into some kind of new life, liberated not only from the Wheel and the Stone, cyclicality and petrification, but from all constraints of the old mythology. Tennyson's understated, provisional attempt to relocate Demeter on the grid of an alien system of myths provides the poem with a remarkable conclusion; we may not have guessed, when, at the beginning, Demeter rejoiced that Persephone's eyes were thawing, becoming once again "human-godlike," how far Persephone would go toward the god-man Jesus Christ. This ending shows that even a goddess feels as the characters in Tennyson's dramatic monologues usually feel as they conclude their speeches: each, as he acquires a definite outline, becomes exasperated or bored with his present lineaments, and tries to reconstitute a different self, in a different place.

We have in Demeter the most elevated persona that Tennyson ever attempted. In his lesser personae the leak of the ocean, the breath of the abyss, gave a certain transpersonal suggestiveness to even the most humble speaker; but in Demeter the ocean itself has been granted a speaking voice, a voice that turned out to be far more unpretentious and subdued, humanly elegant, agreeable, than anyone would have guessed.

Part Three

———✺———

THE THREE

MAJOR POEMS

IX

The Speaker of *Maud* as Adonis

IN TENNYSON THERE IS NO ASYLUM for identity, no resting place, only a passing-across from one's present unsatisfactory state into another, more hopeful condition, a difficult transfiguration. This is why his protagonists are necessarily restless, unstable creatures, preoccupied with making and with unmaking, cloudy beings seeking to disperse. Tennyson likes to discover his personae among the characters of classical mythology, because Ovid, Homer, Quintus Smyrnaeus seem to guarantee the meaningfulness, the precise form, of the speakers they lend him; but, as we have seen, the speakers of Tennyson's monologues, so ratified by precedent, so familiar to educated men, typically wish to be *someone else*. Themselves summoned into being by wishing, they express a wishfulness, a need for a still further act of mythopoeia. In the three great poems of Tennyson's middle years, 1834–55—*In Memoriam, The Princess,* and *Maud*—Tennyson explores the possibilities of giving artistic shape to speakers and speeches that defy all but the most complicated and extenuated kinds of definition; each poem presents an assault on the inexpressible, and in each Tennyson is lead to bizarre aesthetic compromises because of the intractability of his material, the small size of the human mouth, that balks at being forced to utter certain monstrosities.

Of the three poems, *Maud* (1854–55) most closely resembles a dramatic monologue, though it has clearly elaborated beyond any real generic restraint; most of Tennyson's earlier dramatic monologues kept threatening to hyperventilate, shoot off, and in *Maud* exactly that has happened. *Maud* is, as every student of Tennyson knows, an expansion of a lyric called " 'Oh! that 'twere possible,' " begun, like the monologues of 1833–34, just after Hallam's death; but it perhaps owes as much to the advances in the art of poetical characterization Tennyson achieved in "Locksley Hall" (1837–38).

The speaker in "Locksley Hall" is, like the speaker of *Maud,* an emphatic chimera, railing, swooning, thumping his breast, a kind of actor who is known not by what he says—he knows a hundred snatches of plays—but by his style of overemoting. The speaker of "Locksley Hall" is searching for a myth. The poem is loosely based on an Arabic story, but it is not the kind of story which can offer the support, the shoring-up of identity, that, for example, a tale from Ovid could offer; and, in the absence of an informing mythology, the speaker grows wildly eccentric, distracted from his distraction by random memories and presentiments; he cannot terminate the poem, can only stalk off the stage in the hope that mere loudness will substitute for a true finale. *Maud* begins in just this fashion, with the difference that the texture is not continuous raving and panting but is instead broken into a minutely organized hierarchy of sections and subsections, each of which represents a certain group- ing of endlessly readjusting and reaccommodating moods. Tenny- son mentioned that "the pecularity of this poem is that different phases of passion in one person take the place of different charac- ters" (Ricks, p. 1039); but that is little more than a plea that the reader pretend that an anthology of poems, positing a great variety of speakers, is in fact a single poem with a single speaker. The original title of T. S. Eliot's *The Waste Land,* with its incoherently fluctuating personae, was *He Do the Police in Different Voices,* also an invitation to the reader to consider the German quotations of Part 1, the Cockney accents of Part 2, and so forth, as the impersonations of a single speaker; and, as we shall see, *The Waste Land* resembles *Maud* in other ways as well.

Maud is Tennyson's most ambitious attempt to array within a single speaking voice an enormous diversity of feelings, ideas, volitions; and it is also his most ambitious attempt to imbue a character with meaning. Indeed the speaker of *Maud* is so much- meaning, so many-meaning, that he can scarcely fit inside himself all the patterns of significance with which Tennyson charges him. Much of this overcramming with meaning comes from a strategy of allusion to classical mythology; and it will be worth our time to take a preliminary look at Tennyson's customary use, in the *Idylls of the King,* of the sorts of myths with which *Maud* reverberates, myths of natural regeneration that Tennyson loves but darkly suspects of constituting a danger to the Christian soul's well-being.

Tennyson was, like Eliot, fascinated by the notion of some huge, general myth inclusive of many different systems of myths; and, like Eliot, he sometimes employed what we now call a fertility myth for this purpose. Frazer did not publish *The Golden Bough* until just before Tennyson's death, but the tradition of syncretic comparative mythology extends well back into the eighteenth century; what is forward-looking in Tennyson is not his interest in intercultural patterns of myth—this was sufficiently commonplace that his schoolboy prize poem "Timbuctoo" ends with an angel's discourse on this topic—but his ability to devise poetical plots suggestive of no particular story but suggestive nonetheless, full of a blurry plangency, allusive to some deep mythy substructure. In "The Coming of Arthur," the King expects Guinevere to be no ordinary consort but the female principle of natural renewal, a second Persephone whose touch will make the wasteland bloom:

> "for saving I be joined
> To her that is the fairest under heaven,
> I seem as nothing in the mighty world,
> And cannot will my will, nor work my work
> Wholly, nor make myself in mine own realm
> Victor and lord. But were I joined with her,
> Then might we live together as one life,
> And reigning with one will in everything
> Have power on this dark land to lighten it,
> And power on this dead world to make it live."

(ll. 84–93)

Arthur is a kind of farmer who can clear away the weeds, turn the soil, sow the seeds, but who knows it is all in vain unless the annual miracle takes place, unless the goddess of the fields gives her blessing. This agricultural aspect of Arthur is also seen in "Geraint and Enid": the obstinate Geraint decides to test and punish his wife by taking her on a silent tour of the wilderness, of marches, "bandit-haunted holds, / Gray swamps and pools, waste places of the hern" (ll. 30–31); and after all the misunderstandings are cleared up, after

Geraint is a man once more, Arthur sends out a thousand men "To till the wastes" (l. 941), to rid the dark places of bandits.

Arthur is the best of cultivators, but Guinevere is not especially adept at playing the role of Nature; still, there are hints that she had the potential to exert happy influence over the knights and the land; for instance, in "Balin and Balan," when the rough Balin deprecates his lack of finesse, of high courtesy, he thinks that devotion to Guinevere may improve and mollify a man, a Lancelot, even a Balin:

> "But this worship of the Queen
> That honour too wherein she holds him—this,
> This was the sunshine that hath given the man
> A growth, a name that branches o'er the rest,
> And strength against all odds, and what the King
> So prizes—overprizes—gentleness.
> Her likewise would I worship an I might."

(ll. 175–81)

The vegetation that Guinevere inspires, however, is not entirely wholesome; by "The Holy Grail" it seems that Guinevere has made grow not good wheat and fruit but, like Hawthorne's Rappaccini's daughter, a garden of poisonous flowers, as one of Lancelot's speeches suggests:

> " 'in me lived a sin
> So strange, of such a kind, that all of pure,
> Noble, and knightly in me twined and clung
> Round that one sin, until the wholesome flower
> And poisonous grew together, each as each,
> Not to be plucked asunder; and when thy knights
> Sware, I sware with them only in the hope
> That could I touch or see the Holy Grail
> They might be plucked asunder.' "

(ll. 769–77)

Lancelot feels that his adulterous passion has destroyed him, but he still tacitly agrees with Arthur that he is nothing without Guinevere.

In this Idyll it is clear that the regeneration of the kingdom can be accomplished only by Christian grace, by the Grail, if that phantom can stop its distractive flitting long enough to be a responsible ideal; just as Demeter, in "Demeter and Persephone," abdicated her system of myth in favor of Christianity, so Guinevere, a half-pagan goddess of fertility, must be rejected in favor of orthodox supernaturalism; and so Percivale wanders through a whole wasteland of crumbling images, where apples and accomplished women and golden knights and cheering crowds disintegrate into dust, sand, thorns, ruins, dead babies (ll. 379–439), until the Grail intervenes to realize the phenomenal world, give substance and heft to the theater of our souls' redemption. In the realm of Christian Incarnation, Guinevere can survive only as a wraith sickened by the daylight, an involuntary magician who blackens or appals the land:

> she dreamed
> An awful dream; for then she seemed to stand
> On some vast plain before a setting sun,
> And from the sun there swiftly made at her
> A ghastly something, and its shadow flew
> Before it, till it touched her, and she turned—
> When lo! her own, that broadening from her feet,
> And blackening, swallowed all the land, and in it
> Far cities burnt, and with a cry she woke.

("Guine-
vere,"
ll. 74–82)

This sunspot, which swells until it eclipses the earth, reminds us of the optical sublimities of "Armageddon" or "The Coach of Death," Tennyson's earliest visionary style. When Persephone left Enna to dwell in the infernal regions, she did not more effectively devastate the landscape. Arthur's attempt to manipulate the behavior of men and the fruitfulness of the land by the old nature mythologies has gone wrong, and Guinevere is abstracted to a convent, Arthur to Avilion, and priests, politicians, and agronomists are left behind to provide, as best they can, a good life for the human race; in the Epilogue to the *Idylls* (1872), addressed to Queen Victoria, Tennyson becomes studiously antimythopoeic, does whatever he can to avoid parallels between Modred's vanquishing of Arthur and the contemporary fears of the degeneration of the English character:

(ll. 60–66)

> yet—if our slowly-grown
> And crowned Republic's crowning common-sense,

> That saved her many times, not fail—their fears
> Are morning shadows huger than the shapes
> That cast them, not those gloomier which forego
> The darkness of that battle in the West,
> Where all of high and holy dies away.

Tennyson's longer stories are generally informed by some half-concealed structure of mythology, some never explicit movement between desolation and rejuvenation, or desolation and provisional or mock rejuvenation—of course such themes would be hard to avoid in Arthurian material, but similar structures are found in poems other than the *Idylls of the King*—yet Tennyson seems almost afraid of these deep myths, eager to consign them to make-believe while extracting from them whatever shudder, whatever excitement, they may provide. If Guinevere or Merlin dreams of a shadow that devours Camelot, one may be sure that Camelot will be devoured; if a nineteenth-century Englishman dreams that laxity or new warfare will ruin the country, it is no cause for alarm, the shadow is just a shadow and not a presentiment. No poet works for decades on a project that is not important to him, but there is a sense in which the *Idylls* is a toying with myth, a rehearsal of antique potencies performed in order to dismiss them. Percivale tells the monk Ambrosius that no one will ever see the Grail again ("The Holy Grail," l. 532); the novice suggests to Guinevere that her sin has extinguished the glad fairies and mermen from meadow and beach; and similarly Arthur and his court belong to an order of myth that can never return, though certain vestiges may linger:

> O loyal to the royal in thyself,
> And loyal to thy land, as this to thee—
> Bear witness, that rememberable day,
> When, pale as yet, and fever-worn, the Prince
> Who scarce had plucked his flickering life again
> From halfway down the shadow of the grave,
> Past with thee through thy people and their love,
> And London rolled one tide of joy through all
> Her trebled millions, and loud leagues of man
> And welcome!

(Epilogue, ll. 1–10)

As Tennyson concludes his *Idylls,* he remembers Prince Albert, decent not to fail in his public duties even on the brink of the grave; coming just after "The Passing of Arthur," these lines cannot but recall Arthur's vanishing into triumph, his prophesied second coming after a spell as "King among the dead" (l. 449). Arthur and Albert alike seem to allude to a thousand old tales of the god who visits the kingdom of the dead and returns to dispense all felicity and providence—Osiris, Attis, Tammuz—but in the case of Prince Albert this allusiveness is mostly a matter of decoration and graceful praise, rather than a summoning of magical energies; furthermore, when one considers the identity of Albert's wife, any extensive analogy between Arthur and Albert would be scandalous. And yet, though Tennyson carefully sunders every connection between Camelot and Buckingham Palace, he intends for some inarticulate Arthurian glory to inhere in modern England. Tennyson at once embraces mythological implications and avoids them; and similarly the speaker of *Maud* will approximate certain mythological roles and then shy away from them.

In *Maud,* Tennyson's appetite for some unresolved, dubious mythiness is equally great; and the category of myth alluded to is similar to that of the *Idylls of the King.* The speaker of *Maud* is desperate to discover some archetype to ratify, to give significance to his otherwise random fits of mania and depression. Throughout Part 1 he comments continually about the appropriateness or the inappropriateness of the weather to his moods (in the manner of some of Tennyson's early narcissists), as if he expected some consistent correlation, believed that the climate ought to be either friend or antagonist; "the scream of a maddened beach" (1.3.99) seems the proper background to his agony, but it is not always so:

> A million emeralds break from the ruby-budded lime
> In the little grove where I sit—ah, wherefore cannot I be
> Like things of the season gay, like the bountiful season
>   bland.

(1.4.1.102–4)

He wishes to live in a landscape that expresses him, a properly deranged landscape like that of Julian in "The Lover's Tale"; but, as Part 1 continues, he gladly abandons this responsibility and allows

the beautiful spring to be expressive of Maud. At the beginning he
is full of the clenched recklessness of the speaker of "Locksley Hall,"
windy and volatile, fulminating, but slowly he perceives a path by
which he may be given coherence, absorbed into a system of myth.
These clues are at first tantalizing, vague; he half-remembers, half-
imagines a scene of his infancy, when his father and Maud's father
contracted a marriage between their offspring:

> Is it an echo of something
> Read with a boy's delight,
> Viziers nodding together
> In some Arabian night?

(1.7.3.293–96)

As he thumbs through his books of mythology, seeking a story to
embody his life, he finds, not something from the Arabian Nights,
but one or another of the Greek tales of Peeping Toms who prey
upon goddesses, earthly men who yearn for the sublime. Of course
he does not think of himself as Actaeon, the hunter who spied upon
the bathing Diana and was turned into a stag, so that the wrathful
deity might have the pleasure of seeing her violator torn apart by his
own hounds; or as Tiresias, blinded by the apparition of the naked
Athena—the speaker would not willingly invite these results—but
by lingering always at the peripheries of Maud, hopeful when she
waves to him while riding past, delighted when he glimpses her
closing her window, the speaker can slip into a well-defined, conventional, and therefore soothing role, the role of the mortal who
admires a goddess from afar:

> Maud's own little oak-room
> (Which Maud, like a precious stone
> Set in the heart of the carven gloom,
> Lights with herself, when alone
> She sits by her music and books
> And her brother lingers late
> With a roystering company) looks
> Upon Maud's own garden-gate:
> And I thought as I stood, if a hand, as white
> As ocean-foam in the moon, were laid

(1.14.2–3.497–515)

On the hasp of the window, and my Delight
Had a sudden desire, like a glorious ghost, to glide,
Like a beam of the seventh Heaven, down to my side,
There were but a step to be made.

3

The fancy flattered my mind,
And again seemed overbold;
Now I thought that she cared for me,
Now I thought she was kind
Only because she was cold.

He sees her filled with inner luminescence, herself the lamp by which she reads; and she seems about to tremble into pure incorporeal light.

But the speaker cannot fully assent to his own intuition; Maud can shrivel in an instant from a goddess lit by her aura to a tease or a coquette. Imagination can construe a hundred Mauds, because the speaker's acquaintance with her is slight; indeed throughout the poem the world of fact is greatly attenuated, and the reader has only a series of arias from which he can devise whatever libretto suits him best. Though in the 1856 edition Tennyson added a few patches of recitative, such as I.19, to clarify the plot, the speaker's compulsion to construct glamorous dreams and nightmares from the slenderest matter leaves all event shrouded in a plethora of interpretations. The speaker lives an ambiguous life, yet he is singularly intolerant of ambiguity. Maud must be supernal, supreme, sempiternal, the issue of parthenogenesis (1.13.3), or the most trivial woman alive, "A perfect-featured face, expressionless, / Insipid, as the Queen upon a card" (Sonnet ["How thought you that this thing could captivate?"] ll. 13–14). In either posture she is to a large extent a myth; but the clashing of these two irreconcilable archetypes tortures the speaker, and generates much of the psychological complexity of the poem. Maud as goddess and Maud as coquette cannot fuse into a stereoscopic whole; they taunt the speaker with their incompatibilities.

In the beginning, the satirical version, Maud as heartless Queen of Hearts, predominates:

What is she now that to see her a moment provokes me
  to spite?
One of the monkeys who mimic wisdom, whom nothing
  can shake?
One whom earthquake and deluge would touch with a
  feeble delight?
One who can hate so sweetly with mannerly polish, and
  make
Pointed with "love" and "my dearest" a sweet innuendo
  bite?
One who has travelled, is knowing? a beauty and ruined
  with praise?
Well, I was half-afraid but I shall not die for her sake,
Not be her "savage" and "O the monster"! their delicate
  ways!
Their finical interlarding of French and the giggle and
  shrug!
Taken with Maud—not so—for what could she prove
  but a curse.

(Ricks,
p. 1046,
passage b,
ll. [1]–[10])

Tennyson deleted these lines from his manuscript, presumably
because he did not want to give great weight and finish to this
alternative, "incorrect" construction of Maud. It is interesting that
this caricature, a more affected and fatuous creature than the slith-
ery Vivien of the *Idylls of the King,* lives in a Lucretian heaven,
where earthquake and flood inspire a faint refined delight; indeed
she may be said to reside in the Palace of her own Artifice, her brittle
and studied mechanism of gesture. The bad Maud, like the Soul in
"The Palace of Art," seems another member of Tennyson's portrait
gallery of women who represent a spoiled sublimity. Chiefly she is
self-conscious, knowing; her antiself, the divine Maud, is perfectly
ignorant of her beauty.

O beautiful creature, what am I
That I dare to look her way;
Think that I may hold dominion sweet,
Lord of the pulse that is lord of her breast,
And dream of her beauty with tender dread,

(1.16.1.
546–55)

From the delicate Arab arch of her feet
To the grace that, bright and light as the crest
Of a peacock, sits on her shining head,
And she knows it not: O, if she knew it,
To know her beauty might half undo it.

It is of course the goddess that will triumph in the speaker's imagination, and the caricature that will be extinguished; but the caricature intrudes at odd moments to embody the speaker's anxiety, when, for example, he wonders whether Maud would be worth losing if she had engaged herself to her suitor the captain (1.16.2.560–66); and the caricature will reappear in Parts 2 and 3 as the baleful phantom of Maud under whose influence the speaker withers, starves. As I have remarked, *Maud* is an expansion of a lyric of 1833–34, " 'Oh! that 'twere possible,' " written just after "Tithon"; and, as in "Tithon," the poet of " 'Oh! that 'twere possible' " is torn between two versions of the transcendent beloved, one of which irritates and persecutes him, the other of which represents all that is lovable in the universe:

Let the dismal face go by.
Will it lead me to the grave?
      Then I lose it: it will fly:
Can it overlast the nerves?
      Can it overlive the eye?
(ll. 99–110)   But the other, like a star,
Through the channel windeth far
      Till it fade and fail and die,
To its Archetype that waits,
Clad in light by golden gates—
Clad in light the Spirit waits
      To embrace me in the sky.

The Fury, he claims, is a figment, a pathology of the nerves, involuntary, obsessive, while the Archetype is a consciously summoned image of the beloved's "beauteous face" which the poet paints on his "inner eye" (l. 80) in order to ward off the vampire; the poem is part of a rite of exorcism, a dispelling of those aspects

of the dead beloved that are conducive to paralysis, sterility, emaciation. The spoiled sublime is repaired, made ideal; the Erinyes
are changed to Eumenides. The apparition is compelled to change
itself from a maddening and persistent specter, an empty eidolon,
into something actual, consoling, supernatural, something which,
echoing Shelley's Adonais, like a star beacons from the abode
where the Eternal are.

It is not far from Adonais to Adonis. We have seen that the
speaker of *Maud* explored the role, not uncommon in Tennyson's
poetry, of the voyeur to a goddess, the role of Tiresias or of the
blinded churl in "Godiva"; but he finds his most satisfying para-
digm in Adonis. In Greek myth Adonis shared the ardent affections
of Aphrodite and Persephone; they struggled for him until Zeus
decided, in his best Solomonic fashion, that Adonis should spend
part of the year with Aphrodite and part of the year in the underworld with Persephone; finally he was slain by a boar, or by the
jealous Ares in the shape of a boar. The celebrated weeping for
Adonis, first wept by Aphrodite, became an annual Mediterranean
ritual. Adonis, then, is the male version of Persephone, who led a
similarly schizoid life; and it is easy to see why Frazer in 1890 would
take him as a representation of a nature-god, like Osiris or Tammuz, in hell during the winter and on earth during spring and
summer, and why George Stanley Faber, in mythological writings
probably known to Tennyson, would take him, like Arthur, Osiris,
Noah, and Adam, as one version of the Great Father buried as the
world sinks into chaos, reunited with the Great Mother, and then
reborn (W. D. Paden, *Tennyson in Egypt,* pp. 77, 80). The cyclical
nature of the speaker's mental distress, in which euphoria and
elation alternate with grief, despair, and the conviction of ruin,
accords well with Adonis' ups and downs; and in the astral Maud he
has his heavenly Venus; in the trifling Maud, in Maud the abiding
phantom cold, he has his infernal Proserpine. We see, then, that
Tennyson has provided the speaker with a rich critical apparatus for
making mythological interpretations of his state of life; and yet
there is a certain fragility to all this meaningfulness. What most
terrifies the speaker is not the loathsomeness of the world—denun-

ciation is congenial to him, he is so expert at ranting that we must
believe it gives him pleasure—but the meaninglessness of it:

>   4
>   Here will I lie, while these long branches sway,
>   And you fair stars that crown a happy day
>   Go in and out as if at merry play,
>   Who am no more so all forlorn,
>   As when it seemed far better to be born
>   To labour and the mattock-hardened hand,
>   Than nursed at ease and brought to understand
>   A sad astrology, the boundless plan
>   That makes you tyrants in your iron skies,
>   Innumerable, pitiless, passionless eyes,
>   Cold fires, yet with power to burn and brand
>   His nothingness into man.
>
>   5
>   But now shine on, and what care I,
>   Who in this stormy gulf have found a pearl
>   The countercharm of space and hollow sky,
>   And do accept my madness, and would die
>   To save from some slight shame one simple girl.

(1.18.4–
5.627–43)

Mythology offers a refuge from nothingness, from the rigor
mortis of things; in mythology there is, instead of the "passionless
eyes" of the Newtonian stars, a scheme of coherent passions in
which rage and extravagant love are equally valid. Tennyson explains in a note to this passage that the speaker's "sad astrology" is
"modern astronomy, for of old astrology was thought to sym-
pathise with and rule man's fate" (Ricks, p. 1068). Now it is often
the case in Tennyson's poetry that astronomy and other topics of
modern science are fruitful stimuli to the mythopoeic imagination;
but he could not embrace them without reservation. In a late poem,
"Parnassus" (1889), Tennyson presents Astronomy and Geology as
"terrible Muses" who loom above and confound all poetry and
song; these muses are threatening, not because they represent a

scoffing, rationalistic, debunking spirit inimical to art, but because they inspire a superhuman and inconceivable artifice, the "Sphere-music of stars and of constellations" (l. 8). Indeed they are the colossi of "The Mystic" given their final captions. Once again we see that the celestial muse, if she appears without the cooperation of her homelier sister, may disable the imagination utterly. Just as the poet's "evergreen laurel is blasted by more than lightning" ("Parnassus," l. 12), all human myth is swallowed in this abyss of myth-lessness; but it seems that the lightning bolts of Urania, the classical muse of Astronomy, are dangerous, sublime. Art wishes to edge toward states which render art impossible, in which the poet verges on such a coma of awe that he cannot speak. The speaker of *Maud* attempts to extricate himself from this reeling, to withdraw from zones of annihilation into a comfortable and voluble life in which depression and exhilaration enjoy the sanctions of a sympathetic, anthropocentric nature, the nature known from old mythologies.

As we have seen, the world of Tennysonian myth is dominated by Amphion, by Apollo, by Orpheus, by the kinetic singer who can alter and invigorate his environs, by the world-deranger who can impress himself on the landscape he beholds. Though the speaker of *Maud* is not, as far as we are told, a professional artist, he approximates several artistic postures, chiefly the broadside satirist and the troubadour; and certain resemblances to Orpheus may be noted. When he is confident of Maud's love, when "The countercharm of space and hollow sky" has cast its spell, he becomes the resident of an enveloping, sensitive, prelapsarian garden world in which all things move according to his rhythm, in which he is very little discriminated from the flowers around him, from the stars above him: the cedar is like the cedar that shaded "snow-limbed Eve" (1.18.3.626); at his bidding Maud's blush incarnadines the whole earth, until red men across the sea start to turn redder (1.17); and in the great serenade that closes Part 1, the garden chirps, buzzes, exhales in a complex antiphon to his emotions while he waits for Maud to come to him:

(1.22.10.   There has fallen a splendid tear
908–15)   From the passion-flower at the gate.

> She is coming, my dove, my dear;
>   She is coming, my life, my fate;
> The red rose cries, "She is near, she is near;"
>   And the white rose weeps, "She is late;"
> The larkspur listens, "I hear, I hear;"
>   And the lily whispers, "I wait."

It is as if the garden were so caught up in the concentration and intricate violence of his feelings that all its vegetable voices joined into that chorus of vehemencies that constitute the speaker of *Maud*.

Maud is such a radiant, disembodied, incredible figure, appearing only in brief glimpses, a creature of a quick hand-clasp, a hasty blush, a slight murmur of a single Yes, that it is easy to think her little more than a muse, the inspiration and focus of the speaker's orphic delirium, a lyric trance which compels roses to weep and birds to cry out "Maud, Maud, Maud, Maud" (1.12.1.414). Maud is a new Eurydice as well, in the sense that in Part 2 the speaker joins her in the land of the dead, for so he considers the madhouse to be:

> But I know where a garden grows,
> Fairer than aught in the world beside,
> All made up of the lily and rose
> That blow by night, when the season is good,
> To the sound of dancing music and flutes:
> It is only flowers, they had no fruits,
> And I almost fear they are not roses, but blood;
> For the keeper was one, so full of pride,
> He linkt a dead man there to a spectral bride;
> For he, if he had not been a Sultan of brutes,
> Would he have that hole in his side?

(2.5.8.310–20)

In the hell of the madhouse he imagines a deeper, stiller hell, in which the scene of the garden serenade is clinched, frozen, a *tableau mort*. There he and Maud, his "spectral bride," may dwell forever in the Lotos-Eater's aesthetic refuge, an anticipation of Swinburne's Garden of Proserpine, in which a smooth pavane and wax flowers decorate a lapsed world; except that in the speaker's imagination the glossy sterility still threatens to melt into blood, into living passion.

As in "Lucretius" it is at the moment of maximum tension and anguish that the speaker tries to isolate and defend in his memory a vision of sheer calm, what Pound's Hugh Selwyn Mauberley, the greatest twentieth-century proponent of the aesthetic refuge, will call an "Olympian *apathein*," but this reversion from agitation to dead peace fails, and trickles of blood begin to leak from the insipid flowers.

In retrospect it seems that the whole of "Come into the garden, Maud" (1.22), which appeared to take place in an enchanted garden where the speaker's keenness sharpened the flowers, made them responsive, lyrical, in fact took place in the underworld, as if such sublimity were possible only in hell; and the immediate collapse of the speaker's ecstasy, as Maud's brother ran into the garden, to insult the speaker and soon to be killed by him, only seems to make explicit the pathology of the whole scene. As in "The Palace of Art," high bliss is irresponsible, impermissible; Orpheus deserves to lose Eurydice if he experiments with such magical interpenetration. In the Greek myth the Maenads of Thrace grew so exasperated with Orpheus' ceaseless moaning about his dead wife that they tore him limb from limb; and in a sense the speaker of *Maud* suffers a similar *sparagma* in Part 2, the fate he predicted for himself near the beginning of the poem:

> What! am I raging alone as my father raged in his mood?
> Must *I* too creep to the hollow and dash myself down
>   and die
> Rather than hold by the law that I made, nevermore to
>   brood
> On a horror of shattered limbs and a wretched swindler's
>   lie?

(1.1.14.53–56)

The speaker's dismemberment is only psychic, metaphorical, but this wrenching, this disarticulation, may be the proper penalty for one who wrenches nature into a semblance of his own feelings. To make nature pathetic is finally to make oneself the object of pathos.

Orpheus and Adonis have much in common in that both explore hell for the sake of a loving woman, and both have considerable power to alter the natural world, one by the compulsion of song, the other by embodying a principle of vitality. The Romantical poet, who attempts to engage himself with nature so intimately that he and nature can scarcely be distinguished, will easily tend to assume the form of the god whose presence or absence ordains the seasons, determines the forthcomingness of sap and blood; and, because his song is the agency of this access of power, some of the features of Orpheus are likely to enter his mythology of self. *Maud,* then, like much of Victorian poetry, investigates the themes of Romantic poetry in their winter phase, when the god gropes in the darkness for his shattered limbs. Ruskin, in his famous diagnosis of the pathetic fallacy in *Modern Painters,* cites examples from *Maud* of Tennyson's treatment of flowers, though perhaps today we feel, not that an irrational intellect is prevaricating, coloring his environment with his intense emotions, but that his landscape is so deeply imbued with him, so animated by him, that it has its private weather, its private botany, exclusive of any world which the reader might share. The flowers that blush or spring up beneath the feet of Persephone-Maud (1.12.6; 1.22.7), the flowers that carry on a colloquium to edify Adonis the speaker, at last yield to a flower that expresses the speaker with an almost scary immediacy, as pathetic fallacy is abandoned in favor of a metaphor of identity:

> She is coming, my own, my sweet;
>   Were it ever so airy a tread,
> My heart would hear her and beat,
>   Were it earth in an earthy bed;
> My dust would hear her and beat,
>   Had I lain for a century dead;
> Would start and tremble under her feet,
>   And blossom in purple and red.

(1.22.11.
916–24)

Behind this stanza is a whole history of love poetry, like the legend of Tristram and Iseult, who found in death an intermingling of rose and briar sprung from their graves, an aesthetic consolation; or like Shelley's *Sensitive Plant,* in which a poetical weed is carefully tended and pruned by a fair lady. The speaker of *Maud* has become so absorbed in his garden of myth that he has passed out of human form, achieved a metamorphosis into symbol, like Daphne, Narcissus, Hyacinthus; the end of identifying oneself with the natural world, the limit of that sort of deranged sublimity in which the landscape is made expressive of a man, is to become a flower. The trial edition of *Maud* in fact contained two references to the flower narcissus (1.3.101 and 3.6.1.6), though Tennyson altered both to the somewhat more prosaic daffodil; and I believe that Tennyson may have been alluding to a flower similar to the narcissus when he described the dead heart that blossomed beneath Maud's feet. What happened to Adonis after the boar maimed him? According to Shakespeare's *Venus and Adonis,* all nature sympathized with Adonis' wound: "No flow'r was nigh, no grass, herb, leaf, or weed, / But stole his blood and seem'd with him to bleed" (ll. 1055–56). When Adonis died, Venus lamented over him, and he changed into a flower in which the bloody stain became an indelible design:

> the boy that by her side lay kill'd
> Was melted like a vapour from her sight,

(ll. 1165–70)

> And in his blood that on the ground lay spill'd,
> A purple flower sprung up, check'red with white,
>   Resembling well his pale cheeks and the blood
>   Which in round drops upon their whiteness stood.

Venus plucked this flower, and it wept a tear of green sap; she placed it in her bosom and said she would kiss it every minute. The efflorescent heart of "Come into the garden, Maud" and the flower engorged with blood in the madhouse scene both show the easy equivalence of natural and human life; and it is clear that the speaker's wish for a governing mythology has been granted, that he has achieved a passage into a convenient and reflexive world in which metamorphosis is effortless, in which every detail is symbolic and significant, although it is possible that this dwelling in high myth is simply insanity. Tennyson is usually suspicious of the too meaningful.

In the madhouse scene in *Maud* (2.5), we see that the twentieth century has no monopoly on the notion that madness is the mind's attempt at radical cure. Even in Part 1, Maud's suitor's grandfather can plunge into the darkness of a mine and change coal into gold (1.10.1), although this alchemy is as yet only a satirical trope; and in

Part 2, in the madhouse the speaker will descend into hell in order to transform himself into a brighter, more effective creature. Some of the speaker's distention and incoherence will shrink back to more human, manageable proportions; though even after he leaves the madhouse he will be a mythy, ambitious creature. The most notable feature of bedlam is its noise; in its way the asylum is a place every bit as expressive as Maud's garden, though it is the expression of a nightmare:

> See, there is one of us sobbing,
> No limit to his distress;
> And another, a lord of all things, praying
> To his own great self, as I guess;
> And another, a statesman there, betraying
> His party-secret, fool, to the press;
> And yonder a vile physician, blabbing
> The case of his patient—all for what?
> To tickle the maggot born in an empty head,
> And wheedle a world that loves him not,
> For it is but a world of the dead.

(2.5.3.268–78)

Instead of solicitous talking flowers we have the gibbering of the inmates. It is as if the venal and sodden public world at which the speaker vented his spleen at the beginning of the poem—a society which pretended pacific virtue and hid away its squalor, the mothers who murdered their babies for money (1.1.12)—had at last given itself away, grown explicit, loud in its viciousness. In the madhouse there are no secrets. All those feelings that had, in the garden, attained a veiled and private expression through the flowers themselves, here attain a furious declaration:

> For I never whispered a private affair
> Within the hearing of cat or mouse,
> No, not to myself in the closet alone,
> But I heard it shouted at once from the top of the house;
> Everything came to be known.

(2.5.4.285–89)

On Glubbdubdrib, in Book 3 of *Gulliver's Travels,* the spirits of the dead nonchalantly confess to all manner of loathsome crime, for they have nothing to lose, being dead; it is similar in Tennyson's hell, for everything shows itself as it really is, without extenuation or disguise. Maud's father, who cheated the speaker's father, was once called a "gray old wolf" (1.13.3.471); but in the madness scene this epithet is not merely a vituperative metaphor, but the only identity, the only manner of appearing, which Maud's father possesses: the wolf is given a wilderness, a whelp, a howl, some bones to crack, for he is all wolf, in no sense a rich old landowner (2.5.5). Thus in the madhouse the speaker resides in a disconnected and infuriating, imprecise, but unusually real world, in which he passes from sensation to memory to imagination without distinguishing one from the other, yet in which all repressed or concealed things manifest themselves correctly.

Only Maud is silent in the general cacophony of truth:

> Tell him now: she is standing here at my head;
> Not beautiful now, not even kind;
> He may take her now; for she never speaks her mind,
> But is ever the one thing silent here.
> She is not *of* us, as I divine;
> She comes from another stiller world of the dead,
> Stiller, not fairer than mine.

(2.5.7.303–9)

On one hand this disillusioned version of Maud, not beautiful, not kind, not invested with her usual aura of grace, seems more accurate and credible than the swoony apparitions of Maud presented in Part 1; on the other hand Tennyson seems to have perfected for her a different sort of mythic role, the Queen of Hades; and indeed Tennyson may have remembered this passage when, in "Demeter and Persephone," he described the slow emergence of Persephone, "dazed and dumb" (l. 6), clouded and dispassionate, from her infernal stupor.

The madhouse scene presents two different hells, the drugged and painless Lucretian otherworld of Maud and the imaginary garden, and a clamorous, urgent, intolerable place, the locus of unveiling. The first is a state of disengagement, the second of derangement; we have returned to the same two dangerous sublimities that have always haunted Tennyson. By the end of the scene the speaker prays to be buried "Deeper, ever so little deeper" (2.5.11.342), that is, to join faint, demure, dead Maud in her dim confusing garden; but it is only a waking man's prayer for sleep, for the speaker, under the influence of the noisy revelations that he cannot but hear, no matter how much he stops up his ears and groans, is beginning to clarify, to make exact distinctions, to understand moral niceties ("lawful and lawless war / Are scarcely even akin" [2.5.10.332–33]), to reenter the upper world and endure the asperities of public life. His sojourn in the sublime has allowed him to return, refreshed, to the real; though he cannot totally readjust his sense of identity away from high myth, down to the humble and unpretentious. In the brief conclusion after the speaker is discharged from the asylum, in Part 3, it may seem as if he had forsaken the conceits of mythology in order to lead a simple, ordinary, human existence, submerging himself among his patriotic countrymen in the expressive act of warfare, no longer deprecating society but struggling to improve it; but I do not think so. I believe that, having failed to win Venus in his guise as Adonis, the speaker decides to try his luck in the guise of Venus' favorite lover, Mars:

(3.6.1.10–14)
> She seemed to divide in a dream from a band of the blest,
> And spoke of a hope for the world in the coming wars—
> "And in that hope, dear soul, let trouble have rest,
> Knowing I tarry for thee," and pointed to Mars
> As he glowed like a ruddy shield on the Lion's breast.

Having been torn apart, he prefers to be the tearer; it is another stage in the rhythm of action and suffering that dominates his existence. Having eaten his own heart (the phrase is from *In Memoriam* 108) for years, he turns his appetite outward, becomes voracious for war; and Maud, no longer a Fury tormenting him, becomes the avenging angel against England's foes, a role for which she prepared herself at the beginning, when she sang her martial ballad (1.5.1). The monodrama depended on a single speaker who could play or imagine all the roles; it is as if Tennyson tired at last of this claustrophobic, involved art, preferred to relocate the speaker and Maud in the much larger, more public drama of the Crimean war.

Maud, at least its germinal lyric " 'Oh! that 'twere possible,' "

grew, like much of Tennyson's major work, out of his grief at
Hallam's death; it is true that the emotional situation of the speaker
of *Maud* resembles that of Tennyson rejected, circa 1836, by the
beautiful, rich Rosa Baring, but the prime injury is the death of
Hallam, amplifiable, as we know from *In Memoriam,* by any bereavement, any wound. A traditional elegist in the line of Bion's
"Lament for Adonis" and of the "Lament for Bion" attributed to
Moschus would have compared Hallam to Adonis, foully slain but
glimmering in the darkness with latent energies of resurrection.
For instance, Spenser in his "Astrophel" compares his fellow poet
Philip Sidney, who died fighting the Dutch at the battle of Zutpen,
to Adonis, his love "Stella" to Venus, and after the proper pieties
transforms Astrophel into a beautiful red flower, Stella into the
starry carpel of this flower. But Tennyson, the most self-engrossed
of elegists, can never fully elucidate his relation to the object of his
elegy, and so elegist and elegized are blurred together confusingly.
Instead of writing a lament for Adonis, Tennyson lets Adonis
speak, lets him manufacture a lament for himself, masked as a
lament for a vague woman, an ignorant figment, a pretext for self-
mythologizing.

Many readers of *Maud* have found its ending abrupt, or strained,
or irresolute, or even politically reprehensible; I think it is because
the ending is tangential, like the Christian swerve at the conclusion
of that other retelling of an infernal myth, "Demeter and Persephone," an abdication of one sort of divine identity in favor of
another. Mars may indeed be the god worthy of the fair lady, but,
insofar as we can construct a coherent psychology for the speaker,
he is only a wish, a weak man's dream of becoming a bully, and not
a credible role. Tennyson compared the speaker of *Maud* to Hamlet,
and this romantical Hamlet seems so stuck in his agonizing, his
attitudinizing, his loud but unconvinced oratory, that it is hard to
imagine him turning gruff, brawny, blunt, decisive. The shrill
tenor tries to assume the resonance, the vocal weight, of a baritone,
but can only make a hollow and histrionic sound. The myth of
Adonis, the sufferer, seems plausible for him, with its gore, its
stately pathos, its disjecta membra; the myth of Mars, the prepotent
warrior, does not. The dry rustling of Tithon the grasshopper,

wracked each morning by the pain of dawn, cannot easily modulate into the bluster of Hercules. *Maud* is a great poem, but it is thickly, heavily orchestrated, in the manner of Schumann or Brahms, not quite a flexible enough medium for the presentation of a character of such complexity and deviousness.

X

The Muses' Tug-of-War in
In Memoriam

Maud IS THE LOGICAL CULMINATION of "Ulysses," "Tithon," and "Tiresias" in that it goes as far as Tennyson could go toward endowing grief with the authority of myth. But during most of the years between Hallam's death and the publication of *Maud*, 1833 to 1855, when Tennyson was investigating the poses, the attitudes, the fluency, the hoarseness of various lovelorn classical and modern personae, he was also writing brief elegies about Arthur Hallam in which hope and despair are little mediated by ready-made masks; and their aggregate, *In Memoriam A. H. H.* (1850), is an alternative construction to the whole sequence of character studies, in which the griever and the object of grief are presented, not in the context of mythology, but in the context of intimate social life. In such poems as "Tiresias" grief was almost fully siderealized, made vast and world-appalling, noble; *Maud* shows a certain tendency to embed such extremes of emotion in a more modern, recognizably human figure; and *In Memoriam* offers the astonishing spectacle of an earthly muse of such subtlety, grace, and vigor that she can compete with the heavenly muse as a worthy inspirer of elegy.

This seeming masklessness is both a strength and a liability. Sometimes the reader feels that emotion is presented so directly, so simply, so economically, without the usual ingenuity of metaphor, even without the usual rhetorical urgency, that love and desolation must naturally utter themselves in tetrameter stanzas, without any intervening artifice. This effect, like all graces beyond the reach of art, is the result of superior art, just as the effect of masklessness, *mon coeur mis à nu,* is only the drawing of a subtler and more pliable mask. In *In Memoriam* Tennyson did not set out to make an auto-biographical poem, and after it was published he insisted that the

" 'I' is not always the author speaking of himself, but the voice of the human race speaking through him," that "it is a very impersonal poem as well as personal" (Ricks, p. 859). Many years later Yeats, who disliked Tennyson but was as deeply influenced by him as by anyone, would speak similarly of his desire to make his poetry impersonal, "all men's speech," rather than any one man's speech. Tennyson tried various strategies for heightening the feeling of impersonality, discreet anonymity, in the poem: many of the sections are meditations about themes so large that they characterize the speaker, as in "The Two Voices," only by the tonality of his emotional response. In certain sections Tennyson presents his family with gestures toward other families in similar crises—for instance in section 6, where he describes his sister Emily, waiting at home, fussing about how to please her fiancé, Arthur Hallam, who will never return:

(6.37–40)
> And, even when she turned, the curse
>   Had fallen, and her future Lord
>   Was drowned in passing through the ford,
> Or killed in falling from his horse.

Hallam did not die by drowning or by falling, but these divarications into other attendants upon other accidents tend to include, engage a multitude of readers, in the poem's emotional field. Yet despite these motions toward impersonality, the sheer facts of Hallam and the Tennysons—the journey to England of the ship that bore his corpse, Hallam's room at Cambridge, the detailed Christmas celebrations—exert a gravitational pull upon the poet, keep him centered in the specificity of his situation. I think that the poem is strengthened by these restraints against Tennyson's inclination to sublime monumental generality.

Still, for all this diffuse personalness, this minute dwelling upon one's verbal responses to shock and custom, the sequence exhibits exactly that impersonality for which Tennyson strove, because "Tennyson," the ostensible speaker, far from being an incisive, confident character, is only a nervous locus of conflicting and unresolved feelings. Most elegists are impersonal because they adopt the conventional tried-and-true elegiac mask; Tennyson is impersonal for the opposite reason, because, interested in unusual emotional authenticity, he does not impose upon himself the discipline of personality. The speaker of *In Memoriam* is to some degree an expansion of the narcissists, the indeterminant singers found everywhere in his earlier works. His apparatus of feeling and thinking is so distended in time and space—no previous elegy, to my knowledge, ever treated dinosaurs and galactic clouds—that his correct persona is the encyclopedist, not the elegist; and *In Memoriam* keeps swelling beyond any confines of genre because it is in truth not an elegy, or a set of elegies, but a summa of human thought, the utterance proper to the voice of the whole race.

By this strange richness and amplitude of emotion, Tennyson denies himself the consolations of the formal lament. We know that *In Memoriam* was composed in a manner "so queer that if there were a blank space I would put in a poem" (Ricks, pp. 859–60); the trouble with this sort of piecemeal construction—it is like Kafka's version of the building of the Great Wall of China, in which short segments are erected every few miles, so that it is completely useless until the distant future when the whole edifice will be in place—is that it can never properly end. No matter how many brief elegies Tennyson wrote, he could never fill all the cracks, discontinuities, unintelligible transitions, and evidences of arbitrariness in the sequence as a whole. Few readers are much distressed, I suspect, by the disorderliness of *In Memoriam,* because the poet's obsession with Hallam's death and the metrical power of the stanza provide such strong thematic and textural continuity, and because the Christmas poems provide stable points from which many festoons of speculation may depend. But the funeral elegy, perhaps more than any other classical genre, requires structural security to make its effect, and *In Memoriam* is spineless. The speaker of the elegy embodies his shapelessness in the piecemeal construction of the poem.

I invite the reader to look at any old-fashioned funeral elegy, perhaps a slightly unfamiliar one, like Spenser's "Daphnaïda," an orthodox lamentation over the death of Lord Howard's daughter. There the poet begins by asking all unlucky or mournful men to consider the case of sad Alcyon, the most woeful man alive, whom the poet chanced to meet one gloomy evening. Alcyon, once a jolly shepherd, is full of sighs and groans; he explains to the amazed poet that a mild playful lioness had become his pet, had submitted to the role of sheepdog, but a cruel satyr had killed her with his dart and ruined his happiness forever. The poet understands that this is not a factual account but a riddle, and asks Alcyon what it means; Alcyon tells him that Daphne is dead, and faints, but gets up and launches forth on a lament, divided into seven numbered sections: (1) Daphne, though only a lowly primrose compared to rosy Queen Elizabeth, was still the purest, most angelic, most lamentably absent of women; (2) he remembers the counsel of the dying Daphne, who urged him to take comfort in the joys of heaven, soon to be hers, and to love their daughter; (3) he remembers the look of Daphne's corpse and urges nature to be silent, blighted, weeping, to bring forth only monsters; (4) he tells his sheep he will attend no more to their welfare and vows to be spectacularly miserable for the rest of his days; (5) he expostulates that he hates nature, hates the flesh and its sliminess, hates the four elements, hates his five senses, hates all men and women, hates this millwheel the world, driven with streams of wretchedness and woe; (6) he wishes he were dead, for he never sleeps and always wanders, just as the mother of the gods kept wandering heavy-hearted looking for her daughter; (7) he begs rich men, wretched lovers, happy lovers, fellow shepherds, fair damsels, and poor pilgrims to mourn for him. Alcyon grows faint again, and the poet tries to comfort him, even offers his own house as refuge; but Alcyon will not be comforted, will not be sheltered, tears out his hair and staggers into the night.

This elegiac structure is exceedingly rigid, almost mechanical; but precisely because it is so predictable, so foreordained, like a religious ritual, it can bring relief. The whole action of the poem is played out against a background of deep myths of regeneration or succor, with frequent allusions to the dark metamorphoses of Adonis, Philomel, Eurydice; and although Alcyon is obstinately inconsolable, refuses every succor, the logic of his lamentation leads him irresistibly to the consolation he denies himself. Alcyon is a stylized and incredible figure of extravagant grief; in the monodrama of his misery he presents himself as the most lurid, overdrawn, contorted, theatrical figure imaginable. "Daphnaïda," like most elegies, has a double strategy of evasion and confrontation: the poet abstracts Arthur Gorges, the widower of the celebrated woman, into the pastoral caricature of Alcyon, whose hyperbolical outbursts at once give vent to human suffering and deflect it onto someone else, like a hired mourner in a funeral ceremony who satisfies the genuinely bereaved with his graceful imprecations, tremblings, and tears. Furthermore, the real object of lamentation is approached in the most gingerly, roundabout, oblique fashion possible, for Alycon first tells a little fable about a lioness—the white lion was a badge of the Howard family—a myth inside a myth—before settling into the cool, convenient, harmless world of Daphne, oaten pipes, and sad shepherds. The poem is a machine to console. By the end of Alcyon's lament, his woe, which has defoliated the forests and blasted human society, is, despite Alcyon's protestations, spent; he has invited the pity of the companions whom he had previously pronounced hateful, has begun a secret exorcism of the feelings that oppress him, has prepared to rejoin the community of men. "Daphnaïda" is not a great poem; but as magic it is astutely conceived.

When we return to *In Memoriam* we are in the midst of something finer but more ineffectual; the emotion is not epitomized and discharged, firmly stated and dismissed, but instead flickers, writhes, subsides, flares up again, like the sullen apparition in "'Oh! that 'twere possible'" that cannot be expelled until the whole vast mythological apparatus of *Maud* is erected to banish it. I believe, then, that *In Memoriam* fails to be an elegy because Tennyson did not impress upon his material the conclusive shape necessary for psychological relief by aesthetic means. This is not to say that the poem fails, for it is possible that a real elegy would have seemed dishonest to Tennyson, inconsistent with the nature of his peculiarly interminable grief. One might almost say that Tennyson was too imaginative to be an elegist. The role of the elegist is social, ceremonial; an elegy for Hallam should have outfitted the deceased in his most dignified clothes and the bereaved in a proper suit of black, and then announced simply and strongly why the loss of Hallam's friendship left the poet destitute. Instead of this we have a bewildering multitude of experimental statements of their relationship, all of them private, intimate, and eccentric, as if every human affiliation expressed something of Tennyson's closeness to Hallam, but none of them could express the whole. Here is a reason why the subject of the poem is generalized until it encompasses the whole race: Tennyson wishes to claim that everything a human being can feel was pertinent to his relation with Hallam. It seems that Tennyson's intimacy with Hallam grew more obscure the more Tennyson tried to clarify it; where any simile is valid, there is no logical relation between the parts. Thus Tennyson compares himself to a poor girl whose rustic life is spoiled by infatuation with a noble-man (sect. 60); to a dim dwarf jealous of Shakespeare, whose company he imagines the heavenly Hallam will prefer (sect. 61–62); to the wife of a great scientist, whose mind pierces the heavens while she putters about the house (sect. 97); and in a line deleted from section 93 Tennyson implores the ghost of Hallam, "Stoop soul and touch me: wed me." Tennyson keeps struggling to trace the outline of Hallam (sect. 70), to discern the beloved face with its "bar of Michael Angelo" (sect. 87); but though these operations of depiction meet with some success, the image of Hallam continually recedes into a bright haze, in which the poet and his object alike lose all form, depersonalize, boil out into the sublime. The ceaseless abundance of similes and images is required because the contours are so infirm; instead of Spenser's sure-handed caricatures of Alcyon and Daphne we must choose among a whole gallery of effigies, competing versions of the mourner and of the mourned, in which none is exactly the right voodoo doll needed for the elegy to work its magical consolation. Instead of a slow mounting of feeling in the steady vessels of fixed pastoral types, the lightning gathering for discharge, the poem keeps re-turning to the poet's workshop, where Tennyson displays yet another Hallam, yet another griever, as if each section made the previous section obsolete.

Another aspect of the imaginative excess of *In Memoriam* can be seen in the inability of the imaginer to keep himself distinct from his image, the usual debility of Tennyson's deranged characters from Julian in "The Lover's Tale" on. It is common in the elegy for the mourner to undergo a symbolic death out of sympathy for the dead beloved; but it is rare for the elegist to become as confused and involved with his object as Tennyson is with Hallam, as if he did not know where he left off and his beloved began. When Tennyson feels humble, abject, he thinks of his relation to Hallam as that of wife to husband; when Tennyson is excited, he and Hallam become consubstantial, or have the relation of body to soul. Near the beginning of the sequence, when Tennyson gazes at the yew growing over someone grave, he seems "to fail from out my blood / And grow incorporate into thee" (2.15–16), as if Tennyson and Hallam alike were decomposing into vegetation. The yew is a surrogate for an imaginary plant that, like Tristram's and Iseult's briar, feeds on both their bodies. A similar symbolic function is given to the phantom children of Hallam and his fiancée Emily Tennyson, babbling "Uncle" on the poet's knee (sect. 84), for in those unconceived children there could have been mingled Hallam's and Tennyson's blood. Indeed in the later sections Hallam is more vivid as a locus of imaginary potentialities than as a historical man; not only does Tennyson imagine himself and Hallam growing "involved" together into extreme old age, until Christ reaches out to both and takes them "as a single soul" (sect. 84), but he also imagines how Hallam would have felt if he had lived and Tennyson had died young (sect. 80), how much better Hallam would have borne grief. In a related section, addressed to his brother Charles, Tennyson explains that he and Charles were formed, imprinted, by the same upbringing, shared identical experiences, whereas he and Hallam were complementary:

> And so my wealth resembles thine,
> But he was rich where I was poor,
> And he supplied my want the more
> As his unlikeness fitted mine.

(79.17–20)

Again there is the implication that Tennyson and Hallam lose themselves in each other, together constitute a single entity, one all-competent human being, or that, as in the relation of the knights to King Arthur, Tennyson could, through Hallam's generous influence, elevate himself to Hallamdom, even though he must always lag behind on the celestial ascent (sect. 41).

In one section of collegiate reminiscence, Tennyson thinks of Hallam's grave, mollifying integrity in debate, while the young Tennyson remained silent and apart, feeling that "thy triumph was as mine" (sect. 110); it is as if Tennyson dwindled into a mirror reflecting Hallam, as if Hallam led Tennyson's life vicariously. It is as if Narcissus developed an inferiority complex with respect to his own image in the water. This line of investigation, this feeling that Hallam was authentic, possessed reality, while Tennyson was only a copy or simulacrum, led to one of the eeriest passages in *In Memoriam:*

> Whatever way my days decline,
>   I felt and feel, though left alone,
>   His being working in mine own,
> The footsteps of his life in mine;
>
> A life that all the Muses decked
>   With gifts of grace, that might express
>   All-comprehensive tenderness,
> All-subtilising intellect:
>
> And so my passion hath not swerved
>   To works of weakness, but I find
>   An image comforting the mind,
> And in my grief a strength reserved.

(85.41–64)

> Likewise the imaginative woe,
>   That loved to handle spiritual strife,
>   Diffused the shock through all my life,
> But in the present broke the blow.
>
> My pulses therefore beat again
>   For other friends that once I met;
>   Nor can it suit me to forget
> The mighty hopes that make us men.
>
> I woo your love: I count it crime
>   To mourn for any overmuch;
>   I, the divided half of such
> A friendship as had mastered Time.

As best he can Tennyson lives the life denied to Hallam, knowing that he is but a clumsy surrogate prone to every error, but guided by the mysterious hand of the heavenly original, as if he writes the poetry that Hallam should have written, even makes the friends that Hallam should have made. One might say that there is a single being, Tennyson-Hallam, whose earthly component is called by one name, his celestial extension by another.

Tennyson presents his imagination as oddly avid for misery, for domination by a superior entity, for transforming itself into the colorless vessel of a single image, the genius and emotional delicacy of Hallam. Elsewhere in *In Memoriam* it seems that Hallam's early death, the fact that he did little work and gained little fame, allowed him to husband his being, gather himself into a perfection uncontaminated by earthly achievement (sect. 73)—in Yeats's words, triumph would but mar his solitude; but here it seems that Tennyson's life is an expression of what Hallam perforce left unexpressed. In life they shared a telepathic unanimity:

And Fancy light from Fancy caught,
(23.14–16)   And Thought leapt out to wed with Thought
Ere Thought could wed itself with Speech.

In death Tennyson must carry alone the burden of their two lives, in a state perpetually gravid and never giving birth.

There is a danger in such stress of intimacy, such contiguity, such identity between the mourner and the one he mourns; the mourner may feel himself losing shape, staggering from a vertigo of nonidentity. In "The Two Voices" the act of gazing upon the peacefulness of a corpse's face became an invitation to suicide; but the peril of empathy with the dead is different in *In Memoriam*. We have seen that Hallam has escaped the confines of his brief history, has expanded into a creature with a huge repertory of hypothetical terrestrial and celestial lives, no longer a single man but a Kraken of possibilities. This luminous vagueness of identity serves to magnify Hallam, but it also casts doubt over the stability, the distinctness of the human ego. In the course of a sequence speculating on the ego's origin and possible extinction, Tennyson posits a baby who never thinks "this is I":

> But as he grows he gathers much,
>   And learns the use of "I", and "me",
>   And finds "I am not what I see,
> And other than the things I touch."
>
> So rounds he to a separate mind
>   From whence clear memory may begin,
>   As through the frame that binds him in
> His isolation grows defined.
>
> This use may lie in blood and breath,
>   Which else were fruitless of their due,
>   Had man to learn himself anew
> Beyond the second birth of Death.

(45.5–16)

Tennyson approves strongly of an afterlife in which we retain our memories and boundedness, our individuality; and yet he seems to feel a strange nostalgia for those soft and shivery states, the last traces of prenatal glory, in which the baby dwells before "God shut the doorways of his head" (sect. 44), knitted together the bones of his skull to shut out the radical light. Julian in "The Lover's Tale" liked to dream of the womb in which he and his twin sister had once coexisted; and now that Tennyson understands that Hallam was more than a twin to him he turns his attention again to the topic of fetal development, of dreams of superhuman empathy. Rarely in Tennyson's work is the tension between Romantic sublimity—the condition in which the self is smeary, transpierced—and Victorian specificity so manifest:

> That each, who seems a separate whole,
>   Should move his rounds, and fusing all
>   The skirts of self again, should fall
> Remerging in the general Soul,
>
> Is faith as vague as all unsweet:
>   Eternal form shall still divide
>   The eternal soul from all beside;
> And I shall know him when we meet:

(47.1–16)

> And we shall sit at endless feast,
>> Enjoying each the other's good:
>> What vaster dream can hit the mood
> Of Love on earth? He seeks at least
>
> Upon the last and sharpest height,
>> Before the spirits fade away,
>> Some landing-place, to clasp and say,
> "Farewell! We lose ourselves in light."

Tennyson prays that he and Hallam may remain personalized, separable, at least long enough to say a proper farewell; but there is such great pressure of imagery throughout *In Memoriam* urging diffusion, mingling of identities, complete implication of Hallam and Tennyson, that the rejected ending seems the correct one, and double diffraction the most likely outcome. Insofar as Hallam can remain a heavenly example of good conduct, an actual friend whose foibles one fondly remembers, the poem has some hope of being an elegy; but insofar as Hallam and Tennyson become a single intertwined web of nerves, a familiar compound ghost lost in light, the poem veers into a phantasmagoria of provisional and quivering half-things.

Both Hallam and the poet succumb to the disease of narcissism:

> My love has talked with rocks and trees;
>> He finds on misty mountain-ground
(97.1–4)
>> His own vast shadow glory-crowned;
> He sees himself in all he sees.

We are now back in the juvenile world of "Armageddon," of the old illustration of the man who looks at his own vast image reflected in the mists during the eruption of the volcano Cotopaxi. The rest of this section of *In Memoriam* tells the parable of the scientist who ignores his patient wife; but if the scientist sees himself in all he sees—we remember that Ulysses, another explorer drifting into the sublime, was a part of all that he had met—he presumably sees himself in his wife as well, for there is no stopping this delirium of self. When Tennyson attributes such feelings to himself, he recognizes clearly the pathology of the situation:

> I will not shut me from my kind,
>   And, lest I stiffen into stone,
>   I will not eat my heart alone,
> Nor feed with sighs a passing wind:
>
> What profit lies in barren faith,
>   And vacant yearning, though with might
>   To scale the heaven's highest height,
> Or dive below the wells of Death?
>
> What find I in the highest place,
>   But mine own phantom chanting hymns?
>   And on the depths of death there swims
> The reflex of a human face.
>
> I'll rather take what fruit may be
>   Of sorrow under human skies:
>   'Tis held that sorrow makes us wise,
> Whatever wisdom sleep with thee.

(108.1–16)

This suggests that most of the previous 107 sections have been unhealthy, that the poet, while pretending to glorify his friend, has in fact populated a little poetical world with images of himself, pleasantly arrayed in various postures of pensiveness, grief, and pious song. Tennyson understands that just when he would most like to be self-forgetful, to celebrate a genuine Other, to bedeck a tomb with garlands, he has instead checked into his favorite hotel de luxe, the Palace of Art, where all the walls are mirrors. He offers himself the same cure worked upon the Soul in "The Palace of Art," enforced social obligation. But the claustrophobic, stifling quality of *In Memoriam* is not due to excessive brooding solitude; some of the sections are addressed to brothers and friends, in quasi-epistolary manner, and there are many references to a shared, bustling public life—Cambridge, family, even the somewhat balding streets of London. Instead, it is due to the fact that Tennyson's images of Hallam and of himself are ingrown, inextricable; clamorous intimacy has manufactured a cosmos so saturated with the phantoms of the mourner and the mourned, joined at the head like Siamese twins, that all praise directed at its intended object twists into self-congratulation. Well might Tennyson advise himself to choose an earthly muse, the Melpomene of a proper elegy:

> Urania speaks with darkened brow:
> "Thou pratest here where thou art least;
> This faith has many a purer priest,
> And many an abler voice than thou. . . ."

(37.1–4, 9, 13–16)

> And my Melpomene replies . . .

> "For I am but an earthly Muse,
> And owning but a little art
> To lull with song an aching heart,
> And render human love his dues."

Tennyson must consciously delimit his project, concentrate on rehearsing the words and actions of the actual person Arthur Hallam, for the celestial Urania, with her frantic sublimities, her stormy transcendence of all duality and limitation, keeps threatening the poem with an alien inspiration.

Urania is the muse of the aesthete, the visionary, and Tennyson seems to keep her at bay by reaching out his hand to society and by insisting on the inadequacies of art; though, as we shall see, Urania has her place in the economy of the poem. He hopes that even if the rewards, the consolations of art, are shown to be small, they can be shown to be genuine. Indeed there is no theme in *In Memoriam* more persistent than Tennyson's self-criticism, his intricate indictment of himself as an elegist and of the general feebleness of art; but although the poet hopes thereby to clear himself of the charge of too much presuming, his skepticism about his medium may interfere all the more with the magical convulsions and catharsis a proper elegy evokes. *In Memoriam* has scarcely begun before Tennyson calls the whole project into question:

(5.1–12)

> I sometimes hold it half a sin
> To put in words the grief I feel;

> For words, like Nature, half reveal
> And half conceal the Soul within.
>
> But, for the unquiet heart and brain,
>   A use in measured language lies;
>   The sad mechanic exercise,
> Like dull narcotics, numbing pain.
>
> In words, like weeds, I'll wrap me o'er,
>   Like coarsest clothes against the cold:
>   But the large grief which these enfold
> Is given in outline and no more.

This section, evidently not among the earliest written, may be the most Carlylean passage Tennyson ever wrote: the whole of Teufelsdröckh's clothes philosophy—" 'In a Symbol there is concealment and yet revelation' " (*Sartor Resartus,* p. 165)—seems to lie behind these stanzas; though the anxiety about the falsifying necessary to all expression is Tennyson's own. The reader is warned that only a gross impression of the poet's sorrow will be conveyed, only an analogy, not the palpitating thing, the pain, the redness, the swelling; the poetry at once expresses and insulates, protects the reader from the contagion of the poet's chills and fevers. What is more remarkable is that the poet protects himself as well, by interposing words between himself and his emotions. The poem is itself Lotos, and its handler abstracts himself into a state of Lucretian vertigo, in which suffering is drained of all that is not music, delectation. Tennyson wishes to feel largely, to engage himself as fully as he can with the fact of Hallam's death; yet disengagement, Olympian apathy, keeps intruding in many unsuspected places.

If Sorrow is holy ground, as Oscar Wilde was to allege, then poetry writing is an act of deliberate desecration; and Tennyson's chosen muse, Melpomene, announces guiltlessly, suavely, that she "darkened sanctities with song" (sect. 37). It may be argued that the goal of the elegiac experience is similarly anesthetic; but I think that in a real elegy the discharge of feeling arises through a careful reenactment, under laboratory conditions, of all the monstrousness of bereavement, not by this steady dulling, this dribbling palliation, this self-conscious sense of the wrongness of all that is put in words, this refusal to suspend disbelief. At many places in *In Memoriam,* Tennyson seems to feel that the whole exercise is a vast, interminable, pointless game. Sometimes the poetry seems to numb the poet, other times, as a malignant spirit says in a deleted section, "Thy songs are fuel to thy grief" (Ricks, p. 1773); but whether the act of writing conceals or reveals, kindles or quenches, it is all irrelevant to the emotion with which it toys. Again we see how *In Memoriam* fails to be a true elegy, a machine to console by the discharge of feeling, for feeling is largely unchanged, undischarged, by its aesthetic expression. In the same section, perhaps deleted because Tennyson did not wish to face the full implication of what he said, we see that the poet must destroy his poem in order to confront Hallam:

(Ricks,
p. 1773,
ll. 13–16)

> I faltered in my toil, and broke
>   The moulds that Fancy made; and turned
>   To that fair soul that with me mourned
> About his tomb, and sighing spoke.

The teeming of imaginary Hallams has driven away the real man; and poetry, which deals only in images, images that falsely soothe or falsely inflame, leads to an estrangement from the being whom Tennyson would meet honestly.

From the beginning of his career Tennyson had a profound sense that speech is a violation of integrity, that the urge to express is a sign of our fallen state. In "Supposed Confessions of a Second-Rate Sensitive Mind" (1830), the poet envies the trustful infant on his mother's knee because his joy is so little importunate, so little strident, so lacking in urgency, that it leaves no evidence of its existence:

(ll. 47–51)

> He hath no thought of coming woes;
> He hath no care of life or death;
> Scarce outward signs of joy arise,
> Because the Spirit of happiness
> And perfect rest so inward is.

Soon he will change into the sort of man who has to write poems, or otherwise inflict his feelings upon others. In "The Day-Dream" (1830–34), in which Tennyson retells the story of Sleeping Beauty, we find that this self-enclosed infant has elaborated himself into a whole unborn world:

> Here rests the sap within the leaf,
>   Here stays the blood along the veins.
> Faint shadows, vapours lightly curled,
>   Faint murmurs from the meadows come,
> Like hints and echoes of the world
>   To spirits folded in the womb.

(ll. 3–8)

This nostalgia for the unhatched egg, for speechless self-involvement, is strong in Tennyson's work, but it has its disquieting aspects as well; the desire to constitute one's own universe eventually leads to the schizoid detachment of the Soul in "The Palace of Art," who can talk only to herself. A milder version of this syndrome can be seen in Julian in "The Lover's Tale" (1827–28), who would like his affection for Camilla to be as reticent and self-contained, perfect, as that of the infant in "Supposed Confessions." Near the beginning he tells his friends that he cannot explain to them the mysterious, remote origin of his love:

> How should the broad and open flower tell
> What sort of bud it was, when, prest together
> In its green sheath, close-lapt in silken folds,
> It seemed to keep its sweetness to itself,
> Yet was not the less sweet for that it seemed?

(1.146–50)

Later it becomes clear that Julian's obstinate sense that only the unexpressed is pure has been interfering with the progress of his suit:

> I did not speak: I could not speak my love.
> Love lieth deep: Love dwells not in lip-depths.
> Love wraps his wings on either side the heart,
> Constraining it with kisses close and warm,
> Absorbing all the incense of sweet thoughts

(1.455–65, 470–74)

So that they pass not to the shrine of sound.
Else had the life of that delighted hour
Drunk in the largeness of the utterance
Of Love; but how should Earthly measure mete
The Heavenly-unmeasured or unlimited Love,
Who scarce can . . .
Be cabined up in words and syllables,
Which pass with that which breathes them? Sooner Earth
Might go round Heaven, and the strait girth of Time
Inswathe the fulness of Eternity,
Than language grasp the infinite of Love.

Love may resist expression in earthly syllables, but because the childish Julian cannot say "I love you," Camilla turns to a more manly and voluble suitor, Lionel, who speaks "comfortable words" (1.705) while the sound of Camilla's voice "choked all the syllables" (1.700) from Julian's mouth. There is a sinister sense in "The Lover's Tale" that Julian is a miser, a connoisseur of his own emotion, that like the Soul in "The Palace of Art" he has imprisoned himself in a solitary museum where he can enjoy in private the mummified remains of his feelings:

                    Was mine a mood
          To be invaded rudely, and not rather
          A sacred, secret, unapproachèd woe,
          Unspeakable? I was shut up with Grief;
          She took the body of my past delight,
(1.666–76) Narded and swathed and balmed it for herself,
          And laid it in a sepulchre of rock
          Never to rise again. I was led mute
          Into her temple like a sacrifice;
          I was the High Priest in her holiest place,
          Not to be loudly broken in upon.

He is the High Priest, he is the sacrifice, just as the Soul in "The Palace of Art" is both sower and seed. What is unspeakable need not be shared, contaminated by foreign minds; but what is left unexpressed, unborn, will turn fatal, miscarried, a pickled embryo. The soft, bland feelings of an infant remain properly tacit; but as feelings ramify, grow complex, perfervid, abrupt and unsatisfied, they demand expression, or they grow involute and morbid.

In Tennyson's later poetry he usually stresses the dangers of leaving important matters unspoken. "Geraint and Enid" (1856) is a fable in which enforced silence, Geraint's command to Enid never to speak, wreaks all sorts of emotional havoc. The silent world, which Tennyson described with such lavish, wistful doting in "The Day-Dream," is here a condition of damnation: it ought to be easy to clear up the misunderstanding between husband and wife, but instead Geraint and Enid persist in a protacted chafing tongue-tiedness, as we see when Geraint orders Enid to drive the horses of slain bandits before her:

> He followed nearer; ruth began to work
> Against his anger in him, while he watched
> The being he loved best in all the world,
> With difficulty in mild obedience
> Driving them on: he fain had spoken to her,
> And loosed in words of sudden fire the wrath
> And smouldered wrong that burnt him all within;
> But evermore it seemed an easier thing
> At once without remorse to strike her dead,
> Than to cry "Halt," and to her own bright face
> Accuse her of the least immodesty:
> And thus tongue-tied, it made him wroth the more
> That she *could* speak whom his own ear had heard
> Call herself false.

(ll. 101–14)

It is Blake's "A Poison Tree" turned into an Arthurian Idyll. Geraint and Enid have neither verbal nor sexual commerce:

> the two remained
> Apart by all the chamber's width, and mute
> As creatures voiceless through the fault of birth,
> Or two wild men supporters of a shield,
> Painted, who stare at open space, nor glance
> The one at other, parted by the shield.

(ll. 264–69)

In the simile they are translated into artifice, two images painfully impressed upon a shield; and this petrification, this lockjaw, suggests, as in "The Lover's Tale," that what is unspoken will stiffen into pictorial frigidity, will abstract itself from common life. At last Enid, thinking that Geraint is dead, breaks the spell of uncanny silence with "a sudden sharp and bitter cry" (l. 721); and Geraint thaws, springs into action, kills evil Earl Doorm, and vows, in a pretty speech to Enid, never to doubt her again.

The other parable of muteness among the *Idylls of the King* is "Pelleas and Ettarre" (1869), in which a young bumpkin, Sir Pelleas, falls in love with a faithless flirt, Ettarre, who teases him for his speechless infatuation (l. 98); but in this case when Pelleas finds his tongue, it is not to beg forgiveness or to offer it but to curse:

> "O towers so strong,
> Huge, solid, would that even while I gaze
> The crack of earthquake shivering to your base
> Split you, and Hell burst up your harlot roofs
> Bellowing, and charred you through and through within,
> Black as the harlot's heart—hollow as a skull!
> Let the fierce east scream through your eyelet-holes,
> And whirl the dust of harlots round and round
> In dung and nettles! hiss, snake—I saw him there—
> Let the fox bark, let the wolf yell. Who yells
> Here in the still sweet summer night, but I—
> I, the poor Pelleas whom she called her fool?"

(ll. 454–65)

"The Lover's Tale," "Geraint and Enid," and "Pelleas and Ettarre" each present one of the three outcomes of the suppression of emotion: (1) emotion remains suppressed, and compels the rest of one's being to adore the withered splendors of passion; (2) emotion is let out and, in a healthy purge, one is reconciled, readjusted to society; (3) emotion is let out and, in an unhealthy purge, the long-buried passion strives to annihilate all that frustrated it. Pelleas, once overt, expressed, becomes the anti-Arthur, the bad eminence that threatens Camelot. Neither expression nor lack of expression is safe. Each may be a form of dementia, as we see in Tennyson's last great mythopoeic invention, "The Voyage of Maeldune" (1879–80), in which the first two islands, in the series of diseased Arcadias that Maeldune visits, are the Silent Isle and the Isle of Shouting. On the former Maeldune's men are flustered when their voices become "thinner and fainter than any flittermouse-shriek" (l. 22), and in their frustration they begin to slaughter each other; on the latter the cries of wild birds, who scream with human voices, so madden and derange Maeldune's men that they begin to shout too, and begin again to fight. But if silence tends to destroy the mute, and speech the speaker, how can one be a poet, how can one not be a poet?

The ingenious solution of *In Memoriam* is to write half-elegies in which the failure to express becomes one of the chief matters of expression. Expression is muted, never allowed to become extreme, overpowerful; if restraint, propriety, is imposed from without, expression will not get too loud, wander into regions of uncontrolled violence. Two opposing kinds of excess threaten to overwhelm *In Memoriam,* the two competing inspirations which Tennyson denominates as Melpomene and Urania; each would, without the mitigating influence of the other, cause the poem to founder; and the poet frets about the proper balance:

36
Though truths in manhood darkly join,
   Deep-seated in our mystic frame,
   We yield all blessing to the name
Of Him that made them current coin;

For Wisdom dealt with mortal powers,
   Where truth in closest words shall fail,
   When truth embodied in a tale
Shall enter in at lowly doors.

And so the Word had breath, and wrought
   With human hands the creed of creeds
   In loveliness of perfect deeds,
More strong than all poetic thought;

Which he may read that binds the sheaf,
   Or builds the house, or digs the grave,

And those wild eyes that watch the wave
In roarings round the coral reef.

37
Urania speaks with darkened brow:
  "Thou pratest here where thou art least;
  This faith has many a purer priest,
And many an abler voice than thou.

"Go down beside thy native rill,
  On thy Parnassus set thy feet,
  And hear thy laurel whisper sweet
About the ledges of the hill."

And my Melpomene replies,
  A touch of shame upon her cheek:
  "I am not worthy even to speak
Of thy prevailing mysteries;

"For I am but an earthly Muse,
  And owning but a little art
  To lull with song an aching heart,
And render human love his dues;

"But brooding on the dear one dead,
  And all he said of things divine,
  (And dear to me as sacred wine
To dying lips is all he said),

"I murmured, as I came along,
  Of comfort clasped in truth revealed;
  And loitered in the master's field,
And darkened sanctities with song."

Urania tells Tennyson to adopt a less ambitious task, to go home and not to storm the heavens; but from the other side of her mouth she tempts Tennyson to write celestial or profound poetry, the sort of visionary poetry we have in section 36.

As we have seen, the prototype of the sublime poet is Amphion, the poet who can build a city or a world in a trance of song; and when Tennyson describes creation as a book legible in the harvest and the tidal wave—in the manuscript of section 36, line 9, Tennyson wrote "And so the Logos breathed"—he is implicitly comparing his own poetical skills with those of the still more sublime Poet who devised the cosmos. In a previous section Tennyson wondered whether the universe was invented by a more vicious demiurge:

> My own dim life should teach me this,
>> That life shall live for evermore,
>> Else earth is darkness at the core,
> And dust and ashes all that is;
>
> This round of green, this orb of flame,
>> Fantastic beauty; such as lurks
>> In some wild Poet, when he works
> Without a conscience or an aim.

(34.1–8)

It is intolerable to believe that the genius of our fair earth was Zola, or Flaubert, or Lucretius' Venus, a spirit who would not guarantee the soul's immortality, or who devised the earth strictly for the sake of beauty, not for the sake of rewarding virtue. As Tennyson says in an epigram entitled "Art for Art's sake (instead of Art for Art-and-Man's sake)," aestheticism is the philosophy of hell; but it is perhaps natural for Uranian art, for art that challenges the mystery, to regard heaven and earth as a work of art, as something written, whether for good or for evil. Urania is despite her flash and dazzle finally dispassionate, scientific, contemptuous of little prating men, like the Soul in "The Palace of Art." The danger of embracing Urania is that the minute particulars of Arthur Hallam, all the dear things he said and did, will be lost amid ingenious and energetic inquiry into religion, natural philosophy, and geology, and that the elegist as well will vanish into the sublime. The danger of embracing Melpomene is that the flood of human, secular grief may drown the fragile vessel, the "rich shrine" (sect. 57, Tennyson's note) of *In Memoriam*—that is, that Tennyson may not be able to write at all, may have to retreat, like Julian in "The Lover's Tale," into the cave of the unexpressed. For example, in the sequence treating the boat that carried Hallam's body to England, Tennyson

stares at the river Wye and notes how its flow is choked by the tides
in the estuary of the Severn:

> The Wye is hushed nor moved along,
> And hushed my deepest grief of all,
> When filled with tears that cannot fall,
> I brim with sorrow drowning song.

(19.9–16)

> The tide flows down, the wave again
> Is vocal in its wooded walls;
> My deeper anguish also falls,
> And I can speak a little then.

Hallam's corpse entered England at Dover, and was borne overland
to Clevedon, on the Severn (*Letters* 1:105); and so tidal pressure is
equivalent to an engorgement of feeling, hydrocephalus, a great
heartache of sorrow.

The prestige of the inexpressible has always been great, and
became still greater after Wordsworth's Immortality Ode and its
thoughts that lie "too deep for tears"; but here it seems that excessive emotion endangers all corporeal and verbal expression, that
poetry cannot arise from the deepest spells of grief. The soothing,
narcotic effect of elegy writing that Tennyson described in section 5
works only upon that small fraction of feeling which permits itself
to be expressed:

> My lighter moods are like to these,
> That out of words a comfort win;
> But there are other griefs within,
> And tears that at their fountain freeze.

(20.9–12)

There is one kind of grief which naturally melts, grows vocal and
loud; there is another kind of grief which freezes, which introverts,
which shatters the griever; "Break, thou deep vase of chilling
tears, / That grief hath shaken into frost!" (4.11–12). Even the kind
of grief conducive to expression may not, however, be conducive
to poetry writing; in a relatively Uranian section (sect. 54), which
hypothesizes a teleology operant in all things—not even a worm is
cloven in vain—Melpomene appears at the end to dismiss these
lofty speculations:

(54.17–20)

> So runs my dream: but what am I?
>> An infant crying in the night:
>> An infant crying for the light:
> And with no language but a cry.

If Urania is irrelevant to real lamentation, she is at least glib, exuberant, full of elegant tropes; whereas Melpomene, faithful though she may be to authentic suffering, is likely to smother the poet in his own unspeakably involved emotions, or to order him to burst out in languageless wailing, a condition as childish and destructive as the great shout Pelleas utters to shake down the towers of Camelot. Elegy writing, then, can proceed only if the poet can find some precarious middle ground between the state of being choked by grief and the state of the meaningless tantrum. Urania, who behaved so haughtily and unhelpfully in section 37, can be useful in discovering this happy mean:

> I hear it now, and o'er and o'er,
>> Eternal greetings to the dead;
>> And "Ave, Ave, Ave," said,
> "Adieu, adieu" for evermore.

>   58
> In those sad words I took farewell:
>> Like echoes in sepulchral halls,
>> As drop by drop the water falls
> In vaults and catacombs, they fell;

(Ricks,
p. 913,
57.13–16;
58.1–8 and
canceled
stanzas)

> And, falling, idly broke the peace
>> Of hearts that beat from day to day,
>> Half-conscious of their dying clay,
> And those cold crypts where they shall cease.

> The grave Muse answered: "Go not yet.
>> A speechless child can move the heart,
>> But thine, my friend, is nobler Art.
> I lent thee force, and pay the debt.

> "Why wouldst thou make thy brethren grieve?
>> Depart not with an idle tear

> But wait: there comes a stronger year
> When thou shalt take a nobler leave."

I have quoted the last two stanzas of section 58 from a manuscript version; in the final version "The grave Muse" is called "The high Muse," making it clear that Tennyson means Urania. In this section the dialectic of the muses' rivalry is complicated indeed. Melpomene, the sullen earthly muse of wailing and silence, can do little more than bid the poet mutter "Adieu, adieu," and thereby infect his readers with a useless contagion of gloom; a speechless child can move the heart, but a good poem ought to accomplish more, and Urania offers a certain uplifting assistance, so that *In Memoriam* may become more pointed, forceful, significant. If Urania and Melpomene can clasp hands and dance, Tennyson should be able to find the right balance between abstraction and personal emotion, between sublimity and lament, between Hallam the blessed spirit and Hallam as he actually was.

Where in *In Memoriam* do we find this ease, this felicity, this elegiac success? Not in many places. Some of the sections I have cited, such as section 19, concerning the Wye and the Severn, show that Tennyson could compose great poetry on the theme of his inability to write a poem; there and elsewhere we see Tennyson trying simultaneously to obey Melpomene's command to be authentic, terrestrial—he insists that his feeling is too private and intimate to find relief in expression—and to obey Urania's command to be ingenious, noble, speculative, tricky—he finds a pathetic fallacy, a clever metaphorical apparatus of estuaries and tears, to express the condition of inexpressibility. Tennyson's triumph in outfitting the theme of the futility of expression with witty artifices occurs in section 16:

> What words are these have fallen from me?
>   Can calm despair and wild unrest
>   Be tenants of a single breast,
> Or sorrow such a changeling be?
>
> Or doth she only seem to take
>   The touch of change in calm or storm;

(16.1–20)

But knows no more of transient form
In her deep self, than some dead lake

That holds the shadow of a lark
        Hung in the shadow of a heaven?
        Or has the shock, so harshly given,
Confused me like the unhappy bark

That strikes by night a craggy shelf,
        And staggers blindly ere she sink?
        And stunned me from my power to think
And all my knowledge of myself;

And made me that delirious man
        Whose fancy fuses old and new,
        And flashes into false and true,
And mingles all without a plan?

Urania here is assigned to fathom, not the mysteries of infinite time
and boundless space, but the mysteries of the blasted and incoherent
self, the mysteries of grief; she is the muse of anonymity, just as
Melpomene is the muse of historical individuals. I believe that
"fancy," in the last stanza, is used in its exact Coleridgean sense:
Tennyson sees his work as a crazy quilt, artifically and arbitrarily
patched together by mechanical process of association.

    This Frankenstein's monster corresponds nicely to the piece-
meal method of construction of *In Memoriam*. Urania, in her general
role as the heavenly muse, the inspiration of high art, is also the
muse of mythopoeia, of metamorphosis. Now many of the sections
of *In Memoriam* struggle toward various halfhearted or provisional
myths, for the sake of consolation and relief; sorrow seems always
about to turn into something dramatic, momentous, magical, interesting. In the previous part, section 15, Tennyson is tempted to
submit to Urania's blandishments, to see a lurid stormy night as an
expression of his despair, in his best pathetic fashion—but he refuses to do so, because fear for the safety of the boat carrying
Hallam's remains makes him uncomfortable, unexultant at the
sight of a storm. Melpomene, with her concern for the actual and
finite, for the palpable body of Arthur Hallam, checks, quells those

attitudes of mind that Urania inspires. Melpomene is the anti-mythological muse, without conceit, hypothesis, or extrapolation, the muse of debunking. Section 16 is one of her finest labors, for she carefully untangles the basic invariant sorrow, the true theme of the whole, from its embellishments and elaborations, from its temporary expressions as calm despair and wild unrest; Urania's impressive fictions are unraveled, undone.

The metaphor here of the dead lake that reflects lark and sky is related to the metaphors that govern "The Lady of Shalott" and "The Palace of Art": the water images are similarly engaging and unreal, misleading, and the Dead Sea of tears, like the still salt pool to which the Soul contracted in "The Palace of Art," suggests that the imaginer has shriveled into a state of loathing for himself and his images, aesthetic hell. The gifts of the imagination, which had seemed exhilarating, tempestuous, have begun to decay, to smell, to disintegrate; what had seemed an act of high synthesis falls apart into a heap of incongruent parts, for it was only fancy at work after all, not imagination. When the unhappy bark founders, it falls out of hectic, superficial, imaginary life, out of the mirror, and into the static depths of real feeling.

When Tennyson later returns to the themes and images of section 16, he apologizes more explicitly for the disjointed, picturesque, pretty qualities of *In Memoriam:* in section 48 he explains that a certain tact or shame prevents him from making a long, comprehensive explanation of sorrow, that instead he makes "Short swallow-flights of song, that dip / Their wings in tears, and skim away" (ll. 15–16)—Melpomene, as usual, is tongue-tied, so the poet prefers sporadic and superficial expression to none at all. In the next section, 49, Tennyson evaluates his eclectic, mannered, softly graduated style of writing:

> From art, from nature, from the schools,
>   Let random influences glance,
>   Like light in many a shivered lance
> That breaks about the dappled pools:

(49.1–16)

> The lightest wave of thought shall lisp,
>   The fancy's tenderest eddy wreathe,

The slightest air of song shall breathe
To make the sullen surface crisp.

And look thy look, and go thy way,
    But blame not thou the winds that make
    The seeming-wanton ripple break,
The tender-pencilled shadow play.

Beneath all fancied hopes and fears
    Ay me, the sorrow deepens down,
    Whose muffled motions blindly drown
The bases of my life in tears.

The reader is instructed to stop being appreciative of art, to stop thinking that he understands what the poem is about; although *In Memoriam* is informed by the myriad resources of Victorian culture and science, though it is up-to-date and provocative in the best modern way, nevertheless its delicate effects are decorative, trivial, an aimless pattern of ripples and eddies on the surface of a pool. The art does not matter; only the swollen, muffled, imageless sorrow matters, the sorrow as choked as the tide-choked river Wye. W. H. Auden remarked in an essay on Robert Frost that every good poem requires the collaboration of two beings: Ariel, who insists on pure play and earthless delight, and Prospero, who insists on telling the truth about the human condition. If only Ariel rules, the poem becomes insipidly beautiful, the Grecian Urn's cold pastoral, an Arcadia where nothing important can happen; if only Prospero rules, the poem degenerates into squalid sobriety, a Dreiser novel. In *In Memoriam* Ariel and Prospero, who go by the names of Urania and Melpomene, are typically in a state of helpless discord, one struggling to tear down or abrogate the ingenious constructions and transfigurations of the other; but I think that this Pierian rivalry may display a certain unwilling cooperation, just as wrestling or swordplay may reveal a balletic grace. Tennyson gains control of his almost intractable project by his ability to indicate which muse he wants, to specify the nature of his inspiration: if Melpomene becomes maudlin, Urania can console and elevate; if Urania tells lies, Melpomene can make her honest. *In Memoriam* therefore manifests a built-in self-corrective mechanism.

Every elegist must solve in his own way the problem of the elegiac consolation being illusory; while a poem may manifest a character whose grief is soothed by reasoning or intuition or simple habituation, the real man who grieves may well refuse to identify himself with this consolable poetical personage. In "Daphnaïda" Spenser obviates this difficulty by making Alcyon inconsolable and yet subliminally moving toward consolation. Tennyson simply chooses to make Melpomene's objections to artifice and mythology, to the whole intricate mechanism of elegiac relief, less prominent in the later stages of *In Memoriam;* the grief that rejected all extenuation or palliation, insisting that its variations in mood were lies or feeble evasions, slowly becomes infused with an inner hilarity. When the scruples are given sufficient utterance, they may be permitted to grow faint. In section 88 Tennyson says that he tried to constrict the range of his harp playing to woe pure and simple, but, against his will, themes of joy and glory intruded, flashed along the chords; and the nightingale's song suggested to him, as to Keats, that in the depths of sensuous feeling grief mingled with a secret joy. In section 49 contentment, delicacy, and tenderness were superficial; now they have joined sorrow in the deep.

Urania makes grief beautiful, shapely, either by ingenious metaphor and fluent, decorous diction, or by alluding to a satisfying antique myth; and her prompting leads Tennyson to a partial acceptance of a consoling myth, the myth of Hallam's resurrection, after the inferno of mythlessness in the geological section (sects. 50–58) is transcended. As we have seen, Urania has introduced some confusions between subject and object which threaten the formal outlines of the myth, which make the operations of elegiac relief overcomplicated and unsteady; but she also dispatches from her celestial abode an angel to instruct Tennyson in consolatory mythology:

> I dreamed there would be Spring no more,
>   That Nature's ancient power was lost:
>   The streets were black with smoke and frost,
> They chattered trifles at the door:
>
> I wandered from the noisy town,
>   I found a wood with thorny boughs:

(69.1–20)

I took the thorns to bind my brows,
I wore them like a civic crown:

I met with scoffs, I met with scorns
    From youth and babe and hoary hairs:
    They called me in the public squares
The fool that wears a crown of thorns:

They called me fool, they called me child:
    I found an angel of the night;
    The voice was low, the look was bright;
He looked upon my crown and smiled:

He reached the glory of a hand,
    That seemed to touch it into leaf:
    The voice was not the voice of grief,
The words were hard to understand.

Here we are verging on the myth of Adonis. It is not far from this
section to *Maud,* in which an archetype informs nearly the whole
composition, but in *In Memoriam* myths form and disperse so
quickly that one can speak only of an aggregrate mythic tendency,
not of a coherent mythology. Hallam has died, and spring is no
more; but the winter only appears to be endless, and the descent of
Hallam-Adonis-Christ into hell is only a presage of resurrection,
revivification. Like the speaker of *Maud,* the poet is irritated by
chattering and trifling and seeks solitude to dwell upon his, the
world's, grief; and here as in *Maud* it seems that the poet's dwelling
on his own grief is something near to craziness, for, as Tennyson
notes, "To write poems about death and grief is 'to wear a crown of
thorns,' which the people say ought to be laid aside." Tennyson
considered in section 21 the fact that the elegist makes a public
spectacle of himself, that people will deride his "parade of pain";
and in section 49 he seemed to agree with the people's criticism, as
he dismissed his overwrought pictorial effects, his philosophical
speculations, as irrelevance and trickery.

    In section 69 Tennyson called himself fool and child, at Mel-
pomene's urging; but by end of this section we see that the folly, the
childishness, is vindicated, made glorious, and the poet gladly
enters a realm of artifice and high myth, in which the crown of

thorns is resolved first into the badge of a genuine Calvary, then into Dante's laurel wreath. The angel's words of blessing are not quite audible, for we are in a region of aesthetic sublimity in which human speech is no longer valid; it is like the end of "The Vision of Sin," in which the orgy of skeletons is dissipated, appalled, when God makes himself an awful rose of dawn—there someone cries out "Is there any hope?" and an answer peals out "in a tongue no man could understand" (l. 222). In this state of extreme beatitude every metamorphosis, every quickening, every resolution of pain into beauty is feasible, effortless; and Urania becomes the presiding genius of the poem. Tennyson seems to gain in confidence, and the whole poem starts to flower, to elaborate itself, as soon as Tennyson decides to permit himself the elegiac comfort of pretty conceits, mythical embroidery.

The emotion that chaste Melpomene declared submarine and inexpressible, indecorous, suddenly starts to break out in a score of oblique expressions: regret, which was so tacit and deep in section 78 (the second Christmas) that it was almost entirely lost, "Becomes an April violet, / And buds and blossoms like the rest" (115.19–20); in section 83 April scatters flowers over the countryside and the poet "longs to burst a frozen bud / And flood a fresher throat with song" (ll. 15–16). In Shakespeare's *Venus and Adonis,* in the old stories of Daphne and Hyacinthus, great suffering is suffered until it can be suffered no more, and then it veers into loveliness, into anesthesia, into distinctive vegetable energy; and through fitful and unsystematic allusions to such images, through the emblematical flowers that decorate the later sections of his poem, Tennyson evokes a vague mythological world in which he can pass into the efflorescence of his suffering. The imagination, which was in sections 16 and 49 a film of water upon which vain insignificant images formed, is sanctified in section 122:

Oh, wast thou with me, dearest, then,
   While I rose up against my doom,
   And yearned to burst the folded gloom,
(122.1–20) To bare the eternal Heavens again,

To feel once more, in placid awe,
   The strong imagination roll

A sphere of stars about my soul,
In all her motion one with law;

If thou wert with me, and the grave
    Divide us not, be with me now,
    And enter in at breast and brow,
Till all my blood, a fuller wave,

Be quickened with a livelier breath,
    And like an inconsiderate boy,
    As in the former flash of joy,
I slip the thoughts of life and death;

And all the breeze of Fancy blows,
    And every dew-drop paints a bow,
    The wizard lightnings deeply glow,
And every thought breaks out a rose.

This is the perfection of the sublime, of Uranian astronomical vision, this rolling of the zodiac across Tennyson's soul; indeed the whole section is exultant, boisterous. This mythological Hallam has altered considerably from his terrestrial version, and Tennyson's relation to him has altered too—Tennyson was indignant at the thought that anyone supposed that in life he called Hallam "dearest," or even "dear." Hallam is no longer a comrade to Tennyson, a fellow student, but something like the vision-inspiring angel of "Armageddon"; if Hallam will consent to inform Tennyson's faculty of imagination, then Tennyson will trust in his images. The poet's thoughts turn not into a single violet but into a whole garden; and though Tennyson uses the word *fancy,* he seems to mean Coleridge's imagination, in which mind and nature tremble into each other across an ever-shifting boundary, in which common things transfigure, grow chromatically aberrant. Melpomene wishes to bury Hallam, to embalm him in the rich shrine of *In Memoriam;* Urania wishes to reconstruct Hallam in various imaginative guises, in fact to identify him with imagination. As Tennyson opens himself to the wind, becomes an Aeolian lyre, he shakes free of Melpomene's gloomy constrictions on his art, embraces a Uranian elevation, rapture, aesthetic freedom.

The muses make their last explicit appearance in section 103, an odd literary dream in which Hallam is first a veiled statue, around which all the muses sing; then the poet accompanies the muses on a boat ride down a river, on which he and they grow strong and passionate, brilliant; at last the poet boards an ocean ship, and Hallam is already there, as a man "thrice as large as man." The muses weep in fear of being left behind, but Hallam invites them aboard too; the sound of the wailing muses changes into the sound of the wind, "A music out of sheet and shroud," and the ship departs into the sunset. Hallam in his first apparition may suggest the veiled statue at the temple at Sais to which Tennyson alluded in the agonized section 56—to see the truth revealed one must agree to die, and only through the poet's own death will he know the estate of the dead Hallam. Caroling around a veiled statue, lamenting that the beloved is passing beyond the province of art, all this suggests the operations of Melpomene; but when Hallam gestures to the muses to join him and the poet on their final voyage, when the poet feels his body flooded with power, it seems that Melpomene is repudiated in favor of Urania and her supervening mythologies.

That the muses should be the heavenly ancillae of Hallam and Tennyson is the final triumph of art; the afterlife has been transformed into an aesthetic refuge, yet it is in no way stultifying or specular, superb, Lotos-smelling. The Soul in "The Palace of Art" left her palace to mourn and pray, to become worthy to reenter the Palace; and in a sense Tennyson labors through much, much mourning and prayer in *In Memoriam* in order to attain a new ease, direction, and sureness about his role as an artist. I find something moving in Tennyson's hard-won ability to take pride in the glory of art.

In the later parts of *In Memoriam* Tennyson is increasingly confident of his intimations of immortality; but Melpomene's voice, her myth-destroying insistence that images are imaginary, symbols merely symbols and not indisputable truths, is never quite stilled, as we see when the ghost of Hallam materializes to comfort the poet:

" 'Tis hard for thee to fathom this;
(85.90–96)   I triumph in conclusive bliss,
And that serene result of all."

So hold I commerce with the dead;
> Or so methinks the dead would say;
> Or so shall grief with symbols play
And pining life be fancy-fed.

This is as close as Tennyson gets to the mood of the Shakespeare sonnet the most similar to *In Memoriam:*

Nor did I wonder at the lily's white,
Nor praise the deep vermilion in the rose;
(Sonnet 98,   They were but sweet, but figures of delight
ll. 9–14)   Drawn after you, you pattern of all those.
Yet seem'd it winter still, and, you away,
As with your shadow I with these did play.

The imagination ceaselessly teems with various apparitions, memories, enactments, a whole April of flowers in which the force of the absent beloved is felt; but none of these prolific images can satisfy, for the one true image is missing. Yet play is good, though it cannot be more than play.

The Epilogue to *In Memoriam* subtly changes the impression of all that has gone before, for both Melpomene and Urania recede, and a new kind of elegiac strategy takes over. Near the beginning of the Epilogue, Melpomene is sent packing once and for all:

Though I since then have numbered o'er
> Some thrice three years: they went and came,
> Remade the blood and changed the frame,
And yet is love not less, but more;
(ll. 9–16)

No longer caring to embalm
> In dying songs a dead regret,
> But like a statue solid-set,
And moulded in colossal calm.

The themes of section 103, the dream of Hallam and the muses, are here recapitulated, but now the statue is not Hallam, but an image of Tennyson's regret, fully formed and embodied, extracted, finished, petrified. It is the regret that Tennyson once refused to let die (sect. 78) and once expressed as a violet (sect. 115); now it is dismissed. The elegiac method has at last worked: the sorrow that seemed chronic, irremediable, has been discharged by the act of elegy writing, has turned iconic, an artifice extrinsic from the poet. Wailing and mythopoeia, Melpomene and Urania, are spent; and what is left? A homely anecdote, a smiling description of the wedding of Tennyson's sister Cecilia to his friend Edmund Lushington. Many critics of Tennyson have enjoyed the Epilogue but have found themselves uncertain of its propriety, or vice versa; for instance, Dwight Culler notes that "the Epilogue . . . takes the form of an epithalamium, and if it were a better poem it would have fulfilled its function" (*The Poetry of Tennyson*, p. 189); and James Kincaid calls the Epilogue "a brilliant attempt, but . . . essentially disconnected from his magnificent but deeply troubled poem" (*Tennyson's Major Poems*, p. 109). But it is precisely its disconnectedness that gives it force and efficacy. It is a great relief, this turning-aside from the interminable oppression of grief, from the interminable fantasies of eternity, to a simple human ceremony, a tale that little concerns Hallam or Tennyson. Lushington, though he may lay claim to the title of Tennyson's best friend, and thereby Hallam's successor, bears none of the heavy burdens of Hallam's genius, his archangelic severe purity; nor does the gay Cecilia seem very similar to Tennyson's other sister Emily, whose only possible poetical roles were either the eternally blighted almost-widow, or the fickle and compromised creature who decided, over the objections of the historical Tennyson, to marry a man less celestial than Hallam. It is precisely because these resemblances are so tenuous, far-fetched, that the enactment of the death-frustrated wedding of Hallam and Emily is so moving, a rustic pantomime of the marriage which (as King Arthur had hoped of his marriage to Guinevere) would have invigorated the wasteland and improved the human race:

> And rise, O moon, from yonder down,
>   Till over down and over dale
>   All night the shining vapour sail
> And pass the silent-lighted town,
>
> The white-faced halls, the glancing rills,
>   And catch at every mountain head,

(Epilogue,
ll. 109–44)

And o'er the friths that branch and spread
    Their sleeping silver through the hills;

And touch with shade the bridal doors,
    With tender gloom the roof, the wall;
    And breaking let the splendour fall
To spangle all the happy shores

By which they rest, and ocean sounds,
    And, star and system rolling past,
    A soul shall draw from out the vast
And strike his being into bounds,

And, moved through life of lower phase,
    Result in man, be born and think,
    And act and love, a closer link
Betwixt us and the crowning race

Of those that, eye to eye, shall look
    On knowledge; under whose command
    Is Earth and Earth's, and in their hand
Is Nature like an open book;

No longer half-akin to brute,
    For all we thought and loved and did,
    And hoped, and suffered, is but seed
Of what in them is flower and fruit;

Whereof the man, that with me trod
    This planet, was a noble type
    Appearing ere the times were ripe,
That friend of mine who lives in God,

That God, which ever lives and loves,
    One God, one law, one element,
    And one far-off divine event,
To which the whole creation moves.

The baby conceived on this silvery wedding night will be a
simple human child; but just as any infant is a good representation
of the Christ child in a Christmas pagent, so this frail common

thing is a valid link to a race that will surpass our own, an Incarnation. The prologue to *In Memoriam* is a hymn to Christ; the Epilogue, coming after the poet has endured three desolate Christmases, turns to a promising baby. The extraordinary has yielded to the ordinary, the feverish has yielded to the mild and temperate. Hallam, had he lived, might have anticipated, leaped over, a few of the stages in the long phylogeny of mankind; but there is satisfaction in the orderliness, the calm progress, of this immense development in which the child of Lushington and Cecilia will take a small part. The emotion evoked by Hallam's death has resolved itself into something completely disjunct from Hallam, and yet subliminally informed by the ideals he represented; Hallam has become a presence so abiding that he cannot be felt at all, has become a faculty of the poet, illuminating without being itself lit. Tennyson's imagination, animated and illustrated by the spirit of Hallam, perceives vast significance in simple earthly events; the labyrinth of generation, so unintelligible and purposeless in the geological sections, has been pulled taut into a line, a forward movement. Vestiges of Uranian nature myths may inhere—what is seed in us will be flower and fruit in our successors—but this consolation in the Epilogue derives less from sublime mythology than from the successful deflection of feeling from self-preoccupation, endless rehearsals of private sensation, to celebration of other situations, other lives. *In Memoriam* realizes itself as an elegy by abandoning every elegiac theme, by turning into an epithalamion. A convenient couple has been found, who do not know that they suffer from Hallam's death, do not know that they continue a mission he began; and in their unthinking secret obedience to a man who was nothing to them lies the triumph, the passing-away of Arthur Hallam.

As Tennyson matured, he came to see this sort of oblique metamorphosis as the proper purpose of art. The man does not reorganize himself into petal and leaf, like Shakespeare's Adonis; instead he vanishes, and yet something of him is felt indirectly, tangentially, in the actions and emotions of other men. Of course Tennyson did not abandon the method of covert or overt myth; in *Maud,* as we have seen, the injuries inflicted on Tennyson by Hallam's death and Rosa Baring's frivolity work themselves into a mythological shape, though perhaps pertaining less to Urania, the heavenly Venus, than to the other, ampler, Venus. Yet I do not think that Tennyson was ever completely comfortable as a mythologist. When he approached myth he would disguise it, as in *Maud;* or he would preface it, as in "Tiresias" or "Demeter and Persephone," with some amiable, mildly disparaging verse; or he would complain, as he complained of *In Memoriam,* that the result was "too hopeful . . . more than I am myself" (Ricks, p. 859). The fabulous seemed strained, contrived, doubtful, when applied to serious matters; yet how could he be a poet without dealing in fable? The mode of the Epilogue to *In Memoriam,* the swerve into some other, authentic event, a dark semblance, allowed Tennyson to exercise his imagination without alleging too much, without trapping himself in bland statements of hope and happiness. The heavenly Hallam, a muscular radiance helping the angels to sweep and tuckpoint the City of God, is wonderful but unprovable; the Hallam who finds mysterious expression in the marriage of Cecilia and Lushington is invisible but secure. Since he is but a metaphor, the apparatus of poetry is found appropriate, significant.

XI

Disenchantment in *The Princess*

ALL THROUGH THE LATER STAGES of the composition of *In Memoriam* Tennyson was working on another huge project, *The Princess* (1839–47); and *The Princess* was to be Tennyson's furthest investigation into the method of the Epilogue to *In Memoriam,* the method of displacement. Indeed it is probably one of the most original long poems in English; and, though few of the great writers of the twentieth century seem to have paid it close attention, it anticipates many of the self-conscious, self-deflating artifices of a later age. By the standards of classical literature, the last two centuries have produced a nearly uncategorizable body of writings—the only genre is satire, the grab bag, the only meter is logaoedic—but even by the loose generic criteria of modern literature *The Princess* is an anomaly, as its subtitle says, "A Medley." One may regard it—I hope this does not sound too much like Samuel Beckett or Jacques Derrida—as a botched text written by no one in particular. Tennyson goes to great lengths to confuse the reader about who wrote the poem, about how it got written. If we are to believe the Prologue, *The Princess* is a fairy tale conceived by seven college students, who, on holiday at the estate of the father of one of their number, accepted a challenge to invent a legend, to be based on some themes suggested by elements of their present situation. Their heroine was to modeled on the impetuous, beautiful feminist Lilia, the teenaged daughter of their host, and their setting was to be derived from the paraphernalia of Gothic ruins, exhibitions of science and sport, all that they saw around them. Each student was to take a turn, invent a segment, as the seven together managed to extemporize a gangly, disjointed communal myth, interrupted by songs from the ladies present. The responsibility of authorship therefore is dispersed, falls on no one's shoulders. However, there is no perceptible difference in diction or tone or versification or narrative persona from one part to the next; many readers have been puzzled why Tennyson would go to such trouble to make the poem a project of a committee when a single poet would have sufficed—as Edward FitzGerald said when it was published, there was "no indication of any change of speakers in the cantos"—the speakers seemed to be "all of the Tennyson family" (Martin, p. 311). To forestall this objection, Tennyson, who seems to have been more amenable to criticism than any poet in history of comparable stature, has his narrator say in the Conclusion, "The words are mostly mine" (l. 3); so one poet has shaped and versified the story that seven composed.

Therefore the text is both composite and simple; lumpy, bulging, a sack of potatoes, and a coherent, rapid myth; preposterous, unnatural, flippant, and yet full of sober, serious matter. Beckett once said that he began to write in French because of the superior stylelessness available to him in that language; and Tennyson seems to have tried to write in an ambiguous, mush-mouthed, tonally indistinct, mongrel style, orotund without passion, witty without propriety. In the Conclusion the narrator explains that he tried to please both the men, who wanted the poem to be "mock-heroic gigantesque" (l. 11), a jape and a guffaw, and the women, who wanted the poem to be gallant, noble, sentimental, edifying, perhaps a manifesto of women's rights, "true-heroic—true-sublime" (l. 20):

> Then a rose a little feud betwixt the two,
> Betwixt the mockers and the realists:
> And I, betwixt them both, to please them both,
> And yet to give the story as it rose,
> I moved as in a strange diagonal,
> And maybe neither pleased myself nor them.

(ll. 23–28)

"Realists" here pertains not to those who desire verisimilitude, Zola, but to those eager for the sort of fiction that permits suspension of disbelief, that encourages the reader to identify himself with the protagonist.

At one point in the composition of *The Princess* Tennyson wrote links between the parts, brief verses to characterize each of the speakers. The narrator of the Prologue began the fable; Walter, the son of the host, continued it in Part 2, thereby making the initial appearance of the Princess a brother's affectionate malicious caricature of his sister. The steersman of their college boat was forced to take up the tale, against his protests, in Part 3. Part 4 was attributed to a wild clever Irish fellow who liked to write forgettable, mediocre poetry—an odd and self-deprecating choice, because "Tears, idle tears," the least forgettable lyric Tennyson ever wrote, appears in this part, though the Irishman's Cyril-like traits make him suitable for the bawdy song that betrays the identities of the transvestite men. The speaker of the war episode, Part 5, was a flirt who asked Lilia for a favor, a glove, to wear on his cap as if he were a knight going into battle. In the head verse to Part 6, in which the hard hearts of the women begin to soften, the college turns hospital, Tennyson wrote a little pen portrait of himself, "Arthur Arundel the Poet," with dark soft skin, rough soft hair, a mellow soft voice, as if Tennyson could entrust only himself with the task of depicting the crucial mollification of the Princess. Part 7 was ascribed to a ladylike lad, a specialist in female impersonation in college drama, for the speeches of the Princess in full feminine glory clearly required a more adept falsetto than that of the Irishman in Part 4, where everyone derided the cracked singing of "O Swallow, Swallow."

In this version of the manuscript the versification of the whole was accomplished by Arthur Arundel, not by the narrator of the Prologue; we see again the arbitrariness, Tennyson's indifference as to the identity of the author. In the published *Princess* Tennyson retained only the attribution of Part 1 to the narrator of the Prologue, and the little episode of Lilia's glove-favor before Part 5; and it was perhaps best to leave indistinct the speakers of the parts, because the bizarreness of the ostensible method of composition resists any attempt to rationalize it; to call attention to the speakers is only to make the monstrous implausibility all the more glaring. As one studies the various drafts of the Prologue, the discarded links, and the Epilogue, in which Tennyson gropes, stumbles toward a proper explanation of the origin of the fable, one suspects that the author simply did not know how to account for what he had done. *The Princess,* lacking a real genre, must also lack a traditional persona to whom such a discourse could be ascribed; and thus the putative speaker grows complex and blubbery, forked, twisted, choral, jostling for position, so thick with overtones, harmonics, that no primary voice obtains. Here, once again, anonymity speaks.

Why would Tennyson occupy himself with this chimera, this obscure laminated thing so pitifully squeezed, wheezing? I believe that the composition of *The Princess* offered relief from *In Memoriam;* one is a series of jagged, discontinuous, unconnectable moments of pain and revelation; the other is fluent, an endlessly elaborated connective tissue, a huge cicatrice, a glossy integument by means of which all the sharp painful elements discussed in the intercalated lyrics are covered up, partially anesthetized, embedded and half-resorbed into the fabulous. In *In Memoriam* Tennyson haltingly attempts to find an artifice, a fable to hold together the exploding fragments of emotion; in *The Princess* the fable is a membrane tough enough, flexible enough to stretch over anything whatsoever, a whale that has eaten seven Jonahs and much of England, and yet this skin of myth is thin enough that one can feel under it knots and contusions, tangled veins, broken bones, human suffering. In *In Memoriam* asperity reaches out for design, for the consolations of art; in *The Princess* art spreads out its bulk, grows enormous and unreal, until actual pain and love make themselves felt in a shock of disillusion. In *In Memoriam* a battered man needs a masterful heaven to intervene, to make all smooth and artful; in *The Princess* the poor earthly muse at last breaks through the impossible celestial folderol. They are complementary projects, and together they constitute a whole, the major work of Tennyson's life.

The Princess obeys certain rules of storytelling—the personages act within the confines of specific character traits: King Gama is predictably weak and ineffectual, the Prince's father is predictably gruff, domineering, contemptuous of women, Cyril is predictably coarse and courageous, and so on—and anachronisms and inconsistencies are rarer than the apologies in the Prologue would lead one to believe; in fact *The Princess* on matters of narrative technique is not much wilder than the *Idylls of the King.* What makes it seem so incongruous and disproportioned, tonally viscid, muddy, is that it is a fable in which the fabulist feels free to speak of anything at all. Similarly, no subject is excluded from *In Memoriam;* but there the peculiar relevance of all things to Hallam's death imposes a sort of orbital structure upon the multifarious elements, whereas in *The Princess* there is no central force of gravity, and meteors and comets whirl around without a fixed pattern. The ostensible theme of *The Princess* is a university of women, and only a university would be commodious enough to fit all of the topics which Tennyson wishes to broach; and it is proper that a poet with Tennyson's cloistered and self-restricted mode of existence would, when he wished to write a universal myth, choose to write a myth of the university. In *In Memoriam* mythmaking is an earnest but dubious enterprise; in *The Princess* mythmaking is frankly playful, unpretentious, experimental, flighty, rambunctious, a game that can accommodate every digression, a game about playing games. The heavenly muse is given every conceivable license, until she finds herself incapable of sustaining her worldless fantasy-spinning; indeed she is given enough rope to hang herself. A shapeless series of speakers wrestles with shapeless material in order to investigate the possibilities of shape; there is no desired, predetermined denouement—indeed Walter in the Conclusion is dissatisfied with the obvious happy ending of the tale—so each event is arbitrary, each result a willful selection among the many effects possible for a single cause. At the moments when the next speaker tries to take up the tale where the previous speaker left off, we can infer the following rules of narrative succession: the new speaker attempts not to contradict what the old speakers have predicated; he attempts not to be boring; and he attempts to keep the fable Arcadian, free from death or irremediable suffering. Except by these principles, the movement of the narration is ungoverned, spasmodic.

The Prince and the Princess enact their shenanigans in a realm of pure play. The presiding spirit here is Ariel, who is so avid of novelty that he requires hairbreadth escapes, ludicrous costume changes, viragos, flutterers, tame leopards, a giant, cosmological lore, a whole handbook of geology; but who is so ethereal that he cannot stand the sight of real blood. Ariel is not, like Urania in *In Memoriam,* concerned with celestial archetype, with the archaic ordinance of mythology; he is instead a child with a short span of attention, demanding new entertainment, so careless of design that it is all that he can do to remember the story. A universal myth is no myth at all, only a hodgepodge of the elements of traditional fairy tales, of the fairy tales of science. As "The Vision of Sin" attests, Tennyson was fascinated by orgies; and in *The Princess* every shackle is loosed, invention is liberated to play as it wills, but it is an infantile freedom, uncontaminated by serious passion, the children trying to shatter the piñata suspended from the ceiling, running to pick up the gifts that tumble out.

The Mechanics' Institute celebrated in the Prologue is the closest that modern England can come to the Arcadia where everything is interesting and nothing important can happen; the whole culture is displayed—"The nineteenth century gambols on the grass," as the 1847 text has it—but it is all transmogrified into antiseptic wonder. The habitual outlines of things start to blur, to acquire a fringe of the antique, the mysterious, the incongruous, as the spirit of play seizes the gathering. Fossils, claymores, Malayan daggers set the imagination working backward to the prehistoric and mythical; and the hydraulic games, the girls who clasp hands to receive electrical shocks, the fire balloons and clockwork steamers suggest that the staid modern world can easily grow magical, delirious. An actual park can seem to be the locus of realized fantasy, where fiddling and bowling and every harmless delight are embellished with miracle.

At the beginning of the fable proper, when the narrator of the Prologue starts off the outlandish sevenfold tale of the Princess, Tennyson inserted in the 1850 text a passage that has puzzled many readers and irritated some:

> There lived an ancient legend in our house.
> Some sorcerer, whom a far-off grandsire burnt
> Because he cast no shadow, had foretold,
> Dying, that none of all our blood should know
> The shadow from the substance, and that one
> Should come to fight with shadows and to fall.
> For so, my mother said, the story ran.

(1.5–20)

And, truly, waking dreams were, more or less,
An old and strange affection of the house.
Myself too had weird seizures, Heaven knows what:
On a sudden in the midst of men and day,
And while I walked and talked as heretofore,
I seemed to move among a world of ghosts,
And feel myself the shadow of a dream.
Our great court-Galen poised his gilt-head cane,
And pawed his beard, and muttered "catalepsy".

Other descriptions of these weird seizures were intercalated elsewhere in the poem. I do not believe that these additions detract; indeed they serve to make more explicit the condition of imaginative license under which the poem operates. Ariel, Puck, can circle the globe at the speed of light to pluck the particular herb whose juice is required; but despite his omnipotence he cannot discriminate the imaginary from the real, grows easily confused, for all Athenian gentlemen look alike to him. To be expert in shadows is to lose sight of substance. By making the Prince the prey of hallucinatory suspicions that he is only a character in a fairy tale, Tennyson gives the reader, from the beginning, exactly what he needs to discredit the story, to look beneath to the serious suffering world toward which the silliness gestures.

Even in the Prologue the penumbra of the imaginary is threatening to overwhelm the factual estate, to plunge it in myth; and when Lilia dresses up the statue of her ancestor Sir Ralph, who fought with Richard the Lion-Hearted against the Saracens, in rosy silk, an orange scarf, it seems that the boundary between men and the images of men is growing faint. Indeed the fable of the Prince and the Princess is an improvised conflation of Lilia, the modern feminist, with a pretty story found in a book about Sir Ralph and other adventures "Half-legend, half-historic" (l. 30), a story about a Britomart who rode out in full armor from her besieged city and trampled the enemy before her; again, a real woman and a story about a woman are becoming confused, inextricable. If the imagination is to operate unimpeded, in the unnaturally pure laboratory conditions of this poem, it must not be clogged with substan-

tialities, with things recalcitrant to its transfigurations; and so this
Prince becomes a suitable persona, subject to fits of awareness,
knowledge of the utter artificiality of himself and his world. In
addition to these spasms of unreality, the emotional responses of the
Prince are often strangely discordant to his situation: when he is
unmasked and captured, presumably about to be put to death, he
finds upwelling in him "secret laughter" (4.248); and when the
Princess denounces him, orders him thrown out of her palace,
when his suit seems irrevocably lost, he feels only a momentary
sense of misgiving:

> I was one
> To whom the touch of all mischance but came
> As night to him that sitting on a hill
> Sees the midsummer, midnight, Norway sun
> Set into sunrise.

(4.549–53)

We knew that he was the Prince of a Northern land, but we had not
guessed that it lay above the Arctic Circle; of course it is not polar,
frigid, but simply the land of fairy, where the sun never sets and
men amuse themselves in a perpetual summer, appropriate for the
"Summer's Tale" requested in the Prologue. These intuitions that
all is well, no matter how wrong things may appear, are further
presentiments of the sheer imaginariness of the Prince and the events
that take place around him.

If any steady mythopoeia is confounded by the heteroclite,
immiscible elements jumbled together—there is a scarcely a story
about triumphant women from the Bible, Greece, or Rome, that
does not decorate some gate, frieze, or mural in the university of
women, in addition to the topics from romance and science—there
is method in this muddiness. Tennyson uses the fable of the Prince
and the Princess to demonstrate the superior oneness of all discrep-
ant things; and, if his central thesis is this indwelling wholeness, he
must test it upon the most random and unequal materials. In *The
Princess* Urania is such a defective myth inspirer that she often looks
like a stock fool, a fat woman with cellophane wings suspended by a
rope; but she has a serious function in the economy of the poem, for
she is the agency through which Tennyson tries to confirm a

sublime intuition of the integrity of things. During Psyche's lecture on cosmogony the disguised Prince first learns something about origins:

(2.101–4)

> "This world was once a fluid haze of light,
> Till toward the centre set the starry tides,
> And eddied into suns, that wheeling cast
> The planets."

The Prince and the Princess and Psyche and trees and oceans and wrought iron and the moon are congealed light; one single stuff takes a billion shapes, and the sympathetic imagination reels with feelings of universal resemblance and metamorphosis. In the Prologue we noticed the luminous edges of things; this theory well justifies such nimbus and vertigo, the weird seizures in which all sense of substantiality vanishes, for in truth substance is illusion and uniform light is reality. In "The Mystic" Tennyson saw the universe fold itself into a singleness; and such mystical intuitions are made into a fable in *The Princess*.

This delicate feeling-backward toward primordial unity is a common occupation in the poem. Most of the characters, except the Prince himself, are arranged in pairs of brothers and sisters, beginning with Walter and Lilia, whose close indecorous bantering, wrestling, is the nearest approach to strong emotion in the Prologue; later we see Arac, the Princess's rough gigantic brother, yet in whom a simulacrum of his sister is visible—"all about his motion clung / The shadow of his sister" (5.247–48). Friends of the same sex also display this disturbing similarity: Florian is the Prince's "half-self, for still we moved / Together, twinned as horse's ear and eye" (1.55–56); parallel to them are the Princess and Psyche, "inosculated; / Consonant chords that shiver to one note" (3.73–74). *The Princess* is a tissue of tight resemblances, a hall of mirrors; and, as in "The Lover's Tale," a poem similar in many ways, a certain narcissisim is often felt, a sense that entities are collapsing into a single complex creature, self-sustaining, self-admiring. Julian in "The Lover's Tale" adores his own image reflected in Camilla's eye; and, while the Prince is a proper fairy-tale prince, handsome, virile, stout to uphold his honor, and the Princess is a proper fairy-tale princess, beautiful, chaste, devoted to the welfare of others, they nevertheless are unusually androgynous, ingrown, so that self-love and love of another become difficult to distinguish. The Prince has "lengths of yellow ringlet, like a girl" (1.3), and argues so strenuously against war (5.139) that his bellicose father thinks him a sissy; and the Princess is so imperious, so eager to usurp every role of traditional male authority that the allusions of bloodthirsty Semiramis (2.66), Judith (4.207), and Tomyris (5.355) seem fully justified. It is as if the characters were working to abolish all marks of distinction, to become neutral, geminated, epicene, to feel in themselves the shapeless undifferentiated thing comprising all of them before they shattered into sex and divergent paths.

If androgyny is ideal, why does the Princess err in her desire to be lordly and independent, in herself all the man she requires, "sphered / Whole in ourselves and owed to none" (4.129–30)? Even in the Prologue there are hints that something is amiss with Lilia's feminism:

"I hate you all!
Ah, were I something great! I wish I were
Some mighty poetess, I would shame you then,
That love to keep us children! O I wish
That I were some great princess, I would build
Far off from men a college like a man's,
And I would teach them all that men are taught;
We are twice as quick!"

(ll. 130–37)

Believing women oppressed by men, invidious Lilia wishes to compete, to prove the superiority of woman. To Tennyson this is simply to repeat the same age-old mistake, with the sexes reversed; the urge to rival, to dominate will not lead to concord but to endless sexual warfare. We are in danger of reasserting division and friction in a poem that labors in the opposite direction, toward wholeness.

Although Lilia's desire to grow up seems laudable, it also contains a sinister aspect, if adulthood is a license to oppress. To "lose the child" (1.136) is the central tenet of the Princess's university of women; but this means the loss of much that Tennyson values, the loss of playfulness, of pleasantness, of moonshine and malarky and high romance. When, with all panache and high-falutin, the disguised Cyril sings to the Princess the praises of the Prince, she replies icily that "Your language proves you still the child" (2.44). But hyperbole, catachresis, extravagance of metaphor, all these forms of language's self-delight, are the natural manner of expression in a fable; the Princess is struggling to freeze herself out of the fabulous action, grow sober and self-contained. In a facetious world this deadening of language is the greatest sin; but, as Tennyson says in the Conclusion, women are "realists." When the imagination is unrestrained, exuberant, childishness is sacred, and the Princess's attempts to desecrate it in favor of studious philosophical exactitude will fail; the whole premise of the fable works to defeat her, for it is impossible to be scientist or philosopher in the domain of the ridiculous.

The Princess explains to the disguised Prince that love is childish as well:

"To nurse a blind ideal like a girl,
Methinks he seems no better than a girl;
As girls were once, as we ourself have been:
We had our dreams; perhaps he mixt with them:
We touch on our dead self, nor shun to do it,
Being other—since we learnt our meaning here,
To lift the woman's fallen divinity
Upon an even pedestal with man."

(3.201–8)

The Princess thinks that her discipline, the virginal regimen of her university, tends to make her whole and equal; but this integrity, Tennyson implies, is vitiated if it is understood as self-suppression. Instead of liberating all aspects of her being, male and female, instead of becoming a healthy androgyne, she is instead struggling to quell whatever pertains to infatuation, giggly domesticity, those feminine components of which she disapproves. Great deeds are better than children, she avers, because children die (3.236); but this resolute antichildishness will be difficult to sustain as she watches the baby Aglaia, the chief instrument in the fable for instructing the instructress about proper human conduct.

The Prince, on the other hand, is content to seem childish, and employs similes of adolescence and besottedness to describe his love to the Princess:

"I cannot cease to follow you, as they say
The seal does music; who desire you more
Than growing boys their manhood; dying lips,
With many thousand matters left to do,
The breath of life; O more than poor men wealth,
Than sick men health—yours, yours, not mine—but half
Without you; with you, whole; and of those halves
You worthiest."

(4.435–42)

This loud, gimmicky, windy passage is a fair specimen of the blank verse of *The Princess;* it is written in the style deprecated by Gerard Manley Hopkins as "Parnassian," without genius and yet with the resourcefulness of genius behind it. I am not sure that Tennyson did not deliberately write *The Princess* in this style, ornamental and overwrought, fanciful, inefficient, to heighten the artificiality, the fabulousness of the performance; the imagination can achieve only a partial fusion of the heterogeneous elements. The pleading lover who compares himself to a seal is enjoying the act of making a speech, not hoping to persuade; rhetoric is relished for its trickiness, and for that alone. Yet the very preposterousness is a kind of health, a sign that the child has not been lost, that the Prince retains his vision of that neutral thing that both sexes fit to, that primeval creature, which, according to Aristophanes in Plato's *Symposium,* man and woman together constituted, before it split and its severed halves wandered weeping through the world in search of other.

When the Princess replies in a vigorously declaimed, equally fantastical discourse, we suspect, though she rejects the Prince's every claim, that she will sooner or later succumb to his wooing; every silliness in her speech and behavior brings her closer to the Prince, involves her in the spirit of play that informs the poem. She cannot make any real renunciation of the infantile, for she has been playing a child's game from the beginning, with her parody university and its exclusion of men, of male dogs, like a girls' treehouse in which boys enter On Pain of Death; it is only a matter of time before she must acknowledge the fatuousness of her program. The Prince spent his childhood mooning over a picture of the Princess, the Princess constructed a college of butterflies; there is little to choose between them in childishness.

The theme of the movement toward the whole, the undifferentiated, is perplexed by a passage in which the Prince tells his father that women are already whole, while men are all bits and pieces:

> "she of whom you speak,
> My mother, looks as whole as some serene
> Creation minted in the golden moods
> Of sovereign artists; not a thought, a touch,
> But pure as lines of green that streak the white
> Of the first snowdrop's inner leaves; I say,
> Not like the piebald miscellany, man,
> Bursts of great heart and slips in sensual mire,
> But whole and one."

(5.184–92)

The mother, however, like the child, represents a state of vague inarticulate being, something luminous and revered in the dim past; it is not a role available to the Princess, as she protests, puzzled when the Prince seems to require her to become a new mother to him (7.315). Indeed, Tennyson's model for the human equivalent of the clouds of light from which the solar system congealed seems to be an almost intrauterine memory of the union of the male child with his mother, a vision of a featureless human sphere, attained evidently without the stain of sexual congress; out of such namelessness, such an egg, a man slowly particularizes, acquires an identity, desublimes. When the Prince is wounded in the tourney, the Princess converts the college into a hospital and tends him with maternal solicitude; the Prince knows nothing of the hand that nurses him, no "more than infants in their sleep" (7.39).

Modern psychologists sometimes tell us that regression can be a first step toward health; and this regression of the Prince to an ignorant child, the Princess to an ignorant mother, seems a necessary prelude to their marriage; both recede into some mindless, unfocused state, before resolving themselves into the complementary fitting together, the mutual assistance, of mature lovers:

"For woman is not undevelopt man,
But diverse: could we make her as the man,
Sweet Love were slain: his dearest bond is this,
Not like to like, but like in difference.
Yet in the long years liker must they grow;
The man be more of woman, she of man;
He gain in sweetness and in moral height,
(7.259–70)
Nor lose the wrestling thews that throw the world;
She mental breadth, nor fail in childward care,
Nor lose the childlike in the larger mind;
Till at the last she set herself to man,
Like perfect music unto noble words."

Man and woman cannot now be identical, but they differentiate their forked selves out of fetal unity, rehearsed by the Princess and the Prince at the sickbed, and they strive to regain in the distant future the "statelier Eden" (7.277) of the indiscriminate, the androgyne. This is both a phylogenetic and a religious ideal, for Christ, according to the manuscript of "Locksley Hall Sixty Years After," was the "man-woman" (l. 48), emphatic across the gamut of the human; and the Princess too is a would-be Christ, cultivating woman-mannishness in order to "redeem" (4.487) women from ancient bondage by means of self-sacrifice. In the New Jerusalem, as in the old Eden, there will be no fissure between soul and sense, between sweetness and strength, between the imaginary and the real.

In the laboratory of this fable, insulated from the usual shocks of the human, elevated out of earth's gravitational field, art operates backwards, against the grain, preposterously. In the poems of 1830–34—"The Lady of Shalott," "The Palace of Art," "The Lotos-Eaters," "Tiresias"—Tennyson struggles to develop a single myth about the relationship of art to life: in its simplest form this myth concerns a man who envies the artifact its permanence, its beauty, its freedom from pain; he experiments with transforming himself into a work of art, that is, apotheosis, for the gods dwell in this state of delighted anesthesia, but whenever he approaches this state he is blasted, shriveled, made blind, wise, and dull. Most of these elements are retained in *The Princess:* the Prince is, like Tiresias, a voyeur-hero impinging rudely on celestial beauty—to remind him of his rash deed he is forced to climb between the antlers of a gate depicting the metamorphosis of Actaeon (4.185); and the Princess, whom the Prince compares to Persephone (4.419), another deity who subsides in Lucretian stupor, bears many resemblances to the Soul in "The Palace of Art" and to the Lady of Shalott, great rigid superb women who have sequestered themselves in impermeable fantasy—the Princess's chief henchwoman is Psyche, the Soul, and the course of study of the university comprises "Plato, Verulam" (2.144), whose stained-glass faces illuminate the Palace of Art.

Yet, though the Princess dwells in a species of aesthetic refuge, she generally dislikes art; her closest ancestor in Tennyson's poetry is the Athena of "Œnone," who emphasizes self-discipline and bold conduct. She is an Athena with a liberal social conscience, and does not hesitate to banish from her realm the kind of art not conducive to martial vigor, just like Plato in *The Republic*. The Princess's hostility to the finest art can be seen most clearly in the remarkable scene at the beginning of Part 4: it is sunset—"'There sinks the nebulous star we call the Sun, / If that hypothesis of theirs be sound'" (ll. 1–2)—and the women pitch a tent after the geological expedition; the Princess calls for music to pass the time, just as Lilia called for a Summer's Tale to kill the tyrant Time (Prologue, l. 202); a singer takes up her harp:

> "Tears, idle tears, I know not what they mean,
> Tears from the depth of some divine despair
> Rise in the heart, and gather to the eyes,
> In looking on the happy Autumn-fields,
> And thinking of the days that are no more.

(4.21–65)

> "Fresh as the first beam glittering on a sail
> That brings our friends up from the underworld,
> Sad as the last which reddens over one
> That sinks with all we love below the verge;
> So sad, so fresh, the days that are no more.

"Ah, sad and strange as in dark summer dawns
The earliest pipe of half-awakened birds
To dying ears, when unto dying eyes
The casement slowly grows a glimmering square;
So sad, so strange, the days that are no more.

"Dear as remembered kisses after death,
And sweet as those by hopeless fancy feigned
On lips that are for others; deep as love,
Deep as first love, and wild with all regret;
O Death in Life, the days that are no more."

She ended with such passion that the tear,
She sang of, shook and fell, an erring pearl
Lost in her bosom: but with some disdain
Answered the Princess, "If indeed there haunt
About the mouldered lodges of the Past
So sweet a voice and vague, fatal to men,
Well needs it we should cram our ears with wool
And so pace by: but thine are fancies hatched
In silken-folded idleness; nor is it
Wiser to weep a true occasion lost,
But trim our sails, and let old bygones be,
While down the streams that float us each and all
To the issue, goes, like glittering bergs of ice,
Throne after throne, and molten on the waste
Becomes a cloud; for all things serve their time
Toward that great year of equal mights and rights,
Nor would I fight with iron laws, in the end
Found golden: let the past be past; let be
Their cancelled Babels: though the rough kex break
The starred mosaic, and the beard-blown goat
Hang on the shaft, and the wild figtree split
Their monstrous idols, care not while we hear
A trumpet in the distance pealing news
Of better, and Hope, a poising eagle, burns
Above the unrisen morrow."

Tennyson explained that "Tears, idle tears" did not treat real woe, but "rather the yearning that young people occasionally experience for that which seems to have passed away from them for ever" (Ricks, p. 785). But if this amazing poem does not treat real woe, what does it really treat?

This lyric is, I think, one of the greatest descriptions of aesthetic emotion ever written. The tears are idle tears; expressive, but not expressive of anything in particular; without discernible cause, and without discernible effect outside the compass of the lyric, the charmed circle of words in which vague emotion feeds upon its own vagueness. When Borges defined the aesthetic phenomenon as the "imminence of a revelation which does not occur" (*Labyrinths,* p. 188), he similarly understood the strange contentlessness, the unclassifiability, of aesthetic feeling. A teacher will instruct a young poet to be specific and exact when he writes a poem; but Tennyson here avoids denotation as much as possible, speaks only of clouds that grow more cloudy. The origin of the universe, according to *The Princess,* was a haze of light; the origin of mankind was a being simultaneously male and female in whom all human traits were rolled up; and the origin of sentience, according to the lyric, is this spherical yearning, this nostalgia for the ovum, this eerie recognition that the object of feeling is absent, transcendental. Out of the infantile feeling without an object, feeling-in-itself, there will crystallize love and hatred and anger and tenderness and real woe, all the emotions that respond to actual entities in one's environment. The subject of this poem is Uranian emotion in its purest state, emotion before it has discovered a world to be pertinent to.

The sign that this feeling pertains to eternity is the chronological dislocation, the convergence of dawn and sunset, birth and death, beginning and end, as the Ancient Sage tells us in a similar intimation of immortality:

> Who knew no books and no philosophies,
> In my boy-phrase "The Passion of the Past."
> The first gray streak of earliest summer-dawn,
> The last long stripe of waning crimson gloom,
> As if the late and early were but one—

(ll. 218–27)

A height, a broken grange, a grove, a flower
Had murmurs "Lost and gone and lost and gone!"
A breath, a whisper—some divine farewell—
Desolate sweetness—far and far away—
What had he loved, what had he lost, the boy?

This feeling is evoked by stray evanescent things, things that hover at the edge of vision; nothing that is too heavy or palpable, extant, will summon it up, only faint sensations stirred by glimpses, by memory and imagination, "remembered kisses after death" or "those by hopeless fancy feigned." Tennyson once said that Turner could have done a magnificent painting of a certain stanza of "A Dream of Fair Women," a stanza describing the world's early past, the dim red morn smiling with dead lips (ll. 61–64); and there is a quality in "Tears, idle tears" that is Turneresque, what we now call abstract, the sails and the glimmering casements deliberately reduced to red flecks and oblong fields of white; and like most abstract art this lyric can be understand as a description of the operations of an imagination too potent and pure to engage itself with any finite image.

Tennyson further commented on "Tears, idle tears" that the governing feeling was what he had called as a boy "the passion of the past"; "it is the distance that charms me in the landscape, the picture and the past, and not the immediate to-day in which I move" (Ricks, p. 785). It is the virtue of the aesthetic mode that it can impose just this distance, through which all commonplace detail is lost in the blue haze of the sublime; and in the lyric the images keep receding, dancing away, growing oblique and imaginary, feigned. The sail brightens, and Eurydice comes up from the underworld; the sail darkens, and she sinks back down; the ears grow deaf, and the sounds of birds grow louder; the eyes darken, and the dawn brightens. In this heaving and subsiding, this rising and falling, this expansion and contraction, this brightening and darkening, no clear design obtains, nothing is offered to the intellect; there is only a sense of pulse, of rhythm, as if the lyric demonstrated that even the most powerful emotions could resolve into a lullaby, into oblivion. "Tears, idle tears" is to this extent similar to the choric song of the Lotos-Eaters; it suggests, however, not a willful exclusion of emotion, or an escape from it, but some egg or embryo from which the rest of human emotion will articulate itself, and perhaps, if beginnings and endings are one, it also suggests the terminal feeling, what is left when all ordinary emotion is exhausted. Kant, in the *Critique of Judgment,* pointed out that the aesthetic emotion differed from all others in that it was not dependent on any prior appetite: therefore our enjoyment of a steak is different in kind from our enjoyment of the Hermes of Praxiteles. "Tears, idle tears" shows an emotion that is nearly exclusively aesthetic because it is so thoroughly divorced from any ordinary stimulus, a feeling completely self-engorged. Narcissus wept only idle tears. *The Princess* here attains its farthest remove from the earth, its zenith of fabulousness, myth for myth's sake.

"Tears, idle tears" is near the midpoint of *The Princess,* and I think it is permissible to regard the whole fable and Prologue and Conclusion as a vast frame to this lyric. When the pedantic Princess, at the beginning of Part 4, speaks of the nebular hypothesis about the origin of the sun, she reminds us that science as well as art appeals to high states of dispersal, timelessness; at the end of Part 4, when the Prince compares his brief melancholy to the Arctic sun that "Set into sunrise," we see that the fable is groping toward the same union of beginning and ending, the same temporal derangement present in the lyric; and when the Prince, also in Part 4, speaks of ascending to the Princess even if she were "Sphered up with Cassiopëia," of descending to her even if she were "Persephonè in Hades" (ll. 418–19), Tennyson makes explicit the vague mythy Orphic resonances in the second stanza of the lyric. In addition, the 1850 interpolations of the weird seizures tend to intensify the idleness, the fantasticality of the fable; all sensible extremes, whether hope or fear or grief, resolve, flatten into these moods of shadowy insubstantiality, as if to demonstrate that every emotion verges upon aesthetic emotion. The Princess rejects the siren song of "Tears, idle tears," its appeal to vain purposeless indulgence in feeling for feeling's sake; indeed she speaks as if the song would snare its listeners into Lotos dreams, imprison them in a Palace of

Art which she prays will be shattered: let the rough hemlock break the starred mosaic. At this moment it is as if the Princess were Melpomene turned marvelously regal and sneering, but still with the same empirical, antifantastical temperament.

And yet the rest of the poem pronounces her wrong. Whereas in the poems of the 1830s the dream of apotheosis, the dream of the Palace of Art, was always damned, here, in *The Princess,* Tennyson has discovered a kind of art that is valid, prosperous, humane, though it retains something of its transcendental strangeness. The Princess's university, though it ostensibly seeks to make women mature and whole, excludes much of human nature, sets up an intellectual god and tries to dismiss, suppress the imagination; and Tennyson contrives the fable to illustrate the untenability of the Princess's attitude. "Tears, idle tears" is, as the Princess understands, the antithesis of her desire, for it suggests that in the imagination lies the locus of integrity, that sheer fantasy provides the convergence of opposites, the tying together of beginnings and endings, which is our only hope of wholeness. The lyric licenses the fable and validates the meaning of symbols. The Princess, in whom are oddly combined both the she-serpent and the Apollonius in Keats's "Lamia," the illusionist and the rationalist, the beautiful image and the debunker of the imaginary, strenuously argues against fantastical songs, against the propriety of analogues: when she hears the Prince sing "O Swallow, Swallow," the sequel of "Tears, idle tears" in the evening's entertainment, she bristles, tells a story about a maid of hers who died of the consequences of a rogue's serenades (4.118); and she denies the legal value of her proxy wedding, at the age of eight, to the Prince, a ceremony conducted by placing an emissary's leg, naked to the knee, in bed with her (1.33). Against the Princess's rationalism is posed the Prince's healthy confidence in analogy, in aesthetic intuition, in dreams of uncanny commingling, his confidence that the extraterrestrial yearning of "Tears, idle tears" can find a terrestrial fulfillment.

The themes of "Tears, idle tears" are adapted to a love song in another blank-verse lyric, which the Princess reads to the Prince while he is recuperating from his wounds; it is her first verbal acknowledgment that she loves him, an aria, as if the usual Parnassian verse of the poem were not a sufficiently earnest medium for her emotion:

> "Now sleeps the crimson petal, now the white;
> Nor waves the cypress in the palace walk;
> Nor winks the gold fin in the porphyry font:
> The fire-fly wakens: waken thou with me.
>
> Now droops the milkwhite peacock like a ghost,
> And like a ghost she glimmers on to me.
>
> Now lies the Earth all Danaë to the stars,
> And all thy heart lies open unto me.
>
> Now slides the silent meteor on, and leaves
> A shining furrow, as thy thoughts in me.
>
> Now folds the lily all her sweetness up,
> And slips into the bosom of the lake:
> So fold thyself, my dearest, thou, and slip
> Into my bosom and be lost in me."

(7.161–74)

"Tears, idle tears" is based on rhythms of rising and falling, darkening and brightening; "Now sleeps the crimson petal" is based on rhythms of opening and closing. The milky starlight is enfolded in the earth's womb; and the lily slips into the bosom of the lake. In the first it seems that the woman encloses the man, in the second that the man encloses the woman; this double opening and double closing, mutual involution, depends entirely upon suggestive imagery, cannot easily be reduced to rational exposition; it is exactly the sort of fantastical lyric that the Princess angrily deplored in Part 4. She has been converted to the Prince's belief in the sacredness of imagination.

The language is much more concrete than that of "Tears, idle tears," and yet this poem too bears some resemblance to an abstract painting, perhaps an anticipation of Whistler: all the details of the landscape are obscured in the opening lines, as if the nocturnal lovers could draw into themselves the light fading from the world; and against this black background flicker and glimmer fireflies, white peacocks, stars, the trail of a meteor—the poem evolves with a painterly logic, a filling-in of dots and lines—until all these little lights, all particulars, are drowned in sexual oblivion. Since lover and beloved, subject and object, are alike confounded, the emotion of the poem may be said to be aesthetical, detached from any particular circumstance and expressed completely in images and analogies; but here, unlike "Tears, idle tears," consummation is available, and the charmed circle of words is a metaphor, not of the mind that cannot escape from unreal nostalgia, but of the embrace of lovers. Unhealthy narcissism might result from the emotional state of "Tears, idle tears"; but in this poem there is the outward movement, so highly prized by Tennyson, into the realm of family, society, action.

Just as "Tears, idle tears" was the center of many threads of imagery in *The Princess,* so "Now sleeps the crimson petal" imparts a kind of thematic focus as well, for the fable is full of flower imagery. Just before it is read, the Prince rouses himself to ask the Princess to kiss him, but is so debilitated that he cannot do more than whisper—he compares his state to "a flower that cannot all unfold, / So drenched it is with tempest, to the sun" (7.126–27); this may remind us of an earlier passage, where the Prince told Florian that Cyril, though erratic and sometimes coarse, was not evil, just as a water lily may start and slide with every puff of wind, but is still "anchored to the bottom" (4.238). In both cases the flower represents self-expression, blatancy; Cyril goes too far, is boastful and loud, overblossomed, so to speak, while the Prince's proposal is all the more chaste and irresistible because it is whispered, only half-said, half-opened. The water lily of the lyric, which folds itself and submerges, represents an ideal receding into reticence, a dissolved submarine condition of intimacy, indistinctness, wholeness. Insofar as the characters of the fable are Shakespearean orators, self-expressive and self-insistent, declaiming at one another speeches full of high sentence and elaborate figure, they manifest our fallen fractured state, in which we are fierce contentious individuals, red in tooth and claw; insofar as they attend to the lyrics, they intuit a state without division, without personages, Eden. "Tears, idle tears" and "Now sleeps the crimson petal" are, in every technical sense, sublime; and they represent a hope that mundane life can, without being rarefied or contrived, grow instinct with sublimity.

The intercalated songs—the lyrics not written in blank verse, spliced in between the parts of the fable in the 1850 edition—display a similar dialectic between the sublime and the commonplace, Urania and Melpomene. Some of them appeal to transcendental fiction, to the high intuitions that we receive at times; for instance, "The splendor falls," at the beginning of Part 4, nicely prepares us for "Tears, idle tears," soon to follow:

> O love, they die in yon rich sky,
>   They faint on hill or field or river:
(ll. 13–18)
>   Our echoes roll from soul to soul,
>   And grow for ever and for ever.
> Blow, bugle, blow, set the wild echoes flying,
> And answer, echoes, answer, dying, dying, dying.

Distant horns intone like "The horns of Elfland" (l. 10), as the world of experience takes on the character of a fairy tale, as substance starts to seem shadowy; and Tennyson contrasts the dying echoes of our present acoustic with the self-amplifying echoes of the kingdom of the spirit, for the condition of the mortal world is extinction, while the condition of the higher world is increase. This love, growing ever vaster, more interresonant, suggests that the lovers are growing as little individuated as the lovers of "Now sleeps the crimson petal."

But most of the other intercalated songs have quite a different gist; and indeed, if we look at the many poems Tennyson considered and rejected for this sequence, we notice that the rejected songs are generally arch, fanciful things, coerced lullabies, such as "The Baby Boy," in which a moth is importuned to spangle the baby boy's future bride with silver bells, or "Minnie and Winnie," who sleep together in a little pink shell, apprentice cephalopods. Here we have Ariel at his most precious and insipid. The lullaby that Tennyson printed, before Part 3, is altogether more impressive:

(ll. 1–8)
> Sweet and low, sweet and low,
>   Wind of the western sea,

Low, low, breathe and blow,
    Wind of the western sea!
Over the rolling waters go,
Come from the dying moon, and blow,
    Blow him again to me;
While my little one, while my pretty one, sleeps.

The poem imitates the cradle's rocking rhythm, but the repeated phrases, the metrical feet which contain only one prolonged syllable, impart a feeling of intensity, almost of desperation; the mother is far from certain that her husband will come home, and she is lulling her own fears as well as rocking the baby to sleep. Melpomene is the muse of this poem, exactly as in parts of *In Memoriam:* the urgent and earnest, homely muse, the muse of beloved particulars.

Tennyson put great store in the child, who uncomprehendingly sleeps or wakes through the intercalated lyrics: "The child is the link through the parts, as shown in the Songs (inserted 1850), which are the best interpreters of the poem" (Ricks, p. 741). Indeed the sequence of added songs may be thought of as a counterpoem in which the serious passions excluded from the fable find an oblique expression; the usual relation of the lyrical to the narrative is reversed, for the narrative is frisky and outlandish, farfetched, while the lyrics are of such gravity that they threaten to tear apart the fabric of the fable. In the first one, before Part 2, a husband and wife fall out, but are reconciled over the grave of their dead son; at this point in the fable it seems doubtful that the Prince will be able to succeed in wooing the Princess, and the song may express this anxiety from the opposite direction, from the standpoint of long-married lovers abraded and passionate from the blighting of their hopes—the danger, from the Prince's standpoint, is that he will never marry, that the child will never get conceived, let alone born. This is Tennyson's method in *The Princess,* to turn aside to a remote surrogate, in which the factitiousness, the freakishness, of the fable suddenly deflects into something substantial, important; Ariel is interrupted, reproached, by Prospero, who interprets the Prince's mock-worry that his suit will come to naught as a genuine stillbirth. By the time of the second song, the lullaby "Sweet and low," the Prince's suit seems a little more plausible, so the child, buried in the first song, comes back to life, a sleepy half life, attended by deep fear that he will be a ruined orphan. Through the sequence of songs the child slowly realizes himself, as the Prince and Princess struggle through coltish oratory and conventional obstacles to marry. All the childishness that the Princess disdained—she who wished to lose the child, to grow up—materializes in the child of the inserted songs; all the wholeness of marital coupling, the undifferentiated potentiality of our race, is symbolized by him, in whom the blood of husband and wife is joined.

The metachild of the songs appears in the fable as Aglaia, Psyche's small daughter, who is never rash, never wrong, who behaves as one ought to behave, who is not subject to the contrariness, the willfulness, the affectations of the other characters of the fable. When the Princess decides to exile her mother and keep her for herself, Aglaia lets out a "bitter bleating" (4.373), the least histrionic, most honest emotion yet expressed in the poem; when the Princess advises her brother Arac on his conduct at the forthcoming battle, she notes that Aglaia's tender hands "Felt at my heart, and seemed to charm from thence / The wrath I nursed against the world" (5.426–27); and the Princess's surrender of Aglaia to Cyril and Psyche represents the collapse of her hopes of building a feminist Utopia (6.188), for Aglaia is the future of womankind. When the narrator of the Conclusion recommends patience with society because "This fine old world of ours is but a child / Yet in the go-cart" (ll. 77–78), the superior virtue of childishness is assured. Though the French Revolution seems to show that childhood has a petulant, belligerent, demonic streak—"down rolls the world / In mock heroics stranger than our own" (ll. 63–64), it seems that sweetness and blandness, the child's indiscriminate gurgling affection, will win the day, and all things unpleasant will be mere fantasies.

The child of the intercalated songs, this living emblem of the structureless, the inarticulate, the unresolved, the virtual, to whom the whole fable appeals, is properly addressed, as all infants are properly addressed, with a lullaby. As W. H. Auden points out, the lullaby is an unusual musical form in that it works to its own undoing:

But rhythm and tone can also be used to achieve non-musical ends. For example, any form of physical movement, whether in work or play, which involves accurate repetition is made easier by sounded rhythmical beats, and the psychological effect of singing, whether in unison or in harmony, upon a group is one of reducing the sense of diversity and strengthening the sense of unity so that, on all occasions where such a unity of feeling is desired or desirable, music has an important function.

(*The Dyer's Hand*, pp. 504–5)

If the true concord of well-tuned sounds
By unions married do offend thine ear,
They do but sweetly chide thee, who confounds
In singleness the parts that thou shouldst bear.
Mark how one string, sweet husband to another,
Strikes each in each by mutual ordering;
Resembling sire and child and happy mother,
Who all in one, one pleasing note do sing;
Whose speechless song, being many, seeming one,
Sings this to thee, "Thou single wilt prove none."

([Shake-peare,] Sonnet VIII)

The oddest example of music with an extramusical purpose is the lullaby. The immediate effect of the rocking rhythm and the melody is to fix the baby's attention upon an ordered pattern so that it forgets the distractions of arbitrary noises, but its final intention is to make the baby fall asleep, that is to say, to hear nothing at all.

Auden's quotation of Shakespeare's Sonnet 8—Stravinsky made a lovely setting of it in his "Three Songs of William Shakespeare"— seems especially apposite to Tennyson's "Sweet and low," for Sonnet 8, like *The Princess,* is addressed to a celibate beauty who could better, more generously serve the human race by having a child; and the music of Tennyson's songs, both the grave and the acute, is a magical invocation of just this human harmony, this major triad of husband, wife, and child, mutually resonating.

Musical unity is another accession into the wholeness, the

plasmodium, the zone of undifferentiated being, toward which the Prince gropes throughout the fable; the songs tend toward sleep, involution, womby felicity. The other intercalated songs are not lullabies, but are written in simple, sometimes Wordsworthian meters, with strong declamatory accents, the sorts of poems that children like to hear: in "Thy voice is heard," before Part 5, the memory of his child inspires the warrior to excellent feats of war, as if all adult activity were given focus and meaning by the child's existence; and in "Home they brought," before Part 6, the warrior's widow cannot weep or speak or move, is perishing from lack of expression, until the nurse sets his child on her knee, and the tears flow. These scenes of real slaughter, real despair, real consolation, are counterpointed against the tournament in which no one dies; the songs show a world in which no masterful heaven intervenes to patch everything up, in which no fiction mitigates the harshness of life. It seems that there is a narrative about the Prince and the Princess, generally governed by Urania, a spirit of self-infatuated imagination, and a body of intercalated poems, generally governed by lowly, sweet-eyed Melpomene; and that these two strands have only accidental connections. But Tennyson's best surprise is his reconciliation of the two seemingly hostile muses; out of the medley there comes design.

The triumph of *The Princess* lies in the slow convergence of the world of the songs and the world of the fable. In the first song the sorrow and mad kisses of husband and wife over the child's grave could not have been further removed from the Prince's frolics in cloud-cuckoo-land; by the time of the war songs we have what is obviously the analogue of the tournament, a presentation of the emotions it would inspire if it were real war and not a distended game; and by the time of the last intercalated song, "Ask me no more" (before Part 7), the Princess speaks almost in her own person—she could have responded to the Prince's proposal of a kiss in these words, if she had not picked up her poetry book and read aloud, "Now sleeps the crimson petal":

(ll. 6–10)   Ask me no more: what answer should I give?
                I love not hollow cheek or faded eye:

> Yet, O my friend, I will not have thee die!
> Ask me no more, lest I should bid thee live;
>   Ask me no more.

The man to whom the poem is addressed is (like Suckling's lover) pale and wan with lovesickness; now the Princess responds to a lover debilitated not from lovesickness but from wounds, but it is almost the same thing. While the fable has been moving forward in proper chronological order, the beginning, middle, and end of a well-made tale, the songs have been working emotionally backwards, from the hopeless grieving over a dead child, to the consolations provided by a living child even if his father is dead, to a reluctant but wholehearted assent to a proposal of marriage. Amid the general implausibility of the fable the emotions of the songs seem disturbingly solemn, authentic; and as songs and fable converge it seems that grace and lamentation, sequence and interruption blend together as one. It is no surprise that the Prince, after the moment of his engagement, is never again bothered by weird seizures—"my doubts are dead, / My haunting sense of hollow shows" (7.327–28)—for imagination and reality have been united, the shadow has grown substantial fact. Tennyson inserted the songs of the 1850 edition to endow the chimera with mass.

In *In Memoriam*—a true Winter's Tale struggling toward an elusive April—Tennyson discovered how hard it was to try to lift, to arrange, human life into the concinnity of art; he may have felt that the reverse method—the strategy of *The Princess*—was more satisfactory, the deflation of affected artifice into life. Through the strategy of *The Princess,* life retained vestiges of order and fabulous myth, and yet Tennyson was not guilty of falsifying the truth of our condition. In the intercalated songs people suffer and die, and, although the connective tissue—the fable—is deliberately disreputable, a sense of context, of teleology, inheres. The evolution of the Princess herself is especially intriguing. In the beginning she was the Soul in "The Palace of Art," except that she hated art; at the end she renounces her palace, her university, and learns to love art. It is as if Tennyson had learned that the aesthete's stance, that of the involuted narcissistic Soul in "The Palace of Art," had nothing at all to do with real artists, real art; consequently aesthetical emotion could be defended from this haughtiness, this vampirism. *The Princess* is a brief for this defense. When Lilia, in the Prologue, suggests they tell a Summer's Tale, the narrator says wishfully that "we should have him back / Who told the 'Winter's tale' to do it for us" (ll. 230–31). Shakespeare alas is nowhere to be found; but the crucial episode of *The Winter's Tale* is also the crucial episode of *The Princess*.

Tennyson complained in a note to the 1832 printing of "The Palace of Art" that "it is the most difficult of all things to *devise* a statue in verse" (Ricks, p. 405); but I know of no poem so crowded with statuary as *The Princess*. Statues adorn every gallery, niche, finial, fountain, and lawn in the university—statues of winged women (1.207), the Muses and Graces (2.13), caryatids of Art and Science (4.183), Judith and Holofernes (4.207), Mnemosyne (4.250), Miriam and Jael (5.500), Pallas and Diana (6.347–48). The university of women is a museum of statues, images of chastity and graceful wisdom, with a certain tinge of misanthropy, misandry. These statues are amazingly vigorous. In the Prologue the characters chat with the travestied statue of Sir Ralph as if they half expect him to reply; and in the fable this phalanx of statues takes an active part in the machinery of the plot, for instance, when the Prince stumbles on a vine entwined around the feet of the Mnemosyne—his escape from the clutches of the proctors is foiled by an emblem of Memory, his memory of his vow to win the Princess; or when the hubbub that fills the Princess's hall after the Prince's father's declaration of war is set in its place by the pacific, tranquilizing statues of the Muses looking down on the tumult (4.468). It is proper that, in an imaginary world, images should do so much of the work; and the benign statues of the Muses suggests, after all the contentiousness of Melpomene and Urania in *In Memoriam,* that a certain air of cooperation and good will will be present in the rest of the poem. The line between people and statues is thin; if statues are nearly alive, a race endlessly propagating itself in every corner of the university, then people have a corresponding tendency to appear like statues. When the appalling Blanche discovers that the Prince and his friends are males in disguise, Cyril boasts that he will persuade her to keep their secret: " 'I will melt this marble into wax / To yield us farther furlough' " (3.57–58); even Blanche's name suggests a washed-out, marmoreal chastity. Later, Psyche in exile, shocked by the double loss of Aglaia and of the favor of the Princess, is paralyzed, "Like some sweet sculpture draped from head to foot" (5.54), as if all the women in the university could pass effortlessly into artifice; isolated from men and children, they easily grow depraved, imaginary. Indeed everyone who enters the Princess's precincts is threatened with this same petrification: after Arac and his men conquer the forces of the Prince's father, the Princess tells the victorious warriors that in the golden years to come the ladies and heroines will gather flowers and branches "To rain an April of ovation round / Their statues, borne aloft" (6.50–51). It is no wonder that the Prince cannot always distinguish shadow from substance: deceptively real images proliferate rapidly, grow intertwined with deceptively imaginary realities. The imaginary and the real are no longer struggling for supremacy, but coalescing into a single field of operation.

The Princess herself is, of course, the most thoroughly statuelike of all these statuesque women. Just before the Prince is vanquished in battle, he turns his eyes aside from the brawny thews of Arac, catches a glance of the palace, and, at the highest point, the Princess, "among the statues, statuelike, / Between a cymballed Miriam and a Jael" (5.499–500); and later, when every major character pleads with the Princess to forgive Psyche, King Gama denounces his daughter: "see how you stand / Stiff as Lot's wife, and all the good knights maimed" (6.223–24). But, as Gama, who has heard about hemoglobin, says, the Princess has iron in her blood (6.123), and she takes her time before she relents. The Princess has indeed tried to be a statue, to elevate herself into an iconic and mythy splendor, a glorious impermeability consecrated to virgin self-perfection; but in the later stages of the fable she has shown herself to be no Phidian Athena, lifeless and chryselephantine, but only an uglier, feebler sort of statue, a grotesque Jael—who killed Sisera by hammering a nail into his head—or Lot's wife, a cat killed by curiosity, the salty Eurydice of the Old Testament.

The thawing of the Princess is the climax of the poem, and it is accomplished in three stages. In the first she slowly, unconsciously falls in love with the Prince while tending his wounds; he begs her to kiss him, even if she is only a dream, and she consents:

My spirit closed with Ida's at the lips;
Till back I fell, and from mine arms she rose
Glowing all over noble shame; and all
Her falser self slipt from her like a robe,
And left her woman, lovelier in her mood
Than in her mould that other, when she came
From barren deeps to conquer all with love;
And down the streaming crystal dropt.

(6.143–50)

Athena has turned into Aphrodite. Venus has appeared previously in the poem, near the beginning, when the disguised Prince first enrolls in the university and seals his matriculation papers:

This I sealed:
The seal was Cupid bent above a scroll,
And o'er his head Uranian Venus hung,
And raised the blinding bandage from his eyes.

(1.237–40)

The Princess, in designing this seal, seems to intend to make an emblem of love guided by wisdom rather than caprice, a love made studious and sexless; but in the context of the whole the seal has different meaning, for the heavenly Venus opens the eyes of love, and Cupid grows infatuated, wreaks havoc in the world of virgins. The emblem and the Prince's desire both suggest a superior cooperation of Cupid and Urania, earthly and heavenly love. The Princess pretended to be Urania, like the Urania of *In Memoriam* 37, too lofty and gelid, too saturated with ether to descend from her involved mythicality; but by the end she has softened and swollen, grown venereal. Here, as everywhere in *The Princess,* Tennyson works toward wholeness, tries to discover the single Venus before her fissure into heavenly and earthly twins. According to the old Greek story, Psyche was punished in many complicated and tedious ways for daring to lift the bandage, so to speak, from her own eyes, in order to see her lover Cupid; and Tennyson's Psyche seems to suffer

vicariously, almost purposelessly, for the sidelong sexy glances that
the Prince casts upon the Princess.

The second stage of the Princess's thaw is achieved through
lyric analogy; the Princess, mute and shamed after their first kiss,
returns with a book of poetry, and reads aloud, first "Now sleeps
the crimson petal," and then "Come down, O maid":

> "Come down, O maid, from yonder mountain
>   height:
> What pleasure lives in height (the shepherd sang)
> In height and cold, the splendour of the hills?
> But cease to move so near the Heavens, and cease
> To glide a sunbeam by the blasted Pine,
> To sit a star upon the sparkling spire;
> And come, for Love is of the valley, come,
> For Love is of the valley, come thou down
> And find him; by the happy threshold, he,
> Or hand in hand with Plenty in the maize,
> Or red with spirted purple of the vats."

(7.177–87)

Here dalliance with Cupid seems much more attractive than the
role of Urania, for he is the god of abundance and fertility, a tamer
Dionysus; and when the lyric speaks of the monstrous mountain
ledges where water-fumes "like a broken purpose waste in air"
(7.199), it suggests that the whole university was just such a nebulous nonentity. Tennyson has nearly ended his long dispelling of the
life-denying aspects of the fantasy he has erected. Just as in "Lucretius" the sexual gods are the most believable ones.

The Princess so judges it, calls herself the " 'Queen of farce' "
(7.228); and in the last stage of her melting, the Prince reassures her
that there is nothing in her farcical or mocking, that he perceived
from the beginning the warmth, the femininity hidden inside the
icon, beneath the rigid carapace:

> "I [the Princess] have heard
> Of your strange doubts: they well might be: I seem
> A mockery to my own self. Never, Prince;
> You cannot love me."

(7.315–29)

> "Nay but thee" I said
> "From yearlong poring on thy pictured eyes,
> Ere seen I loved, and loved thee seen, and saw
> Thee woman through the crust of iron moods
> That masked thee from men's reverence up, and forced
> Sweet love on pranks of saucy boyhood: now,
> Given back to life, to life indeed, through thee,
> Indeed I love: the new day comes, the light
> Dearer for night, as dearer thou for faults
> Lived over: lift thine eyes; my doubts are dead,
> My haunting sense of hollow shows: the change,
> This truthful change in thee has killed it."

The false self slips away, the male crust shatters, and, in the very last line of *The Princess,* Lilia will remove the girl's apparel from the statue of Sir Ralph. Tennyson removes all the transvestite disguises, according the usual resolution of comedy; but *The Princess* diverges from the usual comic design in that the confusions, the gorgeous vestments, are presentiments of some state in which masks and faces are really interchangeable, in which man and woman, statue and person, are only aspects of a single great colluded being. Such sublimities are a kind of wisdom or health, but only among those who stay low, near the earth, close to the truths of generation and human love.

The naturalness of art, the artificiality of nature, is a theme of Shakespearean romance, of *Pericles,* of *The Winter's Tale,* though perhaps not of *The Tempest,* where Caliban resists any resorption into the fabulous. No scene in Shakespeare seems to have moved Tennyson more than the last scene of *The Winter's Tale,* where Hermione, chilled by Leontes' mad murderous jealousy for sixteen years until she has stiffened into a statue, reveals herself to her astonished husband—how can the sculptor have been subtle enough to carve new wrinkles in her face, how dare he kiss her while the oily raddle is still wet on her lips?—and, as a solemn music strikes, she descends from her curtained niche, resumes her long-suspended life. *In Memoriam* 103, where the veiled statue of Hallam changes to a living spirit, may owe something to this scene; and also the remarkable description in "Gareth and Lynette" of the gateway to Camelot, on which the Lady of the Lake is about as animated as an image can be, "all her dress / Wept from her sides as water flowing away" (ll. 212–13):

> Then those with Gareth for so long a space
> Stared at the figures, that at last it seemed
>
> (ll. 227–31) The dragon-boughts and elvish emblemings
> Began to move, seeth, twine and curl: they called
> To Gareth, "Lord, the gateway is alive."

Yeats may have remembered this passage in the description of the statues in Book 2 of *The Wanderings of Oisin;* and both *The Princess* and *The Winter's Tale* seem to inform the final lyric of Yeats's play *A Full Moon in March:*

> SECOND ATTENDANT. Why must those holy, haughty feet descend
>
> (*Collected Plays,* p. 396) From emblematic niches, and what hand
> Ran that delicate raddle through their white?
> My heart is broken, yet must understand.
> What do they seek for? Why must they descend?
> FIRST ATTENDANT. For desecration and the lover's night.

Works of art aspire to be works of art that come to life; so Galatea and Hermione are irresistible to artists who hope to imbue their work with vigor, sinew, warmth; who hope to reconcile the imaginary and the real.

In a sense Tennyson labored all his life to write a proper ending to "The Palace of Art." We have seen throughout this book how the imagination, in its states of highest activity, kept leading Tennyson to various zones of being that he deemed ethically or psychologically intolerable; and he never could quite persuade himself that his imagination could be disciplined to *want,* of its own volition, what was conducive to the soul's health—simplicity, ease, prayer, human life, good manners. In "The Palace of Art" Tennyson repudiated the concept of an art divorced from the commonplace, the thickly human, but he could not then imagine a genuine alternative: *The Princess* does present an alternative, an art that explicitly verges on life, that renders itself unconvincing in order to give some shock of the real. What vexed Tennyson was that this vision of the truth about art could not easily be sustained, repeated; one had to erect the whole thumping, creaky mechanism of *The Princess* to manifest it. Finally, to Tennyson, art and life were antithetical, reconcilable by such Herculean labor they were scarcely reconcilable at all. In *The Winter's Tale* Polixenes tells Perdita that she should not exclude certain flowers from her bouquet because they were grown artificially:

> Yet Nature is made better by no mean
> But Nature makes that mean; so, over that art
> Which you say adds to Nature, is an art
> That Nature makes. You see, sweet maid, we marry
> A gentler scion to the wildest stock,
> And make conceive a bark of baser kind
> By bud of nobler race. This is an art
> Which does mend Nature, change it rather, but
> The art itself is Nature.

(4.4.89–97)

This easy confidence in the naturalness, the propriety of art, was denied to Tennyson; so he had to content himself with presenting artifices that could not quite get themselves born, and idyllic visions of life that could not quite haul themselves up into art. To claim that art itself is nature is to claim too much; so Tennyson kept studying intensely those brief moments of passage from one state to the other, those sudden discoveries of design, cool myth, in turbulent human life, those instants when old tales grew bright with pertinence. Only in *The Princess* is metamorphosis sufficiently prolonged, does artfulness linger in the presence of the human. Perhaps it was enough for Tennyson, if pure sublimity turned out to be farce, to show the matter-of-fact tinted with these faint touches of the sublime.

INDEX

Index

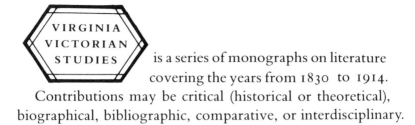

VIRGINIA VICTORIAN STUDIES is a series of monographs on literature covering the years from 1830 to 1914. Contributions may be critical (historical or theoretical), biographical, bibliographic, comparative, or interdisciplinary.

DANIEL ALBRIGHT, *Tennyson: The Muses' Tug-of-War*